Accession no.

D1353011

Visualizing
Social Science
Research

WITHDRAWN

To my darling Elizabeth—Thanks for everything. You amaze me.
—Johannes Wheeldon

Dedicated to Marja for sharing life with me.
—Mauri Åhlberg

Visualizing
Social Science
Research

Maps, Methods, & Meaning

Johannes Wheeldon
Washington State University

Mauri K. Åhlberg
University of Helsinki

LIS - LIBRARY	
Date	Fund
8/6/12	d-ch
Order No.	
2 32121x	
University of Chester	

Los Angeles | London | New Delhi
Singapore | Washington DC

Los Angeles | London | New Delhi
Singapore | Washington DC

FOR INFORMATION:

SAGE Publications, Inc.
2455 Teller Road
Thousand Oaks, California 91320
E-mail: order@sagepub.com

SAGE Publications Ltd.
1 Oliver's Yard
55 City Road
London EC1Y 1SP
United Kingdom

SAGE Publications India Pvt. Ltd.
B 1/I 1 Mohan Cooperative Industrial Area
Mathura Road, New Delhi 110 044
India

SAGE Publications Asia-Pacific Pte. Ltd.
33 Pekin Street #02-01
Far East Square
Singapore 048763

Acquisitions Editor: Vicki Knight
Associate Editor: Lauren Habib
Editorial Assistant: Kalie Koscielak
Production Editor: Astrid Virding
Copy Editor: Barbara Corrigan
Typesetter: C&M Digitals (P) Ltd.
Proofreader: Sue Irwin
Indexer: Diggs Publication Services
Cover Designer: Edgar Abarca
Marketing Manager: Helen Salmon
Permissions Editor: Adele Hutchinson

Copyright © 2012 by SAGE Publications, Inc.

All rights reserved. No part of this book may be reproduced or utilized in any form or by any means, electronic or mechanical, including photocopying, recording, or by any information storage and retrieval system, without permission in writing from the publisher.

Printed in the United States of America

Library of Congress Cataloging-in-Publication Data

Wheeldon, Johannes.

Visualizing social science research : maps, methods, & meaning/Johannes Wheeldon, Mauri K. Åhlberg.

p. cm.
Includes bibliographical references and index.

ISBN 978-1-4129-9104-9 (pbk.)

1. Social sciences—Research—Methodology. I. Åhlberg, Mauri. II. Title.

H62.W448 2012
300.72—dc22
2011012427

This book is printed on acid-free paper.

11 12 13 14 15 10 9 8 7 6 5 4 3 2 1

Contents

Preface

Maps are some of the earliest representations of how people around the world have tried to understand their surroundings. They can represent places, things, components, or even relationships. They allow us a glimpse into how something was understood and capture meaning in an accessible and wholly creative way. By constructing maps, people can transfer their internal perspectives into external illustrations—this has the ability of making the intangible real. As authors, our interest in the use of maps has emerged in different ways. Our backgrounds are very different; however, we both have come to view maps as valuable based on our experiences teaching undergraduate students. Throughout Canada, Finland, the United States, and the United Kingdom, when pressed to explain a relationship or interconnection, we would often revert to diagrams, maps, and graphs. Our interest in their use to teach, learn, and engage in research has emerged from the culmination of theoretical, pedagogical, and practical developments.

This book is an attempt to provide an accessible and student-friendly introduction to research in the social sciences. It is not intended to be a book about the use of concept maps in the health professions or as learning tools in education; it is not intended to be a general overview of research methods. Neither is it a comprehensive description of visual methods in qualitative research nor a primer on statistical analysis. Instead, this book is best seen as a supplemental text, designed to focus on the use of maps, graphs, and diagrams to explore different methods of research and different assumptions about meaning. It is suitable for upper-level undergraduate students, graduate students, and others who seek a novel introduction to the world of social science research. In this text, we connect the theoretical foundations of research with practical examples for students and readers and focus on concept maps and mind maps as useful tools for quantitative, qualitative, and mixed-methods research. As the calls for more participatory research methods increase, the use of maps can guide new approaches to the myriad of research decisions that are at the core of all social science research. In education they offer a means to help students learn while gathering data about learning. In criminal justice, they may offer a means to explore how to implement emergent "what works" practices by capturing the unique processes that operate within institutions. We hope this book can peel back the layers of complexity that surround the social science research process. Using maps may give students, instructors, researchers, and community members another way to "see" research and visualize the processes and decisions that it requires.

The approach taken in the remainder of this book is to provide both theoretical justifications for and practical examples of the use of maps, graphs, and diagrams in social science research. This involves the introduction of the two main varieties of maps used in this book: concept maps and mind maps. The third chapter presents more traditional uses of concept maps and evaluates more deeply the assumptions made by quantitative researchers and the value placed on theory testing, generalizability, and repeatability. The fourth chapter explores the utility of mind maps to the value placed on theory creation, depth of understanding, and the role of the researcher in qualitative research. As mind maps are user generated and more flexible than concept maps, they may be better suited to qualitative research. Based on data within the maps, researchers can create more detailed and relevant interview questions relating to how participants created their maps.

The fifth chapter considers the limitations of quantitative or qualitative research and considers how (and indeed, whether) mixed-methods approaches can address these limitations. By relying on the strengths of each method together, mixed methods can provide a more detailed understanding of what research data are suggesting. The sixth chapter presents how maps can be used to help you write up your research project based on key headings and subheadings. Although approaches will vary by your discipline, class, and research project, most research papers will address the key elements discussed in this chapter, including approaches to, tips for, and strategies for writing up your research project. Finally, Chapter 7 explores some of the limitations associated with concept maps and mind maps, including both conceptual and practical difficulties encountered. In this chapter we consider questions of reliability and validity as well as new approaches to understanding research inferences. In addition, this chapter outlines two new directions in social science research, including evidence-based research through systematic review and participatory-action research models.

Becoming a responsible academic citizen in a rapidly changing world requires that we all take on more responsibility for our own learning, thinking, and theory construction. This requires humility and a means to clearly confront one's current thinking on a topic while allowing that it can and likely will change. By mapping our understanding of an issue or idea, we capture our understanding and investigate how our ideas change over time and as we acquire more knowledge, experience, and reflexive competence. We invite you as students, instructors, researchers, and community members to consider how maps can assist your work. When in doubt, we humbly suggest that you MAP IT!

Johannes Wheeldon & Mauri Åhlberg

Acknowledgments

A number of people have assisted in the development of this book. We would like to thank Pirjo Äänismaa, Vuokko Ahoranta, David Antrobus, Susan Barrett-Landau, Graham Bradley, Alberto Cañas, Robin Cooper, Barbara Daley, Sherika Derico, Stephen Easton, Richard Evans, Jacqueline Faubert, Peter Gärdenfors, Bill Glackman, Robert Gordon, Piet Kommers, David Morgan, Joe Novak, Shannon Portillo, Nahanni Pollard, Ferris Ritchey, Danielle Rudes, Neil Salkind, Richard Shavelson, Elizabeth Suiter, Chris Tattersall, Edward Tufte, Jamie Vaske, Simon Verdun-Jones, Linda Wheeldon, and David Wilson for their support, advice, and assistance. In addition we would like to thank Vicki Knight for her early belief in the value of this project and her support in bringing it from a drafted proposal to a fully conceived introductory research methods textbook.

About the Authors

Johannes Wheeldon, PhD, LLM, is a postdoctoral research fellow at Washington State University and has studied and worked in Canada, the United Kingdom, Latvia, Russia, and throughout the United States. His research has appeared in journals such as the *International Journal of Qualitative Research, Journal of Mixed Methods Research,* and *Qualitative Report.* His work on international justice has been published in journals such as *Crime, Law and Social Change; Law and Justice; Journal of Baltic Studies;* and *Law and Policy.* Other scholarship related to theory, philosophy, and education has been published in journals such as the *Canadian Journal of Criminology and Criminal Justice, Critical Criminology,* and *Contemporary Justice Review.*

He has taught more than 20 courses in criminology, sociology, philosophy, political science, law, and research methods at a variety of institutions. His recent research has focused on the philosophical, pedagogical, and practical utility of visual methods, and he has completed a number of studies that use maps as part of mixed-methods research designs in a variety of settings. For the past 2 years he has been teaching philosophy to inmates at the Coyote Ridge Correctional Center as part of a unique associate of arts degree program.

Mauri Åhlberg, PhD, FLS, is a full professor of biology and sustainability education at the University of Helsinki. He serves as a visiting professor at the University of Exeter, Graduate School of Education. He has taught research methods for decades and supervised hundreds of master's theses and plenty of doctoral theses. He has tested and improved research methods that can be used at the same time as tools for teaching and learning. He has published research on the use of concept mapping and other graphic-representation tools, learning, evaluation, and action research, in particular for teachers and other professionals as researchers and developers of their own work. He has been a referee for research periodicals and for many congresses and conferences arranged by professional organizations. His scholarly interests are in the fields of practical applications of theories and methods of behavioral and social sciences, philosophy of science, and research methods for continually improving teachers' and other professionals' work. His curriculum vita and lists of and links to many of his publications and presentations are online at http://www.mv.helsinki.fi/home/maahlber. He uses his Facebook page for cumulative, collaborative knowledge building, integrating both personal and professional learning, always welcoming new constructive, tolerant, truth-loving Facebook friends.

1

Visualizing Social Science Research

CHAPTER OVERVIEW AND OBJECTIVES

Visualizing social science research refers to the techniques, processes, and tools that allow students, instructors, and investigators to understand, present, and frame research. This includes a variety of maps, graphs, and diagrams used to illuminate processes that may otherwise appear complex and daunting. Visualizing research need not be limited to the presentation of findings. In this book, we explore the potential of graphic illustrations to demystify and clarify designs, collect data, present methods, and explore measurement.

This chapter introduces the research process including major theoretical perspectives, epistemological concerns, and methodological and data-collection choices. A central theme in this chapter is that the assumptions made by different researchers and the resultant approaches inform and influence the research process. By graphically presenting examples of deductive, inductive, and abductive approaches in quantitative, qualitative, and mixed-measures research, this chapter uses visual examples to present an overview of major theoretical approaches to social science research. Finally, this chapter shows how maps can help frame a research project and how they can assist novice researchers when considering the various steps involved in conducting a research project. Through a sample research problem, readers will be encouraged to use maps, graphs, or diagrams to plan a research project. By the end of this chapter, readers should be able to

- define social science research and explain why visualizing the processes involved can be useful;
- understand the steps involved in completing a research project;
- consider how visualizing research can assist students, instructors, and researchers;
- describe how different theoretical starting points influence the research approach taken; and
- explain why it is useful to acknowledge that all research is a series of decisions.

WHY VISUALIZE SOCIAL SCIENCE RESEARCH?

Social science research seeks to understand, explain, and predict human behavior by observing, reflecting, and/or measuring social phenomena. As a branch of science, it focuses on the study of society and the relationships of individuals by exploring meaning from a human perspective and testing and/or constructing theories based on these investigations. Glenn Firebaugh (2008) summarized seven principles for good social science research (see Figure 1.1). The first six are the possibility of surprise, the need to explore differences within your research, the need to compare findings from one group with findings from another, and the need to focus on how, why, and to what extent things change.

Firebaugh (2008) concluded his discussion with an important final rule. Methods must always be the means—never the end—of social science research. Methods serve the

Figure 1.1 Seven Rules for Social Science Research

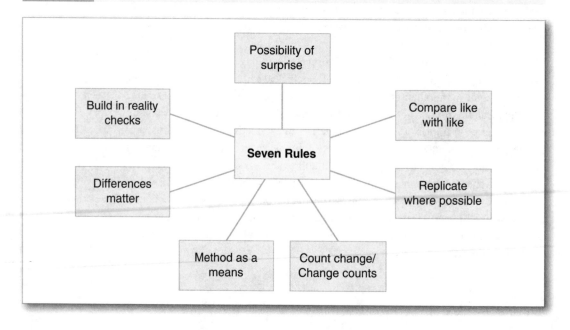

needs of the research, the sample to be studied, and the question(s) to be explored. This may be because all research can be seen as a series of "research decisions" (Palys, 1992). Seeing research as a series of decisions acknowledges that different research problems, data-collection strategies, and methods of analysis shape research findings. All decisions have consequences; it is important to remain humble about the fact that no matter how good the research is, all honest research acknowledges its limitations. Whereas for some, the notion that research cannot provide *the* answer may be disconcerting, when properly planned, conducted, and presented, social science research nevertheless offers us the best means with which to make sense of the world.

This book begins with the assumption that new approaches to research methods are needed to attract students and young researchers into the social sciences in the first place. The tools we explore throughout the book provide a means to channel creativity and investigate how research can assist people to better understand both our world and ourselves (Mintzes, Wandersee, & Novak, 1998). Although images increasingly play an important role in our daily lives, their potential to teach students and to assess learning outcomes have not yet been fully integrated into the social sciences. This may be because we are emerging from an era in which standardized tests were seen as the only means to assess learning, based on a well-intentioned but incomplete one-size-fits-all approach to education. Emergent approaches seek to build teacher education, learning assessments, and measurements of student outcomes by focusing on responsibility and accountability (Shavelson, 2010); however, questions remain about how new integrated assessment systems can be operationalized and incorporated into existing curricula.

One strategy is to view developing social science research pedagogy as not only a means to an end but an end in and of itself. By reading and doing the exercises in this book, the student will become part of a new way of learning through visual and graphic means. Expanding on cognitive approaches to education, in this text we take seriously the need for students to know, understand, integrate, and reflect on what they are learning. In this book we attempt to do this by offering overviews, contemplating debates, and providing examples in ways designed to build critical thinking, research, and reasoning skills among a new generation of college students. To succeed, we think it is time to revisit how research has traditionally been taught. There is evidence that traditional education models have been more successful at ensuring students can recite facts from the past than facilitating the kind of practical skill development and higher order thinking that can enable them to both discover and use knowledge in the future (Blagg, 1991). As Richard LeGates (2004) has noted, undergraduate students who are beginning majors in the social sciences feel inadequate when undertaking rigorous empirical social science research. Unlike their peers in the natural sciences, social science students all too often fear and rarely enjoy research methods courses. Subjecting students to research methods courses they do not enjoy poses motivation and retention problems. It also poses a significant challenge for a new generation of instructors who seek to combine standards with accessibility.

In this text we hope to build on other attempts to demystify the research process (Alvarez & Gowin, 2009) and expand emergent discussions about the use and utility of visual methods (Banks, 2001). Our approach is based on the promotion of practical social science research by making the college classroom a laboratory—a place where research is discussed, conducted, and visualized by instructors and students working together. The notion that visualizing social science research can assist students, instructors, and researchers to see patterns is by no means new (Kaplan, 1964). Yet despite promising developments since the 1970s, visual depictions of exploratory data analysis are only now reemerging, driven in some ways by the wealth of data available to all online. Yet this remains an area of scholarship in which chaos reigns (Åhlberg, 2008) and too few authors acknowledge the shoulders of those on whom they stand. Although we too have likely missed some past visual approaches, we believe there is value in providing a variety of examples. Some predecessors to current mapping efforts include "spider diagrams" (Hanf, 1971), "mind maps" (Buzan, 1974), "box and whisker" charts and "stem-and-leaf" diagrams (Tukey, 1977), "knowledge mapping" (Dansereau, Sells, & Simpson, 1979), "Vee diagrams" (Gowin, 1981), "concept maps" (Novak, 1981), and "clustering" (Rico, 1983).

Despite the wide variety of depictions, visual representations in research are too often limited to the presentation of data and the explanation of findings. A leading expert on the visual display of quantitative information is Edward Tufte. He has written a number of books in his distinguished career, but Tufte is perhaps best known for his detailed analysis of how to display data for precise, effective, quick analysis presented in his seminal book *The Visual Display of Quantitative Research*, first published in 1983. He argued that graphics play an important role in the understanding and interpretation of statistical findings. In the most recent edition of his famous text he wrote the following:

> What is to be sought in designs for the display of information is the clear portrayal of complexity. Not the complication of the simple; rather the task of the designer is to give visual access to the subtle and difficult—that is, the revelation of the complex. (Tufte, 2001, p. 191).

As visualization has been used as part of scientific reasoning, it is often seen as merely another analytical tool for sense making (Viégas & Wattenberg, 2009). In recent years, the availability of online data sources has led to a number of new means to engage in information visualization. These include free online programs such as Many Eyes, Phrase Nets, and Wordle (Feinberg, 2010)—which we have used in this book (van Ham, Wattenberg, & Viégas, 2009; Viégas & Wattenberg, 2009; Viégas, Wattenberg, van Ham, Kriss, & McKeon, 2007). Providing a more accessible means to visualize quantified online data is laudable, but there may be other ways, approaches, and purposes that should be considered. As Johanna Drucker (2009) has noted, for some researchers it is imperative to develop models of knowledge for the digital age that provide a means to capture data that are freely "given" by participants rather than focus solely on presenting data "taken" by researchers.

Although differences among approaches exist, a good starting place is the idea that the bulk of what a researcher does is an attempt to derive meaning from data, requiring the recognition of patterns (Miles & Huberman, 1994). Graphic knowledge representation tools can be especially useful in illuminating this process. This book focuses on concept maps, mind maps, and Vee heuristic diagrams to provide a "window on the mind" (Shavelson, Ruiz-Primo, & Wiley, 2005). We present maps as a distinctive means with which to gather data and facilitate a deeper appreciation of the research process, with the goal of improving teaching, learning, and overall understanding (Entwistle, 2009). To understand the value and potential of maps in social science research, it is important to first appreciate the different aspects of the research process itself.

UNDERSTANDING THE RESEARCH PROCESS

Unlike natural science research, social science research attempts to measure what some consider intangibles. These include perceptions, behaviors, emotions, and/or personalities. It is important to understand that whereas approaches to social science research vary by discipline and approach, all consider in one way or another to what extent we truly are capturing what we say we are capturing. Discussed in detail in later chapters, *reliability* considers the consistency of one's approach to measurement, whereas *validity* involves assessing its accuracy and the conclusions we can draw as a result. These apply in different ways to quantitative and qualitative approaches to research and have traditionally been seen as separate and distinct elements of a research project. It may be useful to see them as integral parts of the research process as a whole (Teddlie & Tashakkori, 2009). For now, let's concentrate on understanding the research process by breaking it into key decisions or elements that inform and affect all research. These include the theoretical perspective, epistemology, methodology, and data collection (Crotty, 1998, pp. 2–3) (see Figure 1.2).

The four elements below are at the heart of the underlying assumptions and differences among researchers from different disciplines. In general, the *theoretical perspective* is the philosophical stance that provides the research context and informs the rest of the process. *Epistemology* refers to the theory of knowledge embedded in the theoretical perspective and attempts to answer questions such as, What is knowledge? How is knowledge acquired? and How do we know what we know? Discussed below, these two concepts might usefully be considered together. Of further practical concern for researchers is the *methodology*—the design, strategy, or plan of action—required to gather and analyze data. This in turn directly affects *data collection,* which refers to the specific methods, techniques, or procedures that you will use to collect or gather data related to a research area, question, or hypothesis. Methodology and data collection can also be usefully discussed together.

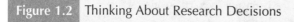

Figure 1.2 Thinking About Research Decisions

Common Theoretical and Epistemological Starting Points

Different approaches to research are based on disparate theories about how people understand reality and develop knowledge about it. Historically, science has relied on the *positivist tradition*. This view held that to establish the truth about the world, knowledge could be quantified and empirically studied through the scientific method. In this view, reality is the same for you as it is for me, and the only research of value focuses on what can be directly observed and measured. In more recent years, many of these assumptions have been revisited through the emergence of *postpositivism* (Slife & Williams, 1995). Unlike positivists, postpositivists see human knowledge as speculative and not based, therefore, on unchallengeable, rock-solid foundations. Influenced by Karl Popper (1968), postpositivists argue that the external world exists independently of an individual's experience of it, and thus human knowledge is always part of a theory, based on general foundations. Although this description is useful to understand how positivism has been updated and revised, some prefer to identify themselves as *critical realists* (Miles & Huberman, 1994). This term refers to the belief that whereas some of our observations of the world are correct, others are not. Regardless of which label is used, however, and in contrast to early assumptions about research, those who value the measurement of social phenomena acknowledge that all research is incomplete in one way or another. For these researchers, the fact that limitations exist should not exclude testing and revising tentative, preliminary, and working theories about the world using the scientific method.

The *constructivist* or *interpretive tradition* is skeptical of the idea of one universalistic notion of truth and instead views meaningful realities as contingent on human practices. Thus, reality is socially constructed and can be different for different people, influenced to varying degrees by the cultural, historical, political, and social norms that operate within a specific context (Crotty, 1998). An emergent tradition based on a more *pragmatic approach* rejects either/or approaches to understanding reality and developing knowledge. Through multiple stages and methods of data collection and/ or analysis, researchers can arrive at a better understanding of a phenomenon by combining the reliability of empirical counts with the validity of lived experience.

These approaches in turn influence how researchers view the process of reasoning. *Deductive reasoning* is sometimes described as a top-down process that tests general premises though a series of steps to reach specific conclusions. Associated with positivism or postpositivism, quantitative research seeks generalizability through controlled, value-free (or value-neutral) processes. *Inductive reasoning* is a process that develops general conclusions based on a series of steps that explore specific premises. Sometimes described as a bottom-up approach to research, qualitative research is associated with constructivism or interpretivism and seeks to understand or make sense of the world based on how individuals experience and perceive it. Figure 1.3 provides one way to think about the differences between deductive and inductive reasoning.

Figure 1.3   Comparing Deductive and Inductive Reasoning

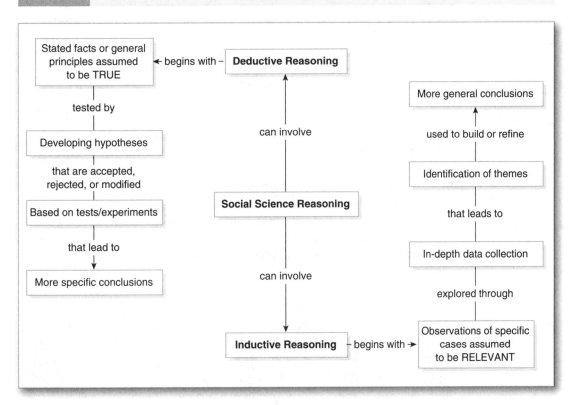

An emergent approach to research is based on *abductive reasoning.* This can be understood as a process that values both deductive and inductive approaches but relies principally on the expertise, experience, and intuition of researchers. Tentative explanations and hypotheses emerge through the research process, and these must be tested theoretically and empirically. Associated with mixed-methods research, through the *intersubjectivity* of researchers and their understanding based on shared meaning, this approach to reasoning encourages the use of both inductive and deductive approaches to research. Mixed methods is perhaps of most interest to a new generation of scholars because it can produce stronger measures of association while allowing that multiple paths to meaning exist. Table 1.1 explores the key issues in social science research.

Table 1.1	Key Issues in Social Science Research		
	Quantitative Approach	Qualitative Approach	Pragmatic Approach
Connection of Theory and Data	Deductive	Inductive	Abductive
Relationship to Research Process	Objectivity	Subjectivity	Intersubjectivity
Inference From Data	Generality	Context	Transferability

Source: Morgan (2007, p. 71).

Methodology and Data Collection

One way to think about the difference between deductive, inductive, and abductive approaches to research is based on their relationship to theory. The deductive approach assumes that researchers are objective and/or value-neutral actors who attempt to draw generalizable conclusions based on cause and effect, the reduction and selection of key variables, and detailed observations and measurement (Creswell & Plano Clark, 2007). *Quantitative methods* can be described as the techniques associated with the gathering, analysis, interpretation, and presentation of numerical information (Teddlie & Tashakkori, 2009, p. 5). Through clearly defined dependent and independent variables, quantitative research relies on *hypothesis testing* to test and validate theories through *falsification,* which requires that one modify or reject certain beliefs based on the integrity and consistency of research findings through a logical investigation. Using deductive approaches to analysis, quantitative studies often begin with a related hypothesis, collect defined categories of data, and objectively analyze the data based on existing assumptions about knowledge. Figure 1.4 provides an example of how these steps are related.

Qualitative methods can be best understood as the gathering, analysis, interpretation, and presentation of narrative information (Teddlie & Tashakkori, 2009, p. 6). Qualitative analysis through inductive reasoning is an approach to analysis that aims to build theory by focusing in more depth on individual cases and context-specific realities. Researchers who use qualitative methods are often dubious about generalization and the neutrality of researchers. Data are collected with the assumption that all knowledge is contextualized and that relationships will become apparent through the subjective analysis of the researchers. Through inductive approaches, qualitative researchers use observational research to observe and record phenomena while acknowledging their own role in the way their analysis unfolded. These studies may include surveys, interviews, or other more detailed ethnographic approaches.

This sort of approach to theory building can be divided into two types. *Classical theory building* is similar to deductive reasoning because it establishes a concept or proposition and then conducts analysis to explore it through the research, as Figure 1.5 presents.

In contrast, *grounded theory building* is a process by which one first collects and analyzes data and, based on the concepts of themes that emerge from those data, attempts to formulate concepts about these relationships. The chief difference between these approaches is how and at what stage researchers identify themes. In traditional approaches, the identification of themes often occurs before data collection. In grounded approaches, themes are identified only after data collection to ensure the researcher keeps an open mind and does not seek to "fit" data into past findings. A visual representation of this approach is presented in Figure 1.6.

Figure 1.4   Testing Theories in Quantitative Research

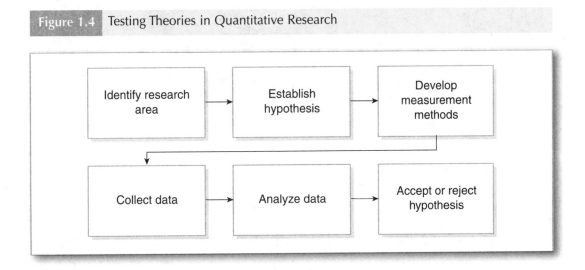

Figure 1.5	Classical Theory Building in Qualitative Research

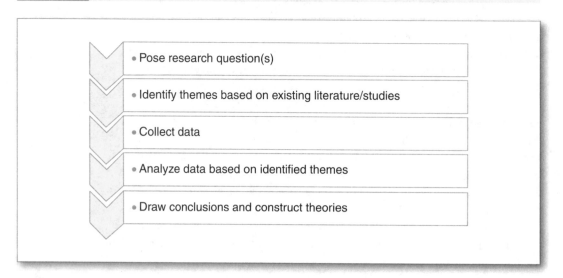

- Pose research question(s)
- Identify themes based on existing literature/studies
- Collect data
- Analyze data based on identified themes
- Draw conclusions and construct theories

Figure 1.6	Grounded Theory Building in Qualitative Research

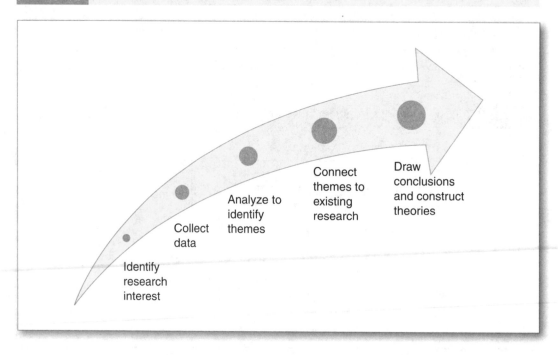

Draw conclusions and construct theories

Connect themes to existing research

Analyze to identify themes

Collect data

Identify research interest

A final methodology is associated with *mixed-methods research.* A central premise is that the use of quantitative and qualitative approaches together can provide a better understanding of a research problem. A variety of types and approaches of mixed-methods research have been defined (Creswell & Plano Clark, 2007). One approach is to use qualitative techniques to develop a theory that can then be tested by establishing a conceptually connected hypothesis and quantitative means with which to test it. Another is to develop a quantifiable means that can test a generated hypothesis and then explore these findings using more qualitative techniques. By using these mixed approaches, research problems can benefit from both qualitative and quantitative approaches to data analysis and the measurement of meaning. Figures 1.7 and 1.8 provide examples of two approaches to mixed-methods research.

Although Figures 1.7 and 1.8 provide examples of how mixed-methods research can be attempted, both conceptual and practical challenges remain. Indeed, no matter which approach to research one takes, each has associated strengths and weaknesses. The question is not which kind of research is better but instead which type of approach is best suited to the kind of research problem under investigation. A key element in this initial stage of research is planning. Maps can be a useful way to see which steps may be involved to complete a research project. This is discussed in more detail in Chapter 5.

Figure 1.7 Quantitatively Testing Qualitative Findings

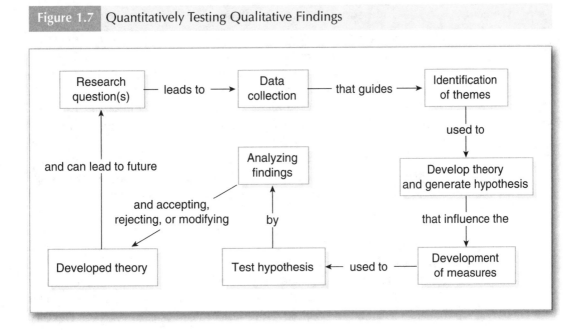

Figure 1.8   Qualitatively Validating Quantitative Findings

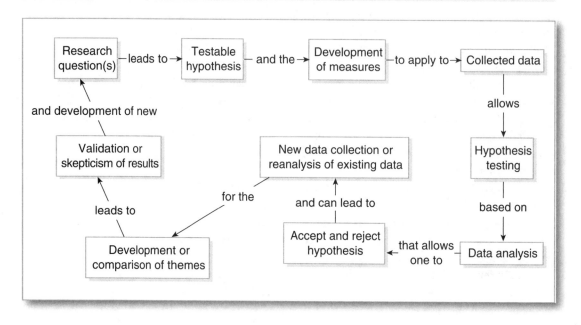

A RESEARCH EXAMPLE

Throughout this book, we will offer research examples to assist you to see the steps involved in research and present practical examples about how maps can be used. In our first example, we consider the question of how one's approach to a research question shapes subsequent decisions. Based on work by Darlaston-Jones (2007), this research example provides an accessible and practical topic about research itself. Its specific value is based on how it demonstrates different ways one might study this topic.

Suppose one wanted to know why some university students complete their undergraduate degrees and others do not. There are a variety of approaches one could take to investigate this phenomenon. Starting from a postpositivist epistemological basis, one might assume that reality is the same for all of us. Thus, students with similar backgrounds or features (age, gender, ethnicity, financial resources) would be equally motivated to complete their degrees. Using a quantitative approach, a researcher might look to existing literature about university retention, develop a hypothesis based on the literature, and set about testing it. For example, by tracking all students over the course of their degrees, one could compare university status (graduated, enrolled, withdrawn) with various demographic data (age, ethnicity, gender, financial resources) to draw general conclusions as to which demographic factors are relevant in explaining and predicting undergraduate degree completion.

On the other hand, starting from an interpretive or constructionist epistemological basis, one might assume that how we perceive reality is contingent on our prior experiences. Thus, depending on how we have been socialized, "university" as a concept may mean very different things to students who otherwise share common demographic features. Consider the student being pressured into a course of study by her university professor parents. She may resent the university and, despite having financial support, may prefer meeting new friends at the local watering hole rather than wrestling with her Introduction to Psychology textbook. On the other hand, consider the student who is the first in her family to attend postsecondary school. She may have fewer means than her bar-hopping colleague but have free reign to find a degree program that is meaningful to her. For qualitative researchers, it is stories and dynamics like these that can lead to deeper meaning about why some students complete degrees and others do not. Although two students of identical age and gender might have completed high school the year before university, their desire to complete their degrees may be completely different. Through in-depth interviews with some students about their university experience and their motivations for completing their degrees, one can understand in a personal way the *how* or *why* around retention rates among undergraduate students.

Because each approach starts from different assumptions about the world, it values and thus seeks different types of data and approaches to investigating this research problem. As a result, neither is a complete account, and thus both are limited. On the one hand, quantitative approaches may miss the nuance of real people's lived experience, their motivations, and their desires, whereas on the other hand, qualitative approaches can tell us about the experiences of only the few individuals interviewed and, by failing to account for larger trends, may miss the forest for the trees. The most compelling strategy may well be a mixed approach. For example, in this scenario, quantitative analysis might show us that men from low-income backgrounds are dropping out of their majors at much higher rates than other subgroups of students. Through qualitative interviews with students in this subgroup, challenges and constraints might usefully be identified. In this way, researchers can get a sense of the *what* along with an understanding of the *why*.

EXERCISE 1.1
Mapping Issues Around College Completion

Based on Figures 1.4- through 1.8, develop two maps that demonstrate how you could approach this research example using a step-by-step approach.

VISUALIZING HOW TO PLAN A RESEARCH PROJECT

Although the above discussion provides a useful conceptual means to understanding the steps one might take to investigate research questions, it may be helpful to link these elements to an actual research project in your field. Organizing your research visually provides a means with which to plan the various aspects of a research project and contemplate which steps are required to conduct a research project. As this chapter has demonstrated, how we plan and conduct research depends to a large extent on the assumptions people make about knowledge, research, and the role of the researcher. Maps, graphs, and diagrams can play a very useful role in assisting researchers to plan their research. Figure 1.9 provides an example of how a mind map can be used to see the elements required to complete a research project. A *mind map* (Buzan, 1974) is a flexible means to show the connections between different ideas within a singular topic.

As another example, Figure 1.10 presents a more complex example of how concept maps can be used to describe the process used in a research project on adult students in higher education (Daley, 2004). A *concept map* (Novak, 1981) is a formal, structured diagram showing relationships among a number of unique concepts. This example clearly demonstrates how the researcher sought to connect existing theory and studies to a research process that involved concept maps.

Figure 1.9 Eight Elements to Consider in a Research Project

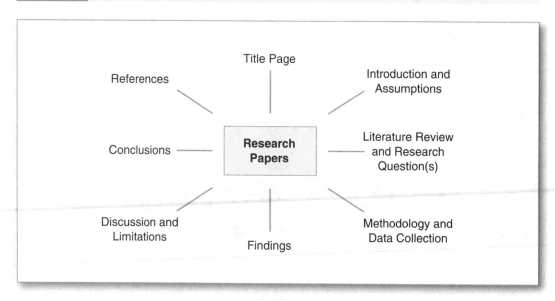

Figure 1.10   Mapping the Scholarship: Understanding Adult Students in Higher Education

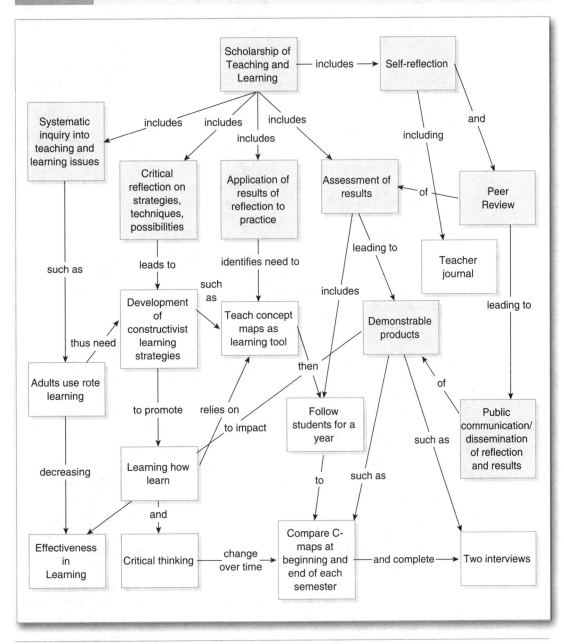

Source: Daley (2004).

Note: C-maps = concept maps.

THE ORGANIZATION OF THIS BOOK

The approach taken in the remainder of this book is to provide both a theoretical justification and practical examples for the use of maps, graphs, and diagrams in social science research. Sometimes the description of a book's organization is placed within the preface and is not used to its full potential. We believe understanding how a book is organized will make it more accessible for readers and have included an overview below. As you have seen, Chapter 1 considers the complexity and numerous choices researchers face when conducting research. We have presented visualizing the research approach as a useful strategy to plan, better understand, and demonstrate the choices you might make.

In the second chapter, the two main varieties of maps used in this book are presented. Through a definition of concept maps and mind maps alongside a discussion of their theoretical bases, these approaches are presented as useful means of data collection in social science research. The third chapter presents more traditional uses of concept maps (Novak, 1981) and evaluates more deeply the assumptions made by quantitative researchers and the value placed on theory testing, generalizability, and repeatability. Used for decades, concept maps can provide data that allow for the measurement and analysis of levels, hierarchies, and relationships. Researchers can use quantitative techniques to count concepts and propositions and can score concept maps based on existing models, scales, and methods.

The fourth chapter explores the utility of mind maps (Buzan, 1974) to the value placed on theory creation, depth of understanding, and the role of the researcher in qualitative research. As mind maps are user generated and more flexible than concept maps, they may be better suited to qualitative research. Maps can provide useful data about how individuals perceive, understand, or remember certain experiences. They can prime the pump of participant reflection and be used alongside other, more traditional, qualitative data-collection techniques. Finally, based on data within the maps, researchers can create more detailed and relevant interview questions relating to how participants created their maps.

The fifth chapter considers the limitations of quantitative or qualitative research and considers how (and indeed, whether) mixed-methods approaches can address these limitations. By relying on the strengths of each method together, mixed methods can provide a more detailed understanding of what research data are suggesting. Using research examples involving concept maps and mind maps, mixed-methods approaches to research are presented and considered. By providing a flexible means both to count concepts generated through more unsolicited data-collection means and to understand how individuals constructed and presented their experience through maps, they offer a logical tool to be used along with other approaches in multimethod, multistage data collection.

The sixth chapter presents how maps can be used to help you write up your research project based on key headings and subheadings, including Research Focus, Literature Review, Methodology, Data Collection, Data Analysis, Results and Discussion, Limitations, and Conclusions. Although approaches will vary by your discipline, class, and research project, most research papers address the above elements. In this chapter, approaches, tips, and strategies to writing up your research project are presented.

Finally, Chapter 7 explores some of the limitations associated with concept maps and mind maps, including both conceptual and practical difficulties encountered. In this chapter we consider questions of reliability and validity as well as new approaches to understanding research inferences. In addition, this chapter outlines two new directions in social science research, including evidence-based research through systematic review and participatory action research models. Applied to criminal justice policy and education, maps offer new ways to capture data and validate existing findings. By suggesting ways that maps can be used in each of these emergent research areas, this chapter presents a tentative integrated action research model that combines the strengths of quantitative systematic review with qualitative participatory action models. This chapter concludes by suggesting that the best way for the use of maps to continue to grow in the social sciences is through their increased use by students, researchers, and community members.

STUDENT ACTIVITY

With the assistance of your instructor, find a recent study in your field. Using the approach used in either Figure 1.8 or Figure 1.9, create a similar map based on how the researcher(s) approached the study. As you read the study, map out the relevant sections based on the elements provided. These might include the research area, literature review, methodology, and so on. Consider how the structure of the paper helps the author to present his or her ideas.

CONCLUSION

Social science research can seem daunting and complex. One way to break it down is to visualize the concepts, processes, and requirements of conducting research. In many ways, research might best be seen as a series of choices researchers face. Visualizing the approach you wish to take to investigate a phenomenon or issue can be a useful strategy, and mapping your research plan can assist your readers to understand the choices you have made. Through this acknowledgment, you demonstrate your understanding of the complexities of research and remain humble.

This chapter has provided an overview of the research process and has presented some examples of how visualizing research may be useful to see the connections between theory and practice, epistemology and methodology. It has also provided some concrete examples of how mapping your research can help when planning and conducting research.

REVIEW

1. Define social science research. Why is it useful to describe research as a series of decisions? What are the consequences of these decisions, and why do they require an acknowledgment of research limitations?

2. How can visualizing social science research be useful for students, instructors, and researchers?

3. Present and define the four major components of social science research.

4. Explain how the research processes vary between quantitative, qualitative, and mixed-methods research.

5. What are the eight major elements of a social science research paper?

SUGGESTED ADDITIONAL READINGS

Crotty, M. (1998). *The foundations of social research: Meaning and perspective in the research process.* London: Sage.

Firebaugh, G. (2008). *Seven rules for social research.* Princeton, NJ: Princeton University Press.

Palys, T. (1992). *Research decisions: Quantitative and qualitative perspectives.* Toronto: Thompson Canada.

REFERENCES

Åhlberg, M. (2008, September 22–25). *Concept mapping as an innovation: Documents, memories and notes from Finland, Sweden, Estonia and Russia 1984–2008.* Paper presented at the Third International Conference on Concept Mapping, Tallinn, Estonia, and Helsinki, Finland.

Alvarez, M. C., & Gowin, B. D. (2009). *The little book: Conceptual elements of research.* Lanham, MD: Rowman & Littlefield Education.

Banks, M. (2001). *Visual methods in social research.* London: Sage.

Blagg, N. (1991). *Can we teach intelligence?* Hillsdale, NJ: Lawrence Erlbaum.

Buzan, T. (1974). *Use of your head.* London: BBC Books.

Creswell, J. W., & Plano Clark, V. L. (2007). *Designing and conducting mixed methods research.* Thousand Oaks, CA: Sage.

Crotty, M. (1998). *The foundations of social research: Meaning and perspective in the research process.* London: Sage.

Daley, B. (2004, September 14–17). *Using concept maps in qualitative research.* Paper presented at the First International Conference on Concept Mapping, Pamplona, Spain.

Dansereau, D., Sells, S. B., & Simpson, D. D. (1979). Evaluation of treatment for youth in the Drug Abuse Reporting Program. In G. Beschner & A. S. Friedman (Eds.), *Youth drug abuse: Problems, issues, and treatments* (pp. 571–628). Lexington, MA: Lexington Books.

Darlaston-Jones, D. (2007). Making connections: The relationship between epistemology and research methods. *Australian Community Psychologist, 91*(1), 19–27.

Drucker, J. (2009). *SpecLab: Digital aesthetics and speculative computing.* Chicago: University of Chicago Press.

Entwistle, N. (2009). *Teaching for understanding at university: Deep approaches and distinctive ways of thinking.* New York: Palgrave Macmillan.

Feinberg, J. (2010). *Wordle.* Retrieved July 28, 2010, from http://www.wordle.net/

Firebaugh, G. (2008). *Seven rules for social research.* Princeton, NJ: Princeton University Press.

Gowin, D. B. (1981). *Educating.* Ithaca, NY: Cornell University Press.

Hanf, M. B. (1971). Mapping: A technique for translating reading into thinking. *Journal of Reading, 14,* 225–230.

Kaplan, A. (1964). *The conduct of inquiry: Methodology for behavioral science.* San Francisco, CA: Chandler Press.

LeGates, R. (2004). Using spatial data visualization to motivate undergraduate social science students. In *Invention and impact: Building excellence in undergraduate science, technology, engineering and mathematics education* (pp. 129–134). Washington, DC: American Academy for the Advancement of Science.

Miles, M. B., & Huberman, M. A. (1994). *Qualitative data analysis: An expanded sourcebook* (2nd ed.). Newbury Park, CA: Sage.

Mintzes, J., Wandersee, J., & Novak, J. D. (1998). *Teaching science for understanding.* San Diego, CA: Academic Press.

Morgan, D. L. (2007). Paradigms lost and pragmatism regained: Methodological implications of combining qualitative and quantitative methods. *Journal of Mixed Methods Research, 1*(1), 48–76.

Novak, J. D. (1981). Applying learning psychology and philosophy of science to biology teaching. *American Biology Teacher, 43*(1), 12–20.

Palys, T. (1992). *Research decisions: Quantitative and qualitative perspectives* (3rd ed.). Toronto: Thompson Canada.

Popper, K. R. (1968). *Conjectures and refutations: The growth of scientific knowledge.* New York: Harper Torch Books.

Rico, G. L. (1983). *Writing the natural way: Using right-brain techniques to release your expressive powers.* New York: Penguin Putnam.

Shavelson, R. J. (2010). *Measuring college learning responsibly: Accountability in a new era.* Stanford, CA: Stanford University Press.

Shavelson, R. J., Ruiz-Primo, M. A., & Wiley, E. W. (2005). Windows into the mind. *Higher Education: The International Journal of Higher Education and Educational Planning, 49*(4), 413–430.

Slife, B. D., & Williams, R. N. (1995). *What's behind the research? Discovering hidden assumptions in the behavioral sciences.* Thousand Oaks, CA: Sage.

Teddlie, C. B., & Tashakkori, A. (2009). *Foundations of mixed methods research: Integrating quantitative and qualitative approaches in the social and behavioral sciences.* Thousand Oaks, CA: Sage

Tufte, E. (2001). *The visual display of quantitative information* (2nd ed.). Chesire, CT: Graphics Press.

Tukey, J. W. (1977). *Exploratory data analysis.* Reading, MA: Addison-Wesley.

van Ham, F., Wattenberg, M., & Viégas, F. B. (2009, October 11–16). *Mapping text with phrase nets.* Paper presented at the IEEE Information Visualization Conference, Atlantic City, NJ.

Viégas, F. B., & Wattenberg, M. (2009, October 11–16). *Artistic data visualization: Beyond visual analytics.* Paper presented at the IEEE Information Visualization Conference, Atlantic City, NJ.

Viégas, F. B., Wattenberg, M., van Ham, F., Kriss, J., & McKeon, M. (2007, October 28–November 1). *Many eyes: A site for visualization at Internet scale.* Paper presented at the IEEE Information Visualization Conference, Sacramento, CA.

2

Concept Maps and Mind Maps

Theory, Definitions, and Approaches

As we saw in Chapter 1, concept maps and mind maps are visual tools that can assist students, instructors, and researchers to understand, present, and frame research. Maps offer other benefits as well. In this chapter, we provide a history of concept maps and mind maps and explore their use in social science research. Defined and coherently developed in the 1970s, maps offer a means to represent experience and can help researchers to explore meaning. To understand how, this chapter focuses on theories of how people learn, considers new cognitive developments surrounding education and pedagogy, and presents maps as a means to help students better engage abstract concepts.

This chapter also introduces the similarities and differences between concept maps and mind maps in more detail. Concept maps provide a more structured approach to explore connections among concepts, using linking words to present clear propositions. By contrast, mind maps are more flexible tools in which a central governing construct is explored using groupings and/or branches. Finally, in this chapter we also consider different approaches to gathering data in the social sciences and how these differences are based on the epistemological assumptions discussed in Chapter 1. Although there are a variety of ways to collect social science data, we think maps offer another useful approach. We suggest that different kinds of maps may be more or less appropriate depending on the kind of research issue under consideration. By the end of the chapter, readers should be able to do the following:

- compare and contrast concept maps and mind maps;
- situate maps historically, theoretically, and practically;
- contemplate research situations for which each approach is best suited;
- explain how visual representations of experience or perception are different from verbal or written data-collection strategies; and
- provide an example of how each map could be used to gather data.

A SHORT HISTORY OF CONCEPT MAPS AND MIND MAPS

Maps that demonstrate visual representations of understanding are by no means new. The use of labeled pictures goes back to medieval times and so-called *mappa mundi,* or early European maps of the world. These maps ranged in size and complexity from simple, small, schematic maps to elaborate wall maps, and they were meant to illustrate different principles as they were understood at the time. Used to remember, to teach, and to learn new ideas, maps included a range of foci including features of distant lands, history, mythology, plants, and animals. As such, early maps represent a unique view into medieval knowledge (Barber, 2005). Maps were used as far back as the third century (Sowa, 2000) to provide a graphic means to represent knowledge structures in philosophy. However, it was only in the 1940s that a renewed interest in diagrams and maps emerged.

In psychology, Edward Tolman first used maps to develop a theory of learning. Based on a number of experiments using rats in a maze, Tolman suggested that we learn by trial and error. When we are successful, we remember the event and create cognitive maps of the places, circumstances, or contexts (Tolman, 1948). Applied in psychology, cognitive maps consider an individual's point of view or how he or she perceives the world. Maps were later applied as visual tools for representing logical concepts and in mathematics (Gardner, 1958). The application of maps to the emergent world of electronics resulted in the development of semantic networks. Used to assist in the development of early computers, semantic networks are a graphic notation for the representation of knowledge based on interconnected nodes and arcs. During the next decade, a variety of semantic networks were developed (Ceccato, 1961; Masterman, 1957; Quillian, 1967) and used in early machine-based linguistic translation systems and to assist in the development of artificial intelligence. Semantic networks continue to be explored as a means to use computers to better sort data, make connections, and organize available information. They are often discussed in relation to the future of the Internet (Berners-Lee, Hendler, & Lassila, 2001).

Maps and diagrams were integral in the development of information and communication technology, but by the 1970s the utility of maps was being considered in other contexts. Like the mappa mundi of old, mental maps are today often associated with geography and consider how people conceive of the geographical world around them (Gould & White, 1974). Mental maps often focus on spatial awareness and have been applied to practical issues such as driving directions, the way we view where we live, and people's recall of the physical features around them (Aberley, 1993). Maps may provide a window on how the mind's eye uses visual images to reduce cognitive load and enhance both recall and the absorption of information. Although all maps provide a means to make invisible internal maps of understanding apparent, in this book we are specifically interested in concept maps and mind maps. Based on a variety of research in the social sciences, concept maps and mind maps can be used to focus on the meaning an individual associates with a topic or idea. Both are visual representations of experience, knowledge, perception, or memories, but important differences exist between them. These are related to the way the maps are structured, what they may represent, and the ways in which their meaning might be interpreted. Let's take a closer look.

Understanding Concept Maps

A *concept map* can be defined as a graphical tool for organizing and representing knowledge. First presented by Novak (1981), this approach was usefully expanded and developed in the seminal book *Learning How to Learn* (Novak & Gowin, 1984). Concept maps include unique concepts, usually enclosed in circles or boxes. Lines and linking words between concepts suggest hierarchical relationships through clear propositions, as presented in Figure 2.1.

Joseph Novak developed concept mapping in the 1970s and remains the central authority on the utility of maps, concept mapping techniques, and analysis. Originally designed as a means to assist people to produce patterns of how they organized and structured their thoughts (Novak, 1981), concept maps were later developed into metacognitive tools for learning and teaching (Novak, 1990, 1998). Traditionally, concept maps required hierarchically labeled nodes denoting concepts and links demonstrating how independent concepts are linked to form meaningful propositions and claims about the map's theme (Åhlberg, 1993, 2004). The use of concept maps is most common in quantitative research, based on the idea that concepts and propositions are basic elements or building blocks of our learning and thinking. Studies that use concept maps often calculate the number of relevant concepts and relevant propositions within them.

Figure 2.1 A Simple Concept Map

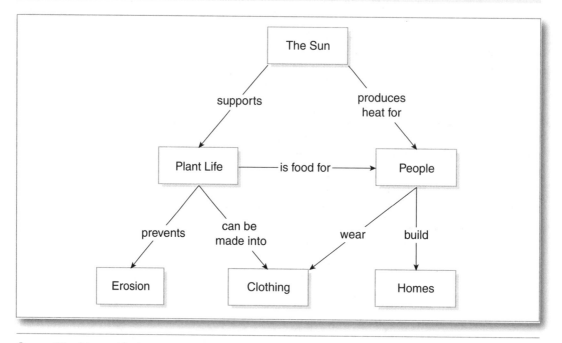

Source: Wheeldon and Faubert (2009, p. 70).

As we shall see in Chapter 3, concept maps can provide data that allow the measurement and analysis of levels, hierarchies, and relationships. Quantitative researchers may use maps to count and analyze data presented through created maps using existing scales, models, and measures.

Exploring Mind Maps

A *mind map,* by contrast, is a diagram used to represent words, themes, tasks, or other items linked to and arranged around a central key word or idea. First described by Buzan in 1974, they were further defined and developed during the next decade. Mind maps are structurally more flexible and often less formal than concept maps. They offer a means to represent different associations between a central theme and key words. They may include the use of images, pictures, colors, or bolded lines (Buzan & Buzan, 1996). A key focus in mind maps is that they represent an individual's personal style and can therefore be unique. Qualitative researchers may use mind maps as a

Figure 2.2   Some Uses of Mind Maps

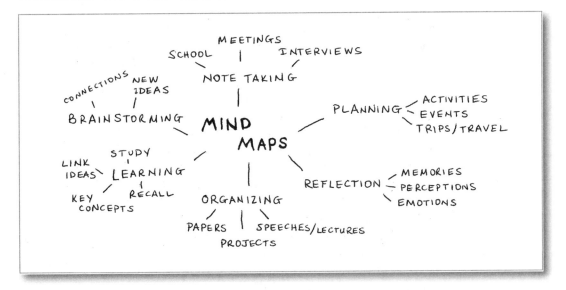

means to gather unique, personal, and user-generated data to explore perceived relationships and unfiltered associations. Figure 2.2 provides a mind map of some of the uses of mind maps, beginning with a central idea and building outward.

Interest in the use of maps in social science research is clearly increasing. Nesbit and Adescope (2006) discovered that more than 500 peer-reviewed articles in the field of education and psychology have been published on the application of concept or knowledge maps. Although most of these publications came after 1997 (Nesbit & Adescope, 2006, p. 413), in recent years debates have emerged about what is and what is not a concept map (Åhlberg & Ahoranta, 2004) or a mind map (Buzan & Buzan, 2010). For example, Nesbit and Adescope (2006) referred to concept, knowledge, and mind maps as though they were interchangeable in their otherwise useful literature review. This definitional flexibility has arguably facilitated the wider use of maps; however, there has been push-back as one of the most well-known researchers in the field continues to promote the stricter definition of a concept map (Novak & Cañas, 2008). Whichever approach to mapping one chooses to use, it is important to recognize that all approaches share similar theoretical considerations. Åhlberg (1993, 2008a) provided a more detailed account of some of the theoretical comparisons of what he called different kinds of "graphic knowledge representation tools."

MAPS AND COMMON THEORETICAL STARTING POINTS

In general terms, mapping knowledge is a technique that can demonstrate how people visualize relationships between various concepts. Whether one calls the maps knowledge maps, mind maps, concept maps, spider maps or cognitive maps, they can be said to provide a visual representation of dynamic schemes of understanding that exist within the human mind (Mls, 2004). Åhlberg (1993, 2008b) has suggested these tools could be usefully combined and called "external graphic knowledge representation tools." Although this would be a useful definitional development, for now let's consider how to understand the justification for the use of maps in social science research. This might be usefully explored by weaving together a number of theoretical strands.

The cerebral cortex in the brain is responsible for abstract thinking and complex cognitive activity (Bowsher, 1973; Luria, 1996). To use the full power of the brain, maps use a combination of words, graphics, and images to represent meaning. In this way, the brain works more effectively by integrating and linking concepts in new and different ways (Buzan, 1997). This view is based on a modern understanding of cognitive science (Murphy, 2002; Thagard, 2010) in which concepts are seen as having distinct criteria. Meaningful understanding requires a determination about which objects belong together and which do not. Concepts are often part of a network and can be combined with other concepts and/or examples to show interrelationships and connections. Yet the same concept can be verbally expressed differently by different people, in different situations, and in different languages. Data gathering that does not consider this aspect of language may be inherently limited and based on assumptions that researchers and participants share similar understandings of the terms, concepts, or constructions under investigation. What should we make of these sorts of challenges?

Cognitive theories of learning are concerned with processes that occur inside the brain and nervous system as a person learns. They share the perspective that people actively process information and learning takes place through the efforts of the learner. Internal mental processes include gathering, organizing, storing, retrieving, and finding relationships between information. New information is linked to old knowledge, and greater understanding results. *Gestalt learning theories* view perception, insight, and problem solving as key processes in learning. Individuals are seen as perceptive; they organize, interpret, and give meaning to the events in their lives. In short, the learner makes sense of things by thinking about them. Although cognitive theories are quite diverse, they are unified by the desire to focus on people's internal mental processes as the site of learning.

One starting place is the work of Alfred Korzybski. His theory of general semantics argued that individuals think more clearly and effectively if they can avoid the assumptions and inherent limitations built into language (Korzybski, 1933). Although this may be difficult or perhaps impossible given the interplay between thinking, concepts, and language (Åhlberg, 1993), it is possible to promote activities and approaches that avoid, challenge, or revise unnecessary assumptions. This observation appears connected to the cognitive theories of Jerome Bruner and Ulric Neisser. Bruner's (1960) work on categorization and concept formation provides models of how the learner derives information from the environment. Bruner's theoretical framework is based on the theme that learners construct new ideas or concepts derived from existing knowledge. Bruner suggested that learning is an active process, and his theories emphasize the significance of categorization in learning. By recognizing that interpreting information and experiences is predicated on a search for new information based on understanding similarities and differences between concepts, Neisser (1976) presented a good model demonstrating how people continually create, test, and improve their internal maps of the world around them.

David Ausubel (1963) was also interested in the way people integrate information from their environment into their own understanding of the world. Like Bruner, Ausubel built on the early work of Piaget, who suggested that children recognize patterns in the world and symbols for what they perceive (McNamara, 1982). Yet for Ausubel, new learning is often heavily mediated by language and takes place primarily through a receptive learning process in which new meanings are obtained by asking questions and receiving clarification through verbal interactions (Novak & Cañas, 2008). Yet the focus on verbal interactions and the social aspects of learning—although useful in learning social norms and customs (Akers, 1998)—may undermine more autonomous learning processes. Indeed, these types of interaction often mean that individual human experience gets filtered and mediated by linguistic constructions (Whorf, 1956). More accurately, it might be said that our concepts are like lenses, or perhaps nets, through which we see the world around us while we gather new information (Åhlberg, 1993). For example, it is widely accepted that the way in which teachers use language affects how concepts are transmitted to students. By developing an awareness of the multiple ways in which understanding exists beyond mere linguistic processes, we can become more autonomous, flexible, and reflexive individuals (Freire, 2000). In education, this has led to the impression that instead of focusing on learning through rote memorization (Bloom, 1956; Holden, 1992), meaningful learning requires an interaction between the individual and the material and an acknowledgment of the role of prior knowledge.

For data collection in social science research, this may mean that maps in their various forms offer a means to break out of conventional representations of experience through language. This view is based on the acknowledgment that people learn in different ways and think using a combination of words, graphics, and images. It avoids the sole reliance on data collection based on psycholinguistic assumptions about the meaning of syntax, semantics, and context (Cassirer, 1946). People live their lives both in their own heads and as part of a social, cultural, and linguistic collective

(Habermas, 1976). If consciousness is a combination of individualized experiences and those based on interactions with others (Husserl, 1970), maps may provide one strategy for breaking out of conventional and linguistically limited representations of experience, rehearsed narratives, and canned responses (Hathaway & Atkinson, 2003). In this way, maps may be able to assist people to access other kinds of information, connections, and relationships often ignored through more verbal or written means of data collection (Legard, Keegan, & Ward, 2003).

EXERCISE 2.1
The Revenge of Theory

Read through the Maps and Common Theoretical Starting Points section again. Make a concept map or mind map that demonstrates how the theories and approaches discussed provide a justification for the use of maps in social science research.

MAPS AND ENGAGEMENT

Using maps in social science research can help to bridge some of the inherent challenges faced by students. Based on the work of Swedish cognitive scientist Peter Gärdenfors (2010), there are four perspectives on learning (see Table 2.1). Each can be connected to the kind of learning that occurs and the pedagogical method that often results.

Table 2.1   Basic Perspectives in Learning

Perspective	Form of Knowledge	Learning Method
Students who do	Know how	Imitate
Students who know	Know that	Acquire facts
Students who think	Know why	Construct new knowledge
Students who research	Know how to know	Manage their own learning

Source: Gärdenfors (2010, p. 121).

Using this framework, in early stages of development, students learn how to do something by imitating others around them. Later, students begin to know things about the world by acquiring facts and comparing and contrasting existing knowledge presented to them. As students' cognitive abilities grow, they begin to think for themselves and understand why the world operates as it does through the construction of new knowledge. Finally, students who learn how to research begin to know how to manage their own learning by applying and challenging existing knowledge and their own past beliefs. One approach to understanding how maps can help students move through these learning methods is to consider the work of Paulo Freire. Identified with more critical approaches to education, Freire (2000) argued that true education encourages individuals to take responsibility for their own potential. By thinking critically about the ways in which our past experience informs our current way of thinking, new kinds of personal connections can be made. Although this involves exposing people to different experiences more generally, the research process can be used to challenge their own preconceptions, beliefs, and assumptions. Seen in this way, the purpose of education is to create autonomous persons who engage in a project of emancipation, reflection, and evaluation.

We believe engaging in research may be the best way to approach systematic thinking, to understand your own approach to knowledge, and to achieve academic success. There may be other benefits as well. Learning to visualize the concepts, processes, and requirements of research may also help us to understand how the choices we make are connected to our relationship with the environment, our health, and the role of wealth. In one way or another, these choices are often connected to our attainment of a meaningful life. By providing a visual record of how you understand a topic at one moment in time, maps allow a means to capture understanding in the short term. They can also assist in longer term reflection, reconsideration, and more meaningful learning.

MAPS, DIFFERENCES, AND APPROACHES TO RESEARCH

Maps share a common theoretical basis, but their development has been characterized by a wide variety of approaches (Åhlberg, 1993, 2008b). Despite this variety, as Alkahtani (2009) pointed out, too often the term *concept map* is used as a blanket term for mind maps, knowledge maps, and other sorts of graphic/visual organizers. Although similar in many ways, there are important differences between different sorts of maps. Figure 2.3 provides a means to understand some differences between concept maps and mind maps.

Figure 2.3   Differences Between Concept Maps and Mind Maps

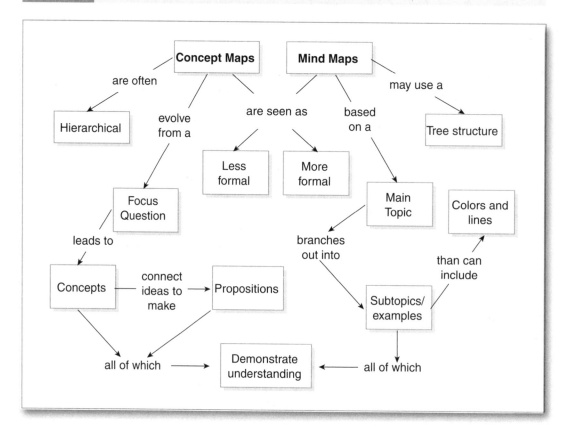

As Figure 2.3 illustrates, there are a number of important differences between concept maps and mind maps. Traditionally, concept maps were organized hierarchically, with the most important terms on the top and less important terms underneath. As we shall see in Chapter 3, this view is based on assumptions about knowledge construction and has since been qualified in a number of important ways. However, most authors who work with concept maps do require that maps include linked concepts that form clear propositions or meaningful phrases. In contrast, mind maps have the potential to be far more creative. As we shall discuss in Chapter 4, mind maps are often less formal, do not require linking phrases, and generally focus on one topic at a time. They may use color, graphics, bold lines, or other, less conventional techniques in the creation of very personal maps that reflect their authors' individual views. They often begin in the center of the page with central ideas or themes and radiate out, connecting associations and examples with the central topic on the page. It is the free-form possibilities of mind maps that may be of most interest to qualitative researchers seeking new kinds of data-collection tools.

One way to reflect on the differences between concept maps and mind maps is to consider the kind of research methods employed by researchers who use them. One important distinction relates to quantitative and qualitative approaches to research. Although qualitative researchers have explored the use of concept maps to clarify relationships identified through interviews (Raymond, 1997), concept maps have been most widely used in quantitative research. This may be because earlier versions of concept maps were first used to explore science education (Stewart, Van Kirk, & Rowell, 1979). Today, some require that a number of steps occur in the creation of a "good" concept map. These include the generation of an initial ranked list of concept maps, a hierarchical presentation in the map with general concepts at the top and specific concepts at the bottom, and the use of linking words to show how the various concepts are related (Novak & Cañas, 2008). This often requires some training by researchers to ensure participants understand how to construct a concept map.

Useful explorations of qualitative research using concept maps exist (Daley, 2004); however, one issue for the use of concept maps in qualitative research is the requirement that participants be taught to create them. Collecting data through concept maps that follow strict construction criteria and require a uniform structure may be in line with the quantitative focus on measurements and generalizability, but it is at odds with the qualitative focus on capturing unique, individual perceptions, reflections, and experiences. Thus, instead of ensuring compliance with defined precepts, some qualitative researchers seek data that are grounded in a participant's knowledge and favor techniques that provide as unfiltered a view as possible (Wheeldon & Faubert, 2009). For this reason mind maps may be more appropriate for qualitative research, as discussed in Chapter 4.

Recently, the authors most often associated with different approaches to maps and mapping have attempted to clarify, streamline, and make more consistent what they mean by concept maps (Novak & Cañas, 2008) and mind maps (Buzan & Buzan, 2010). Although we understand the arguments each makes, ultimately we believe these efforts represent an attempt to shut the barn door after the horses are long gone. The contributions of these authors can and should not be underestimated; however, it may be better to favor more flexible approaches to both concept maps and mind maps rather than insist on a uniform standard that favors the perfect over the good. Strict standards may have the effect of rendering these tools impractical and difficult to rely on in real research situations (Wheeldon & Faubert, 2009). This text builds on more flexible approaches to both concept maps and mind maps; it is integral for students and researchers to clarify how they are using each term and to acknowledge the relevant limitations where appropriate. The reliance on greater definitional flexibility is of practical importance to researchers and can allow maps to

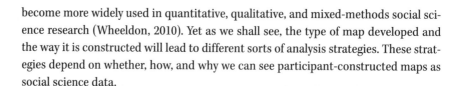

become more widely used in quantitative, qualitative, and mixed-methods social science research (Wheeldon, 2010). Yet as we shall see, the type of map developed and the way it is constructed will lead to different sorts of analysis strategies. These strategies depend on whether, how, and why we can see participant-constructed maps as social science data.

MAPS AS SOCIAL SCIENCE DATA

In later chapters we will explore how different sorts of maps have been used as part of specific research designs, to plan projects, gather data, and present analysis strategies. For now, let's focus on how maps can be used to gather data. Grady (2008) suggested visual data can be understood as any visual objects produced by people who record human doings of one kind or another. Based on our theoretical discussion above, creating concept and mind maps requires people to make decisions about how topics relate to each other. These decisions provide a way to understand how participants view the topic and the nature of the connections between relevant issues, ideas, and concepts. They also allow researchers to see these connections, consider what the organization of these concepts means, and assess the hierarchical and multidimensional levels of different sorts of relationships. In different ways, both concept maps and mind maps offer a means for people to connect different sorts of material into a coherent body of knowledge. Ebener et al. (2006) suggested that

> mapping offers an opportunity to elucidate and assist with analysis of complex processes and hence play a role in knowledge translation. . . . [It] has the advantage of being concrete and tactical . . . [and] makes tacit and explicit knowledge graphic and visual. (pp. 638–640)

Maps have been used to collect data in a variety of ways within social science research (Wheeldon, 2010). Although some suggest visual images enjoy "authority" within social science research (Harper, 1994), for those new to their use, it may be useful to compare them to other forms of data collection. Traditionally, quantitative data are based on instruments that measure individual performance and attitudes or use interview or observational data based on clearly predefined categories. Instruments might include surveys, questionnaires, or achievement tests. In contrast, qualitative data are generally based on themes that emerge through open-ended interactions, such as interviews and observations. Another approach of interest is using data collected from so-called unobtrusive measures, such as the review of documents or other kinds of data that have been created with less involvement by the researcher. Mixed methods might use some or all of these strategies based on the research design and the approach to mixing data analysis that is taken. So, where do concept maps and mind maps fit?

Concept maps might be seen as another approach to testing or perhaps as another means to assess change among research participants. As discussed in Chapter 3, this analogy is not perfect. However, concept maps offer a structured way to gather information from people about how their understanding of a concept changed over time based on predefined terms, concepts, or ideas. Concept maps can be used in other ways to gather data, but it may be useful to see them as a tool that can be used in place of other kinds of pre-/postsurvey instruments. On the other hand, mind maps might best be seen as another example of the move toward more unsolicited approaches to data collection based on unobtrusive measures. Data videotapes, photographs, sound, and even e-mail and text messages are acceptable (Creswell, 2005), but other forms of this approach including vignette- or scenario-based responses, participant-operated cameras/videos/sound recordings, journaling, and visual life history interviews are becoming more popular (Wheeldon & Faubert, 2009). Mind maps might be seen as a new form of visual interview or as another way to conceive of an unobtrusive or perhaps less intrusive measure.

Although nonverbal communications and visual images are equally valid symbolic expressions (Harper, 1994; Weber, 2008), we believe the credible use of maps as social science data depends entirely on how the researcher uses them. As discussed in Chapters 3 and 4, in practical terms this means that the kind of analysis that might result from maps must consider how explicitly directions are given to participants and how involved the researcher becomes in the process of teaching people to make them. As with everything else in social science research, the use of maps is simply one more decision to make. Using maps properly, however, requires an understanding of the research problem, the relative benefits of different kinds of maps, and the recognition of limitations that result. Nevertheless, we believe maps offer a variety of ways to see research, and this visual process can be useful for students, instructors, researchers, and others.

STUDENT ACTIVITY

Professors spend a lot of time designing their lectures and class activities to assist students to learn topics of interest. They hope that their efforts will result in their students' learning that material and retaining that knowledge during their course, throughout their academic careers, and indeed throughout their lives. Suppose you wanted to investigate how well students in your class could recall a lecture provided by your professor. Let us say that your professor were willing to provide you his or her lecture notes and, working together, the class identified 10 important concepts from the lecture or assignment. How might you use maps to investigate student recall of the lecture? Which kind of map(s) would be most appropriate for this research question? Perhaps you are more interested in which elements of the lecture were most valuable for the students in the class. How might you use maps to investigate student perceptions? What kind of map(s) would be most appropriate for each of these research issues?

An interesting class activity is to have your professor divide the class into two groups. Group 1 should investigate student recall of a lecture or activity, and Group 2 should investigate how useful students perceived the lecture or activity to be. Develop some hypotheses about the similarities and differences between Group 1's and Group 2's maps. Do you think they will look the same? Is recall influenced by perception of utility? Does the excellent, fair, or poor level of recall say something about the students in your class, your professor, or both? Do student perceptions of the utility of the lecture vary by age, gender, academic major, or other factors? If you were trying to draw conclusions from this exercise, what limitations might exist?

CONCLUSION

People have made maps since the beginning of civilization for different purposes and to present different things. Concept maps and mind maps should be understood with this history in mind. Like other approaches to mapping, they continue to develop and change based on our practical needs. This chapter has provided a theoretical basis for the use of maps as graphic knowledge representation tools and acknowledged that all maps have important features that make them similar in some ways and very different in others. Although traditional definitions of concept maps require a host of structural elements within maps themselves, they are of great utility in quantitative research because they provide a means to quantify the differences in knowledge or understanding between different groups.

Although concept maps have been used in qualitative research, their more formal and strict requirements may limit their ability to allow participants to express themselves in more individualistic and user-generated ways. As such, mind maps may be better suited to qualitative research as part of new developments in data collection that attempt to privilege the views of participants by collecting data in less obtrusive ways. Whichever approach is used, visual and/or graphic representation of concepts, propositions, and ideas provides an underexplored means to gather data in social science research. Using concept maps offers a means to more fully engage with participants and collect data in more active ways. Mind maps offer the potential to collect data using less obtrusive approaches, allowing individuals to make connections in their own ways based on their unique understandings of the world. This chapter has provided a basis for the general principle that the kind of map you use depends on the kind of research question you explore.

REVIEW

1. Define concept maps and mind maps. How are they similar, and how are they different?

2. Explain some of the theories presented for the use of maps in social science research. Do these explanations make sense to you?

3. How might the differences between concept maps and mind maps be connected to different assumptions within social science research?

4. Why are concept maps best suited to quantitative research? Provide an example of a research situation in which they could be useful.

5. Why are mind maps best suited to qualitative research? Provide an example of a research situation in which they could be useful.

SUGGESTED ADDITIONAL READINGS

Åhlberg, M. (2008, September 22–25). *Concept mapping as an innovation: Documents, memories and notes from Finland, Sweden, Estonia and Russia 1984–2008.* Paper presented at the Third International Conference on Concept Mapping, Tallinn, Estonia, and Helsinki, Finland.

Buzan, T. (1974). *Use of your head.* London: BBC Books.

Nesbit, J. C., & Adescope, O. O. (2006). Learning with concept and knowledge maps: A meta-analysis. *Review of Educational Research, 76*(3), 413–448.

Novak, J. D., & Gowin, J. B. (1984). *Learning how to learn.* Cambridge, UK: Cambridge University Press.

REFERENCES

Aberley, D. (1993). *Boundaries of home: Mapping for local empowerment.* Philadelphia: New Society.

Åhlberg, M. (1993, August 1–5). *Concept maps, Vee diagrams and rhetorical argumentation (RA) analysis: Three educational theory–based tools to facilitate meaningful learning.* Paper presented at the Third International Seminar on Misconceptions in Science and Mathematics, Ithaca, NY.

Åhlberg, M. (2004, September 14–17). Varieties of concept mapping. In A. Cañas, J. Novak, & F. Gonzales (Eds.), *Concept maps: Theory, methodology, technology* (Proceedings of the First International Conference on Concept Mapping, Vol. 2, pp. 25–28). Retrieved from http://cmc.ihmc.us/papers/cmc2004-206.pdf

Åhlberg, M. (2008a, September 22–25). *Concept mapping as an innovation: Documents, memories and notes from Finland, Sweden, Estonia and Russia 1984–2008.* Paper presented at the Third International Conference on Concept Mapping, Tallinn, Estonia, and Helsinki, Finland.

Åhlberg, M. (2008b, October 10–17). *Practical methods and techniques of knowledge representation in particular those related to concept mapping and mind mapping: History, theoretical background, software, and comparison table.* Invited discussion paper presented at the Instructional Technology Forum, Atlanta, GA.

Åhlberg, M., & Ahoranta, V. (2004, September 14–17). *Six years of design experiments.* Paper presented at the First International Conference on Concept Mapping, Pamplona, Spain.

Akers, R. L. (1998). *Social structure and social learning: A general theory of crime and deviance.* Boston: Northeastern University Press.

Alkahtani, K. (2009). *Creativity training effects upon concept map complexity of children with ADHD: An experimental study.* Unpublished doctoral dissertation, University of Glasgow, Scotland.

Ausubel, D. (1963). *The psychology of meaningful verbal learning.* New York: Grune & Stratton.

Barber, P. (2005). *The map book.* London: Walker.

Berners-Lee, T., Hendler, J., & Lassila, O. (2001, May 17). The semantic web. *Scientific American Magazine, 284*(5), 29–37.

Bloom, B. S. (1956). Taxonomy of educational objectives. In B. S. Bloom, M. D. Englehart, E. J. Furst, W. H. Hill, & D. R. Krathwohl (Eds.), *Taxonomy of educational objectives: The classification of educational goals* (Handbook 1, pp. 201–207). New York: McKay.

Bowsher, D. (1973). Brain, behavior and evolution. *Brain, Behavior and Evolution, 8,* 386–396.

Bruner, J. (1960). *The process of education.* Cambridge, MA: Harvard University Press.

Buzan, T. (1974). *Use of your head.* London: BBC Books.

Buzan, T. (1997). *Use your memory.* London: BBC Books.

Buzan, T., & Buzan, B. (1996). *The mind map book: How to use radiant thinking to maximize your brain's untapped potential.* New York: Plume.

Buzan, T., & Buzan, B. (2010). *Mind map book: Unlock your creativity, boost your memory, change your life.* London: Pearson International.

Cassirer, E. (1946). *Language and myth.* New York: Harper & Brothers.

Ceccato, S. (1961). *Linguistic analysis and programming for mechanical translation.* New York: Gordon and Breach.

Creswell, J. W. (2005). *Educational research: Planning, conducting, and evaluating quantitative and qualitative research.* Upper Saddle River, NJ: Pearson.

Daley, B. (2004, September 14–17). *Using concept maps in qualitative research.* Paper presented at the First International Conference on Concept Mapping, Pamplona, Spain.

Ebener, S., Khan, S., Shademani, R., Compernolle, L., Beltran, M., & Lansang, M. (2006). *Knowledge mapping as a technique to support knowledge translation.* Geneva, Switzerland: World Health Organization.

Freire, P. (2000). *Pedagogy of the oppressed.* New York: Continuum International.

Gärdenfors, P. (2010). *Lusten att förstå: Om lärande på människans villkor* [The desire to understand: On learning in a human way]. Stockholm: Natur & Kultur.

Gardner, M. (1958). *Logic machines and diagrams.* New York: McGraw-Hill.

Gould, P., & White, R. (1974). *Mental maps*. London: Penguin.

Grady, J. (2008). Visual research at the crossroads. *Forum: Qualitative Social Research, 9*(3), Article 38.

Habermas, J. (1976). *Communication and the evolution of society*. London: Polity.

Harper, D. (1994). On the authority of image: Visual methods at the crossroads. In N. K. Denzin & Y. S. Lincoln (Eds.), *Handbook of qualitative research* (pp. 379–399). Thousand Oaks, CA: Sage.

Hathaway, A. D., & Atkinson, M. (2003). Active interview tactics in research on public deviants: Exploring the two-cop personas. *Field Methods, 15,* 161–185.

Holden, C. (1992). Study flunks science and math tests. *Science, 26,* 541.

Husserl, E. (1970). *The crisis of European sciences and transcendental phenomenology* (D. Carr, Trans.) Evanston, IL: Northwestern University Press.

Korzybski, A. (1933). *Science and sanity: An introduction to non-Aristotelian systems and general semantics*. Fort Worth, TX: Institute of General Semantics.

Legard, R., Keegan, J., & Ward, K. (2003). In-depth interviews. In J. Ritchie & J. Lewis (Eds.), *Qualitative research practice: A guide for social research students and researchers* (pp. 138–169). Thousand Oaks, CA: Sage.

Luria, A. (1996). *Higher cortical functions in man*. New York: Basic Books.

Masterman, M. M. (1957). The thesaurus in syntax and semantics. *Mechanical Translation, 4*(1/2), 35–43.

McNamara, J. E. (1982). *Technical aspects of data communication* (2nd ed.). Bedford, MA: Digital Press.

Mls, K. (2004, September 14–17). *From concept mapping to qualitative modeling in cognitive research*. Paper presented at the First International Conference on Concept Mapping, Pamplona, Spain.

Murphy, G. L. (2002). *The big book of concepts*. Cambridge, MA: MIT Press.

Neisser, U. (1976). *Cognition and reality: Principles and implications of cognitive psychology*. San Francisco: Freeman.

Nesbit, J. C., & Adescope, O. O. (2006). Learning with concept and knowledge maps: A meta-analysis. *Review of Educational Research, 76*(3), 413–448.

Novak, J. D. (1981). Applying learning psychology and philosophy of science to biology teaching. *American Biology Teacher, 43*(1), 12–20.

Novak, J. D. (1998). *Learning, creating and using knowledge: Concept Maps™ as facilitative tools in schools and in corporations*. London: Lawrence Erlbaum.

Novak, J. D. (1990). Concept maps and Vee diagrams: Two metacognitive tools to facilitate meaningful learning. *Instructional Science, 19*(1), 29–52.

Novak, J. D., & Cañas, A. J. (2008). *The theory underlying concept maps and how to construct and use them*. Pensacola: *Florida Institute for Human* and *Machine Cognition*.

Novak, J. D., & Gowin, J. B. (1984). *Learning how to learn*. Cambridge, UK: Cambridge University Press.

Quillian, M. R. (1967). Word concepts: A theory and simulation of some basic semantic capabilities. *Behavioral Science, 12,* 410–430.

Raymond, A. M. (1997). The use of concept mapping in qualitative research: A multiple case study in mathematics education. *Focus on Learning Problems in Mathematics, 19*(3), 1–28.

Sowa, J. F. (2000). *Knowledge representation: Logical, philosophical, and computational foundations.* Pacific Grove, CA: Brooks Cole.

Stewart, J., Van Kirk, J., & Rowell, R. (1979). Concept maps: A tool for use in biology teaching. *American Biology Teacher, 41*(3), 171–175.

Thagard, P. (2010). *The brain and the meaning of life.* Princeton, NJ: Princeton University Press.

Tolman, E. C. (1948). Cognitive maps in rats and men. *Psychological Review, 55*(4), 189–208.

Weber, S. (2008). Using visual images in research. In J. G. Knowles & A. L. Cole (Eds.), *Handbook of the arts in qualitative research: Perspectives, methodologies, examples, and issues* (pp. 41–53). London: Sage.

Wheeldon, J. (2010). Mapping mixed methods research: Methods, measures, and meaning. *Journal of Mixed Methods Research, 4*(2), 87–102.

Wheeldon, J. P., & Faubert, J. (2009). Framing experience: Concept maps, mind maps, and data collection in qualitative research. *International Journal of Qualitative Methods, 8*(3), 68–83.

Whorf, B. L. (1956). *Language, thought and reality: Selected writings of Benjamin Lee Whorf* (J. B. Carroll, Ed.). Cambridge, MA: MIT Press.

3

Scoring and Statistics

Using Concept Maps in Quantitative Social Science Research

In Chapters 1 and 2 we discussed some of the differences between quantitative and qualitative research. These differences are based on different theories about how people understand the world and develop knowledge about it. Understanding the distinction between quantitative and qualitative research is important; however, sometimes the differences between them are overblown. Most research contains both quantitative and qualitative elements. Whether you are counting the number of sources that support one view or assigning numeric values to the responses of participants, quantitative considerations are ever present. Although many students fear the complexity of statistics, being quantitatively literate is both useful and practical. So what is quantitative research? Quantitative research methods focus on gathering, analyzing, interpreting, and presenting numeric information and/or quantities (Teddlie & Tashakkori, 2009, p. 5). Data might be gathered using pre-/posttest scores, ratings on a survey or questionnaire, or the amount of time it took to complete an activity.

Quantitative research tries to answer the question What? by measuring characteristics of individuals, groups, states, countries, and so forth. Although quantitative researchers often focus on theory testing based on empirical data that can be observed and measured, they also require an ability to count, compare, and describe data quantitatively. Based on the view that the external world is observable and knowable independent of an individual's experience of it, this approach to research attempts to test certain hypotheses about the world through the scientific method. Often through deductive or top-down analytical approaches that rely on a series of steps, specific conclusions are based on general premises and the results of earlier theoretical and empirical research. Using clearly defined dependent and independent variables, quantitative research relies on hypothesis testing to validate theories by modifying or rejecting certain beliefs based on the results of research findings. To help researchers understand what their data suggest, statistical tools such as distributions, cross-tabulations, and statistical indicators of centrality (mode, median, mean) or variation (range, standard deviation) are often useful. Concept maps can be used in all phases of research to provide a theoretical framework, describe a research design, gather data, present results, and map further discussion and conclusions from the research. By the end of this chapter, readers should

- understand some of the assumptions made in quantitative research;
- list some of the strengths of concept maps for quantitative research;
- consider how concept maps can assist researchers to gather and analyze data;
- be able to teach three people to make a concept map about a topic of interest; and
- develop a concept map to present to the class based on the three collected maps.

THEORETICAL JUSTIFICATION

As discussed in Chapter 1, quantitative research draws on postpositivist ideas about human knowledge and the notion that the external world exists independently of an individual's experience of it. As a result, it is possible to make tentative and/or provisional theories of how the world works. These theories are continually tested and can be improved over time. An important starting place for concept maps in quantitative research is the idea that mapping concepts can assist in learning, understanding, and demonstrating knowledge about how the world works.

Joseph Novak is a noted authority on concept maps. So-called Novakian concept maps are representations of regularities of the world in one's mind (Novak & Cañas, 2008; Novak & Gowin, 1984). Novak's thinking and writing about concepts is based on

Professor Bob Gowin's work that suggests concepts exist as representations of regularities. Gowin defined a concept as follows: "A concept is a sign/symbol pointing toward regularities in events, or to [a] record of events" (1981, p. 29). We often make a distinction between a spoken or written term (sign/symbol) and a concept as it exists in the mind, but Gowin combines the two. In his view, one's understanding of an idea can be inferred from how it exists in relationship to other ideas.

An important theoretical starting point for the creation of concept maps is David Ausubel (1963). As discussed in Chapter 2, his theory of meaningful learning provided an important basis for Novak and his research group at Cornell University in the 1970s (Novak, 1981). Ausubel held that an individual's subject-matter knowledge is mentally represented in a hierarchy of concepts, and as a result, concept maps were developed using strict hierarchies. The topmost concepts were more abstract than lower level concepts. However, Novak and Gowin (1984, pp. 16–18) subsequently challenged this imperative by showing how three different concept maps could be made from the very same 11 concepts. Although each map began with different concepts (e.g., water, living things, and molecules), the common interrelationships between the maps changed, but the meaning did not require a fixed hierarchy to emerge. Nevertheless, Novak (1998) has continued to use this approach and its assumptions. Many users of concept maps think they require a clear hierarchical structure (Novak & Cañas, 2008). There may be a movement to qualify this less flexible approach to mapping (Wheeldon & Faubert, 2009).

As Åhlberg (1993, 2004, 2008) has demonstrated, concept maps can be seen as a language in and of themselves. He has suggested that many learning theories can use concept mapping because everything that can be written can be transformed into a concept map. Maps, in turn, can be transcribed back into ordinary text. In these cases, maps can be created starting from anywhere on the page. Yet the important idea here is that your approach to maps depends, to a large extent, on what is to be mapped. A useful example might be an abstract general concept, such as organisms. It includes the following kinds of narrower concepts: unicellular (single-celled) organisms and multicellular organisms. The concept of multicellular organisms covers still narrower concepts such as plants, animals, fungi, and so forth. Mental hierarchies can be useful in these sorts of cases. In general, it is important to remember that concepts are often related and meaning can be presented through links and connections. Figure 3.1 provides an example by considering people and their relationships to the broader world around them.

In the concept map in Figure 3.1, the central concept is transformed nature based on the number of links (six) between it and other concepts. The map suggests that humans are a part of nature but have transformed themselves through culture and the development of science and technology. What are other central concepts that can be identified using the same criteria?

Figure 3.1   Humans in the World

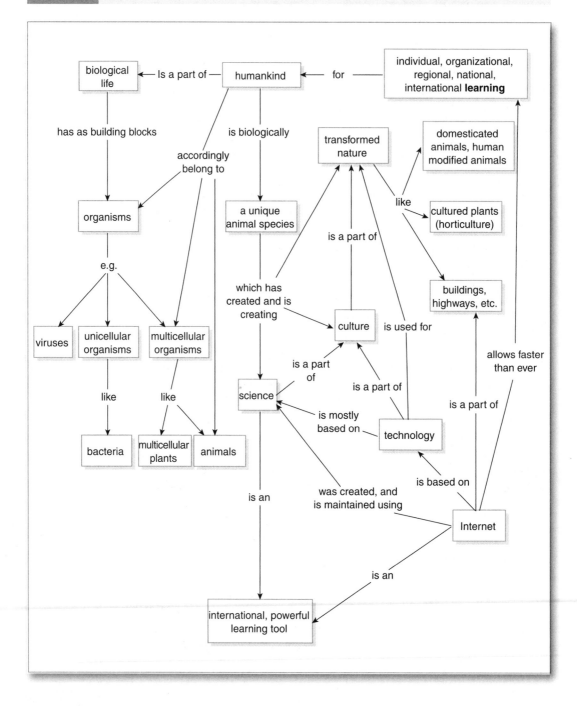

KEY TERMS AND THE LANGUAGE OF QUANTITATIVE RESEARCH

Before exploring how concept maps can be used in quantitative research, we need to understand some key concepts. The first is the idea that quantitative research is concerned with general principles. As discussed in Chapter 1, postpositivists believe it is possible to make speculative or provisional theories of how the world works. This *ontological* view is based on the idea that we can tentatively assume certain facts and that these facts can be grouped together. One of the most basic assumptions is that the universe is a system and that it contains subsystems that are connected or linked in one way or another. These connections allow us to acquire new knowledge and relate it to what we already know.

Although absolute certainty may not be attainable, quantitative social research is based on the idea that we can estimate the probabilities implicit in different sorts of actions and interactions. This *probabilistic* approach to research is one reason why quantitative social scientists use statistics to help them understand social situations and measure relationships between different phenomena. To understand how quantitative researchers measure data, it is useful to start with the idea that all properties in the world around us change or vary, either slowly or quickly, in response to some things and not others. These properties can be measured, but there is an enormous variety of data to consider. It is important, therefore, to make some decisions about which kinds of data should be collected and in which ways their collection can lead to meaningful and useful analyses. When systematic observations and measurements are condensed into numerical data (figures/numbers) they are called *quantitative data.*

One way to do this is to explore how different variables act on, or sometimes interact with, other variables. According to Field (2009, p. 795), "variables are anything that can be measured and can differ across entities or across time." In simplistic terms, a *variable* is an entity that can take on different values or anything that can vary. Variables can include age, weight, height, gender, eye color, level of school completed, and income, among others. They can be single entities or can comprise multiple variables that are combined into a new variable a researcher develops. In general, almost anything that can vary can be considered a variable. An easy place to start is *dichotomous variables,* or data that can be divided into two categories. These categories are often assigned an arbitrary value of 1 or 0.

Categories like these can be very useful when describing groups within your data such as married/unmarried, male/female, or owns books/doesn't own books. Of course, some people own many books. To speak about the number of books a person owns, researchers talk about *discrete variables,* which are those that take on a specific numeric value (e.g., 2, 3, 8, or 12) and do not have meaningful quantities between the response numbers. By contrast, *continuous variables* are those that involve measurement values such as time or distance, which do have meaningful quantities between the response numbers. Continuous variables have an almost limitless number of values depending on the precision of the measurement. For instance, if you count children, the number of children you have would be a discrete variable. There is no inherent meaning (or sense) in counting ½ children—in reality people have 2, 3, or 4 children. You never have 2.73 children. However, with age, the quantities are meaningful within the numbers. If you are recording how old people are, it may make sense to record the fact that someone is 35.5 years old.

Science that deals with numerical data in social and behavioral sciences is called *statistics*. The word *statistics* is used in several senses, but in its broadest it refers to a range of techniques and procedures for describing and displaying data and making decisions based on data. Statistical tools can be used to describe data, such as calculating distributions, tables, cross-tables, central statistics, and different kinds of averages. *Mean, median,* and *mode* are three of the most common measures of central tendency, or the middle of your data. The mean is the average many of us are accustomed to and is calculated by summing all the observed numbers and dividing the total by the number of observations. The median is the middle value (50th percentile) in the list of numbers when you place them in numerical order. The mode is the value that occurs most often. If no number is repeated, then there is no mode for the list.

The importance of averages in statistics is that when you both have a sample mean and know the variance of a random sample, you can use this information to estimate the mean and variance within the entire population. This process is known as *statistical inference*. It is based on the real-world challenges associated with obtaining data for the entire population. Think about teachers in the United States or students in China. Although we may want to analyze data about these groups, it would be impossible to collect data from them all. Instead, researchers pick samples or groups to represent the whole. Ideally, these samples are *randomly selected* so that each member of the population has an equal chance of being selected. Because it is often very costly and time consuming to obtain a real random sample of a large population, nonrandom samples are more common. We will discuss some of the implications of this below, but for now, let's consider in basic terms how social science researchers think about the ways variables can affect one another.

A relationship between variables may be a direct cause-and-effect relationship, or *causal* relationship. It may also be a *correlative* relationship. This denotes the presence of a relationship but can't tell us whether one variable causes the other. It is not as powerful a technique to help explain the relationship, but it might justify further testing to assess cause-and-effect or direct relationships. One way to think about this is to consider cigarette smoking. Public health messages often imply that everyone who smokes gets cancer. This suggests a direct cause-and-effect relationship. It is more correct to say that smoking increases

LIBRARY, UNIVERSITY OF CHESTER

your risk of getting cancer. If the first statement were true, there would be a causal relationship between smoking and cancer. Although smoking is rarely a good idea, it is only correlated with cancer. In the social sciences, *partial correlations* test whether there are *mediating* variables that are actually the cause of the correlation between two other variables. For example, education can be seen as a mediator variable between poverty and crime.

To undertake any sort of quantitative study, it is important to develop a *hypothesis.* This refers to a specific statement of prediction that describes what you expect to happen in your study, based on the variables you have identified or developed and the relationship you expect to see. To develop a hypothesis about what you expect to see, you first need to consider another aspect of how different variables interact. This requires the identification of what are traditionally called *independent variables* (IVs) and *dependent variables* (DV). The IV is what is hypothesized to be the causal variable in a relationship and is what people, places, or things manipulate. In experimental research, it is the variable the researcher manipulates to assess its impact on other variables. By contrast, DVs are those that are affected by the IV. They can and often do change as a result of the IV. In some cases the same variable can be an IV in one research question and can act as a DV in another question. Although the terms *IV* and *DV* have a historic pedigree, we agree with Field (2009), who suggests that it would be wiser to use the general and unambiguous terms *predictor* and *outcome* variables in place of *independent* and *dependent.* We will discuss more about these variables and hypothesis testing later in this chapter.

To understand why concept maps are especially well suited to quantitative research, a few additional terms are relevant. The first is *semantics.* This refers to the difference between terms or words, and concepts or ideas. Often, new phenomena are found as a pattern in the external world. These might include a new organism, relationship, or connection. Once a concept is discovered, a term or word is developed to give it a label. Ideas with the same meaning may have labels or terms associated with them in different languages; however, the concept itself remains the same. Another is *axiology.* This refers to the study of values such as truth, beauty, quality, or value. When applied to research, it invites us to ask questions about which sorts of research are valuable, which kinds of research are useful, and which ethical assumptions are being made when we study people, places, and things. In Chapter 6, we will cover in more detail ethical responsibilities of researchers and important concepts to guide your own future research. For now, let's think about axiology and semantics as they apply to maps.

These terms are important for concept map researchers because they get at the heart of two important issues. The first idea is that people visualize relationships between different kinds of concepts as a way to make sense of the world. As discussed in Chapter 2, using maps to gather data may be of value because maps allow researchers access to creative and more unfiltered data. We think concept maps can be treated like other kinds of social science data, but a second issue surrounds their practicality. Although concept maps come with more rules for their construction than other approaches, the data that emerge are still more personal than data collected through surveys, questionnaires, or perhaps even interviews based on literature reviews. Concept maps offer both a means to get to the heart of how people understand the world around them and a way for researchers to see this understanding. This requires that we find ways to meaningfully count concepts, connections, and structure.

CONCEPT MAPS AND QUANTITATIVE STUDY: EXISTING STUDIES AND SCORING MAPS

Historically, concept maps have been used primarily in quantitative research as a means to assess knowledge integration (Besterfield-Sacre, Gerchak, Lyons, Shuman, & Wolfe, 2004). Mathematics educators have used concept maps as a way of teaching subject matter to students and prospective teachers, as a means of identifying misconceptions (Huerta, Galan, & Granell, 2003), and as an assessment instrument (Bolte, 1999). Science educators have used them extensively as a tool for formative student assessment, for identifying student knowledge prior to instruction, and for looking at change in knowledge as a result of instruction (Jones, Carter, & Rua, 2000; Jones, Rua, & Carter 1998; Novak, 1998; Novak & Msonda, 1991).

Some argue that concept maps can affect concentration and overall test performance because they promote interaction and engagement between the student and the material (Hall & O'Donnell, 1996) and suggest there may be an easier way to communicate one's knowledge when compared to text writing (Czuchry & Dansereau, 1996). According to Kommers and Lanzing, "constructing concept maps stimulates us to externalize, articulate, and pull together information we already know about a subject and understand new information as we learn . . . [while] . . . stimulating a learner to find contours of his/her knowledge" (1997, p. 424).

Alkahtani (2009) identified more than 50 studies that empirically tested concept maps in education and concluded that concept maps appear to be useful for learning and teaching because they allow different kinds of information to be connected in an organized way. By making use of our visual perception system, concept maps allow people to quickly and easily scan a picture, identify key words as well as similarities or differences between different maps, and provide a means to develop a pictorial overview or a concept or idea (Kommers & Lanzing, 1997, p. 423). Figure 3.2 is a concept map exploring the traditional features of concept maps.

Åhlberg (1993, 2004, 2008) has discussed, in addition to the uses of concept maps described above, how concept maps can be used to provide a theoretical

Figure 3.2   Traditional Features of Concept Maps

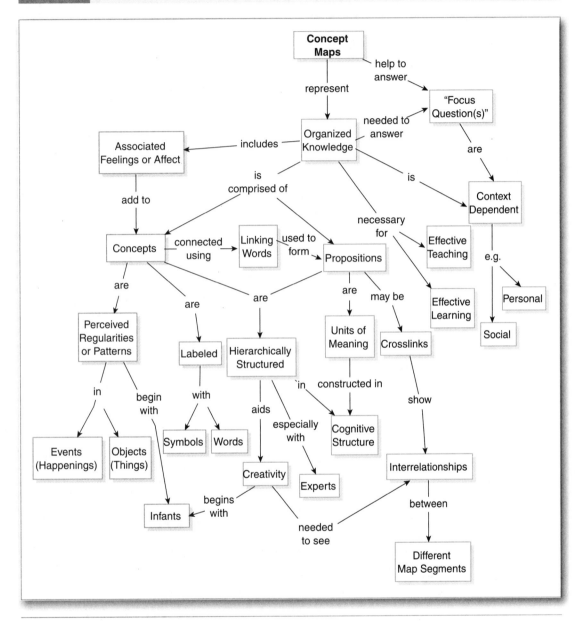

Source: Novak and Cañas (2008).

framework, describe a research design, gather data, present results, and map further discussions and conclusions based on the research. Some examples are outlined in Figure 3.3.

Figure 3.3 Using Concept Maps in Social Science Research

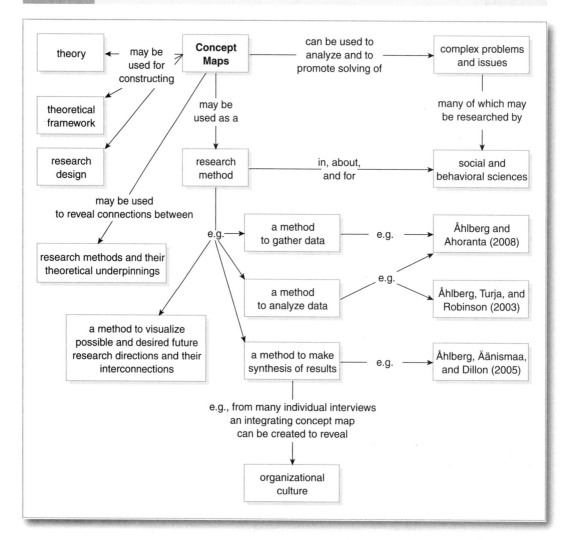

EXERCISE 3.1
Interpreting a Concept Map

Look at Figure 3.3 and interpret the concept map yourself. According to the authors' calculations there are two equally central or important concepts, based on the number of links to and from each concept. What do you think the most important concepts in the map are? Would the map make much sense if these two concepts were removed?

Using Concept Maps to Gather Data

Concept maps can help to organize research projects, reduce data, analyze themes, and present findings (Daley, 2004). They can also be used as a means to collect data (see Figure 3.4). Concept mapping used as a data-collection method facilitates a global understanding of the topic under consideration. Because it is less common to collect data through visual representations, mapping may uniquely demonstrate the way in which people connect knowledge and experience. Within the fields of science education, engineering, mathematics, nursing, psychology, statistics, and medicine, concept maps have been the subject of a number of studies (Wheeldon, 2010). In education, they have been shown to be more effective in assisting knowledge retention than attending class lectures, reading, and participating in class discussion (Poole & Davis, 2006).

One approach is to use maps in place of other sorts of pre/post data-collection strategies. In one study, student-constructed pre- and postlaboratory concept

Figure 3.4   Concept Map of Data Collection

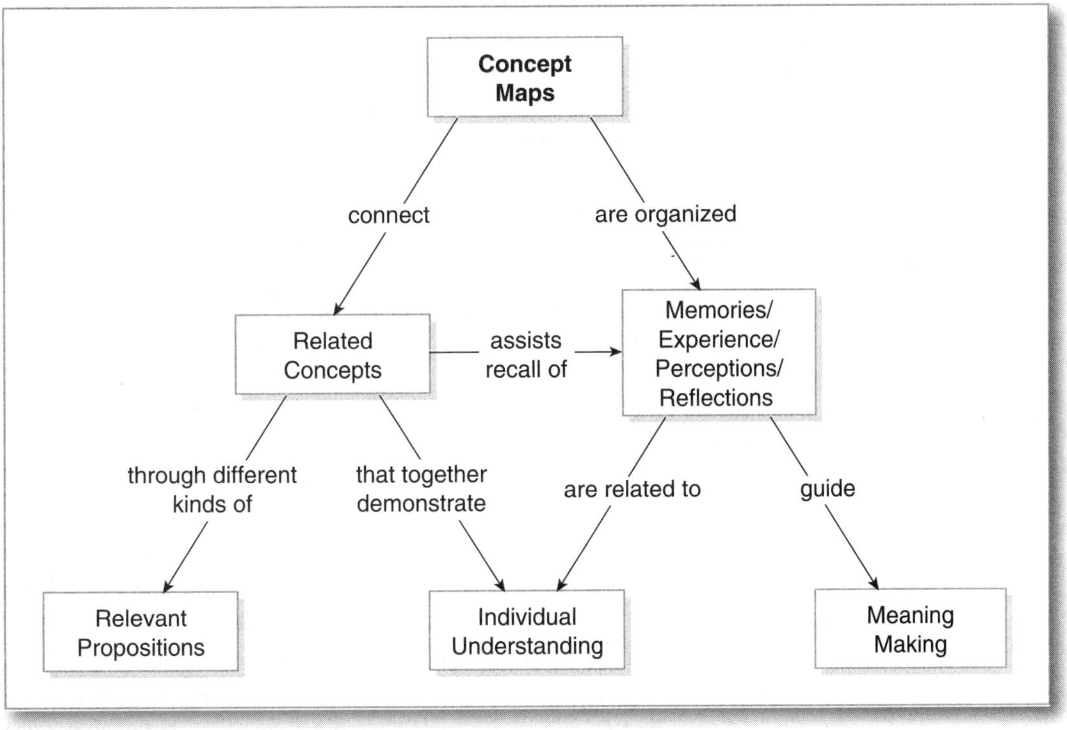

Source: Wheeldon (2010, p. 90).

maps were used as a means to uncover how understanding, views, and/or perceptions can change over time (Kilic, Kaya, & Dogan, 2004). Based on a procedure that involved instruction about how to construct and quantitatively score a concept map, student maps were used as a basis for subsequent peer-to-peer discussions about chemistry. Used in this way, concept maps can offer important data about common understandings among students as well as areas of disagreement or confusion.

Using Concept Maps to Assist in Data Analysis

As Figure 3.3 suggests, concept maps can be used to assist in data analysis in a variety of ways. This might be done by generating tables based on data drawn from concept maps to assist in the assessment of different maps. Key concepts and the number of direct links with other concepts can be ordered by frequency (Åhlberg, Äänismaa, & Dillon, 2005). In addition, this approach to concept mapping was used in a similar way by Åhlberg, Turja, and Robinson (2003), who compared key similarities and differences based on the concept maps of administrators in Helsinki, Finland. Identifying common views and shared concepts in the minds of experts and decision makers, they modeled an approach to research that sought to build proposals for sustainable development as part of the 10-year City of Helsinki Program (2001–2011).

Concept maps can assist in data analysis in other ways as well. As Figure 3.5 suggests, concept maps can be transformed to and from ordinary text and can assist researchers to see explicit, implicit, and even hidden meanings and assumptions. This is an important aspect of quantitative research because it may allow concept maps to serve as a reliable tool for the measurement of an individual's knowledge structure. In this way, maps can assist in data analysis by providing a novel insight into data gathered through the map, allowing researchers precise justification for additional assessments (Srinivasan, McElvany, Shay, Shavelson, & West, 2008).

Scoring Maps

Once created, maps can be assessed, scored, and/or compared. Scoring systems are understood as either structural or relational (West, Park, Pomeroy, & Sandoval, 2002). Structural assessments consider physical characteristics such as number of valid concepts, number of links, number of hierarchical levels, and number of cross-links (Turns, Atman, & Adams, 2000). In education research, Novak and Gowin (1984, pp. 97–108) first considered how to quantitatively score a concept map by proposing that different elements be worth more than other elements. Although various

Figure 3.5   Concept Mapping Data Analysis

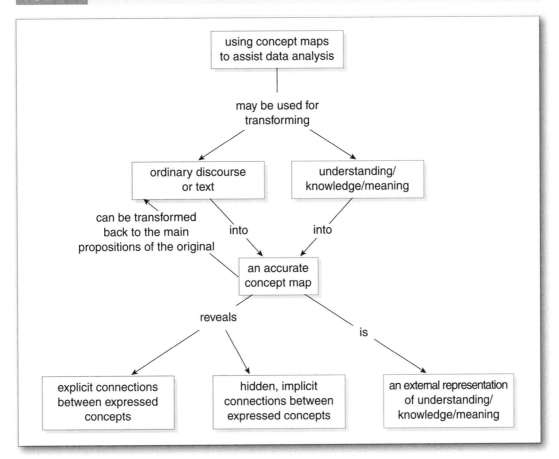

refinements have been proposed since (Åhlberg & Ahoranta, 2008; Besterfield-Sacre et al., 2004), Figure 3.6 provides a traditional example of how a concept map might be scored based on its structure.

In addition to individual concepts and labels that make clear propositions, the example in Figure 3.6 relies on Novak's approach to map measurement. Because this approach views cross-links as an important part of meaningful learning, concept maps that include cross-links receive higher scores than maps that include other kinds of links between concepts. According to Åhlberg's (1993) theory of high-quality learning, it is the quality of cross-links that matters, not the existence or total number of cross-links. Instead of attaching different weights to concepts, cross-links, or examples that may appear arbitrary, Åhlberg's approach requires that all relevant links between concepts be treated as equal in value. Using this approach, it is the

Figure 3.6   Scoring Concept Maps

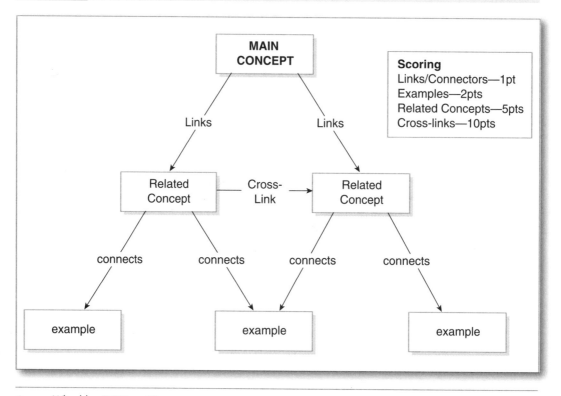

Source: Wheeldon (2010, p. 92).

Note: pt = point.

number of relevant concepts and propositions that is crucial. The relevance of a concept map is connected to how closely it corresponds to how the map's maker understands the issue being mapped. Åhlberg's approach is outlined in Figure 3.7.

Another approach to scoring concept maps is based on relational assessment. Relational assessment is more subjective than the structural method, but it has some advantages over structural methods due to its greater emphasis on map correctness and overall quality. Relational assessments have revealed valuable information about learning and changes in understanding over time (Edmondson, 2000) and are often used in the classroom to assess student learning about a particular subject (Goldsmith & Davenport, 1990; Ruiz-Primo, Shavelson, Li, & Schultz, 2001; Rye & Rubba, 2002). Whether we are using an expert map as a basis for comparison or an actual expert to examine and/or assess a student map, the quality of concepts and propositions is of utmost importance. To make sense of data, quantitative research is also concerned with developing and testing theories about the world.

Figure 3.7   Åhlberg's Approach to Scoring Concept Maps

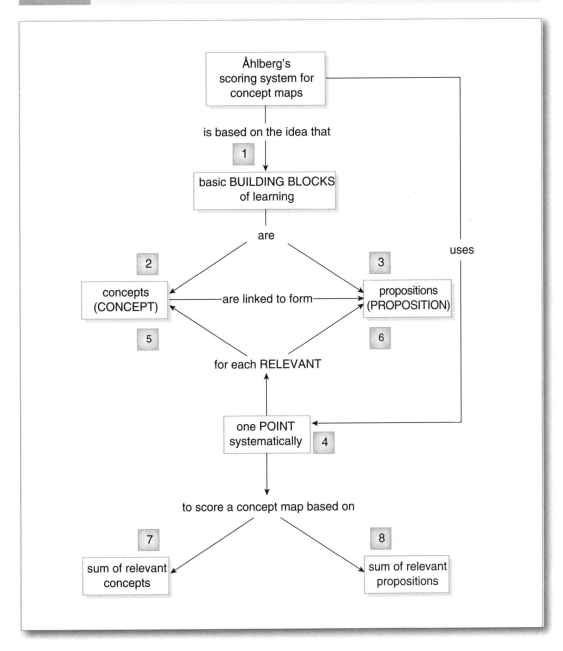

BASIC STEPS IN HYPOTHESIS TESTING

As discussed above, quantitative approaches to research require that we accept, to some extent, a probabilistic approach to making inferences about the data we study. This requires us to think about samples and populations. In statistics, a *sample* is usually picked because populations are generally too large to be analyzed as a whole. It is important to distinguish between a *population parameter* and a *sample statistic*. A population parameter is a numerical summary of an entire population that would be almost impossible to obtain. Imagine we wanted to know what percentage of American university students took part-time jobs in addition to their studies. If we could ask all university students in the United States, the data we gathered would be for the entire population. Given the challenge of doing this, we might instead try to acquire a sample of 1,000 students and ask them. Ideally, this sample would be a random sample. If a sample is truly random and sufficiently large, then it can be considered representative of the whole student population. Any numerical measure computed from this sample of the population is called a sample statistic. Once we understand in general terms concepts such as variables, populations, and samples, we can try to pull them all together and explore how quantitative researchers can design studies to test hypotheses. A useful way to organize the hypothesis-testing process is to see it as a series of steps. In Chapter 1, we introduced a simplified view of how some of these steps are related. This figure is reproduced as Figure 3.8.

Figure 3.8 Testing Theories in Quantitative Research

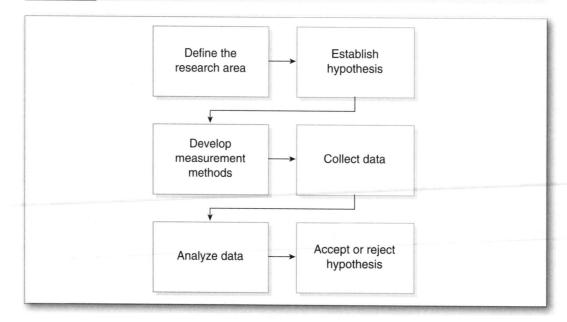

Although this is a good starting point, to understand hypothesis testing, it might be useful to see each of these broader steps in more detail. Figure 3.9 outlines eight key steps in hypothesis testing. Let's take each of these steps in turn. Step 1 requires that we identify a research area and develop an *overall hypothesis*, or a prediction about the state of the world that we want to test through our study. Hypotheses are often developed based on theoretical assumptions, past experiences, and previous research findings. To develop a hypothesis about what you expect to see, you first need to identify the *predictor* and the *outcome* variables (Field, 2009, p. 792). As previously discussed, in some contexts, predictor variables are referred to as IVs, and outcome variables are called DVs.

In Step 2, we need to define the null and alternative hypotheses. What are these? When testing hypotheses, it is always possible that there is no effect of a predictor variable on an outcome variable, that there is no difference of means, or that there is no relationship between variables. The idea that any observed relationship between variables is the result of pure chance is called the *null hypothesis* (often represented as H_0). The alternative is the *research hypothesis* (often represented as H_1), stating that the observed relationship or difference is not due to chance. The null hypothesis and research hypothesis ought to be mutually exclusive.

Figure 3.9   Detailed Steps in Hypothesis Testing

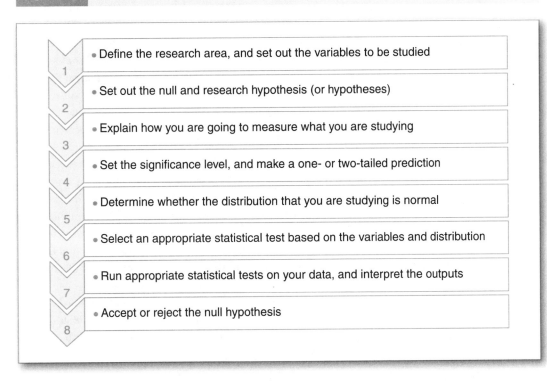

1. • Define the research area, and set out the variables to be studied

2. • Set out the null and research hypothesis (or hypotheses)

3. • Explain how you are going to measure what you are studying

4. • Set the significance level, and make a one- or two-tailed prediction

5. • Determine whether the distribution that you are studying is normal

6. • Select an appropriate statistical test based on the variables and distribution

7. • Run appropriate statistical tests on your data, and interpret the outputs

8. • Accept or reject the null hypothesis

In Step 3, we need to clearly outline what we are studying and how we are trying to measure our defined variables. In quantitative research, *reliability* is concerned with questions of stability and consistency. In short, reliability asks if the same measurement tool can yield stable and consistent results when repeated over time. In contrast, *validity* considers how well we were able to design methods or measures to investigate the broader constructs under investigation. Although we will discuss this in more detail in Chapter 7, in general it is important to consider these concepts as we develop a research project and define what we are attempting to study. It is also important for the kind of data we collect and the test statistic we choose to test the null hypotheses. Keep in mind we are testing the null hypothesis only when we're conducting hypothesis testing—we may ultimately accept the research hypothesis, but we do this by first testing the null. Testing the null requires that we think about the kind of data that can be collected. It is crucial to remember that the kind of statistical test you use depends on the data you have. In quantitative research, we often refer to data in terms of *levels of measurement.* There are four main kinds of levels of measurement in the social and behavioral sciences.

The lowest level is called *nominal level of measurement,* sometimes called *categorization.* It simply refers to data in which we have used numbers to represent a category. For example, within the variable eye color we could divide the data into these categories: 1 = *brown,* 2 = *blue,* 3 = *hazel,* and so forth. There is no implicit order in these numbers; instead they are just arbitrarily selected as a numeric code for categories and used systematically within your analysis. Because research requires systematic knowledge testing, once you have decided on a code, you must use it consistently.

The next level of measurement includes real order and is called *ordinal level of measurement.* This refers to numbers assigned to objects or events to represent the rank order. A simple example of this is measures of time, as in a race wherein the person who finished first was the fastest, the person who finished second was a bit slower, and so on. Ordinal variables, like nominal, are still categorical and do not have intrinsic numeric qualities. A common level used in the social and behavioral sciences is *interval level of measurement.* Unlike ordinal levels of measurement, it assumes equal intervals between measurement scores and has no absolute zero. So, for example, in an interval scale the difference between 1 and 2 must be the same as the difference between 4 and 5, or 25 and 26. In practice, some of these measurements are closer to ordinal-level measures because ensuring equal intervals is difficult. It is a common assumption, however, that if we can assume that equal intervals exist, we can treat ordinal data as interval data. *Ratio level of measurement* is also very common in the social sciences. Ratio-level data have an absolute zero, which (unlike with interval-level data) denotes an absence of the phenomenon under study. Figure 3.10 provides a useful concept map of the levels of measurement.

In Step 4, we need to set the significance level and make a one-tailed or two-tailed prediction. Only two outcomes of a hypothesis test are possible: Either the null hypothesis is rejected, or it is not. The z score is one kind of *test statistic* that is used

Figure 3.10   Levels of Measurement

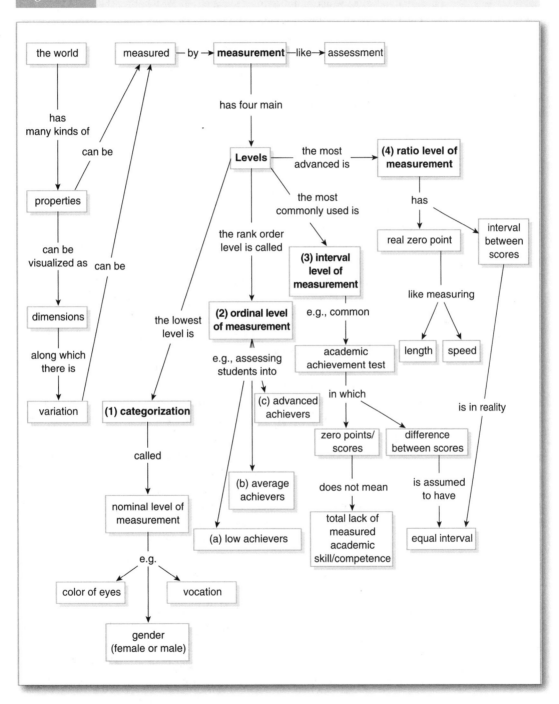

to determine the probability of obtaining a given value. To test hypotheses, you must decide in advance which number to use as a cutoff for whether the null hypothesis will be rejected. This number is called the *critical value* or "*p* value" because it represents the level of probability that you will use to test the hypothesis. If the computed test statistic has a probability less than our critical value, the null hypothesis will be rejected. This is done to avoid a *Type I error,* which occurs when the null hypothesis is rejected when it should not be rejected. Although there is always a possibility that an observation in our study could have arisen by chance, we want to make the significance level as small as possible. Usually, the significance level chosen is .05, and this refers to the probability we would wrongly reject the null hypothesis when it is true. There may be cases in which we set the significance at $p \le .01$, which represents a smaller chance that we would wrongly reject the null hypothesis, and $p \le .001$, which represents an even lower chance that we would wrongly reject the null hypothesis.

Next, in Step 4, we make a *one- or two-tailed prediction.* This refers to the kind of relationship we expect to see. A one-tailed prediction often indicates that you believe your outcome variable will be affected by the predictor variable in one direction, either positively or negatively. There may be some research questions in which this assumption is built into your research hypothesis. For example, in education we often assume that all students will have more knowledge about a subject area after learning about it. In other fields, assumptions like this may be problematic. When making a two-tailed prediction, we are suggesting we cannot make a choice about the direction of the relationship under investigation, whether it will affect the outcome in a positive or negative way. A one-tailed or two-tailed prediction influences at what point you could reject the null hypothesis. A one-tailed test might occur if we have good theoretical or empirical reasons to make a directional research hypothesis (H_1) that the mean of one data set (M_1) will be larger than the mean of another data set (M_2). This can be represented as $H_1: M_1 > M_2$. If we set the significance level (α) at .05, that would correspond to the critical value of $|1.64|$, here expressed as absolute value, meaning that the value can be -1.64 or $+1.64$, depending on the direction of our prediction.

A two-tailed test occurs when we are less sure about the relationship within our data. The null hypothesis usually states that there is no difference between the values of the same statistic such as a mean or correlation. For example, let's suppose that our research hypothesis (H_1) is that the mean of one data set (M_1) will not be equal to the mean of another data set (M_2), represented as $H_1: M_1 \ne M_2$. The region of rejection would consist of a range of numbers located on both sides of the sampling distribution because it is possible that the mean of one data set may be either larger or smaller. To achieve a significance level of .05 for a two-tailed test, the absolute value of the test statistic ($|z|$) must be greater than or equal to the critical value 1.96—which corresponds to the level .025 for a one-tailed test. If we think of probability as an area, then in the one-tailed test the critical area is bigger than in the two-tailed test, in which the critical area has been divided on both tails of the theoretical distribution.

In Step 5, we need to determine whether the distribution that we are studying is normal. This determination has implications for the types of statistical tests that you can run on your data. As discussed above, whereas ideally we could gather data from everyone we were interested in studying, populations are generally too large to be analyzed as a whole. As a result, we often pick a group to represent the whole. The science of statistics is to evaluate how well the statistic estimates the true population parameter. To make estimations, it is necessary to accept that the normal (or Gaussian) distribution or bell curve is a reasonable description of human behavior. Using this approach, some people will be above average, most will be average, and some will be below average. Used in both natural sciences and social sciences, it is a simple model for complex phenomena. Many parametric statistical tests have been developed assuming a normal distribution. How can you tell if your sample is normal?

The best way is to compare what is observed in your data and what would be expected by chance. For example, the *sample mean* for research data would give information about the population mean, and the *standard deviation* of the sample could give the best available information about the standard deviation of the researched variable in the whole population. The *correlation coefficient* between two variables is also an example of a statistic indicating how much variation of one variable can be predicted from another variable. From the sample correlation coefficient, the population correlation coefficient can be estimated. It is important that the researcher carefully—and as completely as possible—define the population before collecting the sample, including a description of the members to be included. The *sampling frame* is the list of all members of the group who could possibly be selected for the study.

A *random* sample means that each member of the population has an equal chance of being selected into the sample. Often the probability of being selected is the same for each member. Usually, in real-life research practice, researchers have to use nonrandom samples (purposive samples, even convenience samples) because of financial and other obstacles, usually because there is not a sampling frame from which to randomly sample. A variety of statistical tests can be used to calculate how probable it is that obtained data come from a certain population. These include *t* tests, analyses of variance (ANOVAs), and *F* tests. These are based on accurate assumptions of distributions of population-level data, like bell-shaped random distributions or *t* distributions, which have different shapes depending on the size and attributes of the sample in question. Let's assume you have a normal distribution: How should you choose from the many available statistical tests? Good question. One issue is your research question. Another is the kind of data you have collected.

In Step 6, we can finally select an appropriate statistical test based on your research question, the defined variables, and whether the distribution is normal. When you have larger samples, a number of powerful parametric statistics and statistical tests can be used. Although the size of the sample required for each test statistic varies depending on the sample frame, we often associate parametric tests with larger samples ($N > 120$). These assume a normal distribution and require quantitative DVs that can be presented as interval- or ratio-level data so that we can calculate means, medians, and modes or standard deviations. Larger samples reduce the chances of both Type I and Type II errors. Type I errors occur when the null hypothesis is rejected when it is in fact true. By contrast, a Type II error occurs when we fail to reject the null hypothesis, even when we should. This is often a result of a small sample size or differences between the sample data and the population in general (Salkind, 2010). Although discussing Type 1 and Type II errors is a common feature of many statistical courses, Howitt and Cramer (2008, p. 100) suggested that these terms may be less practical given that statistics deals primarily with probabilities and not certainties. As such, there is always a chance that any decision you make is wrong. We will discuss more about the importance of acknowledging limitations in Chapters 6 and 7. For now, let's focus on statistical tests.

There are numerous statistical tests that might be appropriate for the kind of data you have available. Let's look at a few key parametric tests provided by Neil Salkind (2010, p. 211). His useful introductory chart is a good starting place and has been adapted for this book in Figure 3.11. If you cannot be sure that your data follow the normal distribution, special so-called *nonparametric* statistical tests can be used on both nominal and ordinal levels of measurements. According to Siegel and Castellan (1988, pp. 35–36), nonparametric methods make no assumptions or fewer assumptions about whether the data are drawn from a given distribution and do not require large samples to be robust. Although they reduce your ability to generalize to the population, they can be useful validation measures and can be used when your sample is smaller and based on more flexible parameters. Key nonparametric tests are outlined in Figure 3.12.

Once you have selected the appropriate test, Step 7 involves running the statistical test on your data and interpreting the outputs. Depending on the test you run, there are a number of relevant outputs that will result. One starting place is to think of the normal distribution as a distribution of probability mass of 1.00 or 100% spread over the whole area between the horizontal X-axis and the bell-shaped Gaussian curve. The 68/95/99 rule refers to the idea that in a normal distribution almost all values fall between +3 and −3 standard deviations of the mean. Although this is an approximate estimate, in general this means 68% of the values lie within 1 standard deviation of the mean, 95% of the values lie within 2 standard deviations of the mean, and almost all (more than 99%) lie within 3 standard deviations of the mean.

For now let's use the simple *z* test to demonstrate statistical reasoning. Any interval-/ratio-level data can be transformed into *z* scores by subtracting the data scores from the mean and dividing that value by the standard deviation. This shows how much variation there is from the mean within your sample. A low standard deviation indicates that the data points tend to be very close to the mean, whereas a high standard

Figure 3.11   Which Parametric Statistical Test Should You Use?

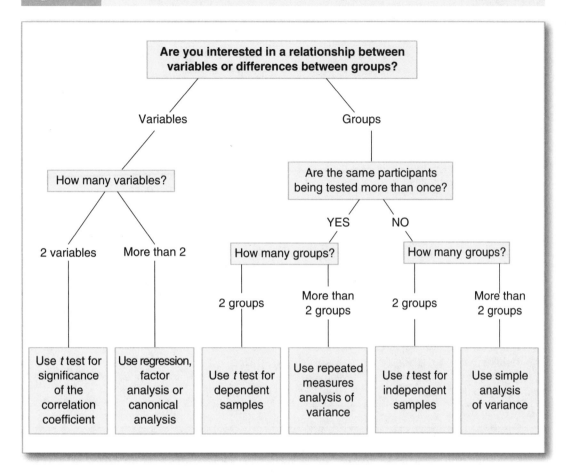

deviation indicates that the data are spread out over a large range of values. The resulting new z-score distribution's mean $= 0$, and its standard deviation $= 1.00$. If the z score is more than 3 standard deviations from the mean, we would say that the observed z score is very improbable and accordingly the test result is statistically significant. As Field (2009, p. 26) reminded us, important z values are $+1.96$, because it cuts off the top 2.5% of cases, and -1.96, because it cuts off the bottom 2.5% of the cases. This corresponds to the common significance level or p value of .05. As discussed above, this means that 95% of cases are between -1.96 and $+1.96$ z scores, or 2 standard deviations from the mean.

The second important benchmark is z scores -2.58 and $+2.58$, or 3 standard deviations from the mean, between which 99% of all cases would occur within a normal distribution. This corresponds to a significance level of .01. The third important

Figure 3.12 Which Nonparametric Statistical Test Should You Use?

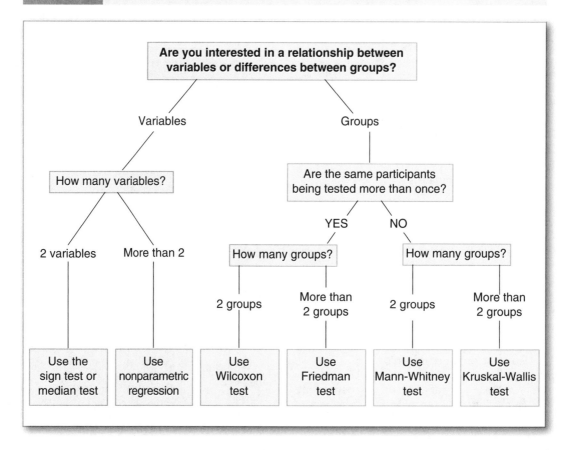

cut point is between −3.29 and +3.29. Between these scores, 99.9% of all cases would occur. This corresponds with a significance level of .001. Arriving at a z score that is greater than 3.29 by chance is very improbable, and it differs very significantly ($p < .001$) from the other z scores. In the social sciences, we usually accept the .05 level, or ±1.96 standard deviations from the mean.

Of course, there are many other statistical tests. Some common additional tests are the *F* test or ANOVA, *t* test, and chi-square test. All these statistical tests have their own sampling distributions and tables of critical values. Field (2009, p. 52) explained that the basic idea of test statistics is to first calculate variance explained by the statistical model—called *effect*. Next, you calculate variance not explained by the model—called *error*. When effect is divided by error, this ratio of systematic to unsystematic variance (or effect to error) is a test statistic. *Effect size* is an objective and standardized measure of the magnitude of an observed effect. For example, the common Pearson's correlation coefficient, *r*, is at the same time a measure of strength of association between pairs of values of two variables and a measure of effect size (Grissom & Kim, 2005, p. 70).

As we will see below in the research example, in the context of ANOVA, *eta squared* can be used to measure the effect size of a relationship between two variables. Effect sizes are often presented to emphasize or connote *practical,* rather than statistical, significance. Another output that is worth mentioning is *sampling error.* As Kinnear and Gray (2010, p. 20) remarked, random sampling implies sampling variability as each sample gives us a different estimate for population parameters of any variable. This variation is often called sampling error and estimates how much variability there is in this statistic across samples from the same population. A low sampling error means that we had relatively less variability within the sampling distribution.

Finally, in Step 8, we are in a position to accept or reject the null hypothesis. This involves interpreting the value indicated by your statistical test and determining whether it corresponds to a relevant significance level called the critical value. This cutoff value determines which test statistics lead to rejecting the null hypothesis and which lead to a decision not to reject the null hypothesis. If the calculated value from the statistical test is greater than the critical value, then the null hypothesis is rejected in favor of the research hypothesis. In the *z* test, critical values are 1.96, 2.58, and 3.29, corresponding to *p* values of .05, .01, and .001, respectively. In Table 3.1, basic error types in statistical testing are presented (Field, 2009, pp. 55–56). To reduce the chance of wrongly rejecting the null hypothesis (Type I error), set your significance level accordingly (typically at .05). To reduce the chance of wrongly failing to reject the null hypothesis, ensure your sample size is adequate to the research question under investigation (Guilford, 1965, pp. 207–220).

Table 3.1   Decisions in Hypothesis Testing

Our decision		Reality	
		H_0 false	H_0 true
	Reject H_0	Correct, $p = 1 - \alpha$. We can be 95% sure that we made a right decision, because $p = 1 - \alpha$. In our case: $1 - .05 = .95$.	Type I error $= \alpha$ level, $p = \alpha$, probability of error is commonly set at .05.
	Fail to reject H_0	Type II error, β level = maximum accepted probability is suggested to be set to .20.	Correct. Probability: $p = 1 - \beta$. In our case $1 - .20 = .80$. We would make a right decision based on our analyses 80% of the time.

Note: H_0 = null hypothesis.

A RESEARCH EXAMPLE

Based on a study from Åhlberg and Ahoranta (2008), this example is useful because it highlights how concept maps can be used in education to test three hypotheses. The first is whether we can show that concept maps do demonstrate student learning by comparing the pre/post maps of students. The second is whether students have more knowledge of a topic than they were able to represent through the maps they created. The third concerns whether we can explain the variation between pre/post maps based on a student's past academic achievement. As you read through these examples, keep in mind the research questions, the kind of data that were analyzed, and the statistical tests used.

To understand how concept maps can be used in quantitative research it is necessary to understand how variables inform measurement. One such variable is learning in education. As discussed above, concept maps have been used widely in science education. Åhlberg's (1993) theory of high-quality learning includes an idea that the more relevant concepts and propositions we have, the more relevant distinctions we can make, and thus the more we know about a specific field. This requires a means to measure the differences between students to understand why some students appear to learn concepts easily whereas others struggle. One approach is to look at how they represent their understanding of a topic using a concept map (Stoddart, Abrams, Gasper, & Canaday, 2000; Thompson & Mintzes, 2002). When using this approach, however, questions remain about how much a student's structured knowledge can be represented in concept maps.

According to Åhlberg (1990), all concepts become accurate only in relation to other concepts and as part of a developing conceptual structure. That is why it is important to monitor and promote development of students' conceptual structures. To consider some of these questions, data were collected in a variety of ways. Students learned to make concept maps as a group and created their first concepts maps on March 26, 2001, before beginning a unit of their course that focused on the earth's atmosphere. The second concept maps were created a month later, in April 2001, after the unit was completed. A month later, in May 2001, an instructor map was created for each student based on his or her short-answer test results. Figure 3.13 provides the preunit concept map for Student 208.

Figure 3.13 is a simple example of a concept map that provides an appropriate hierarchy and identifies 4 relevant concepts and 3 relevant propositions. There are no clear misconceptions. In Figure 3.14, the postunit concept map for the same student is provided, and the hierarchy of concepts is once again clear. There are 11 relevant concepts, 12 relevant propositions, and no clear misconceptions listed. Based on the number of links to and from each concept, we find 3 equally central concepts in this concept map: phenomena, rainbow, and thunder.

Figure 3.13 Student Preunit Map of Atmosphere

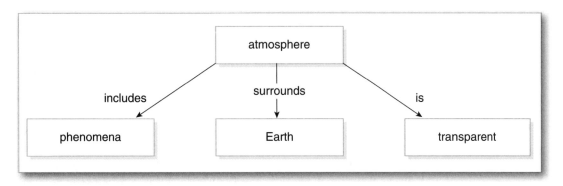

Figure 3.14 Student Postunit Map of Atmosphere

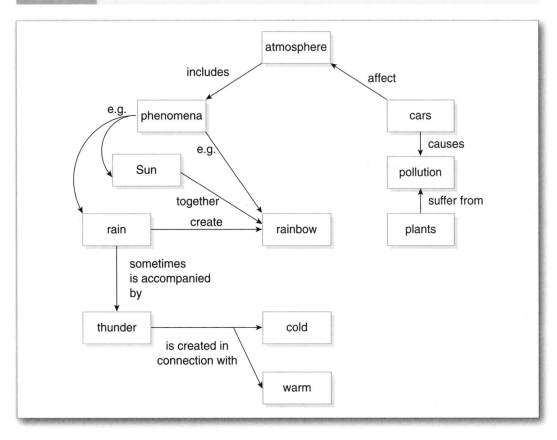

Each of them is connected to other concepts by three links. It is likely that these concepts were the most prominent in the student's thinking when he or she constructed this concept map.

In addition to assigning the maps (which were treated as data), following the completion of the unit, the instructor delivered a short-answer test to students that focused on the topics covered during the atmosphere unit (see Table 3.2). Based on their earlier preliminary results and observations, the researchers hypothesized that students have much more knowledge than they are able to express with their own concept maps.

Based on the answers provided by the students, each student's test was transformed into a concept map by the teacher. Student 208's short-answer test was transformed into the concept map shown in Figure 3.15. A central concept for this student was gases. It has seven links with other concepts. Whereas atmosphere has nine links with other concepts, four of them are inferred implicit links, represented by the dotted lines. In this experiment, although the number of concepts in the postmap increased from the number in the premap, it is the teacher's map of the student's test that resulted in 31 concepts—by far the most. It appears, then, that all students were able to provide much more information when explicitly asked questions connected to the atmosphere in the short-answer test than they could on their own. These two methods of gathering knowledge about how and what students learn

Table 3.2 Questions for the Short-Answer Test

Question Number	Test Question
1	What are the atmospheric gases that make up the air?
2	What are the most important indicators that the wind is blowing?
3	Define air pressure.
4	What are the most important uses of the atmosphere by humankind?
5	How is a rainbow created?
6	How are the northern lights created?
7	How do humans specifically use aspects of the atmosphere?
8	What causes air pollution, and how can it be prevented?
9	In what kinds of conditions do thunderstorms occur?
10	How is combustion linked to the earlier questions and their answers?

Figure 3.15 Teacher-Made Concept Map From Student Test

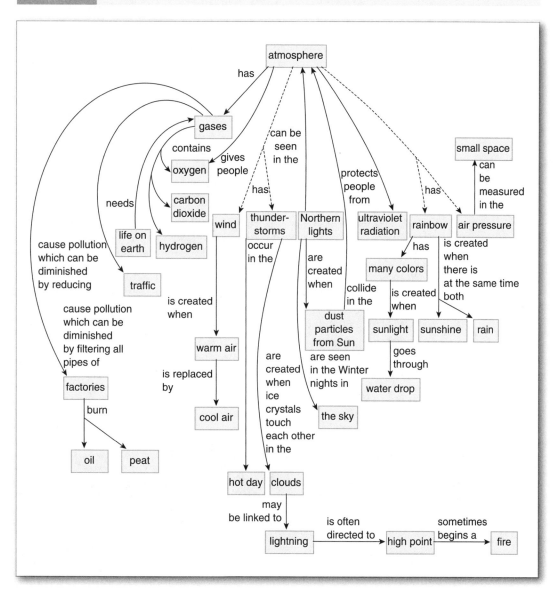

might be seen as complementary because both provide useful knowledge for the pupil and teachers. Using these data, it is possible to develop a simple chart that provides readers with important demographic data about the students (gender, academic level) along with compiled numeric data from all three maps.

DATA-ANALYSIS STRATEGY

The underpinning of all sound measurement is that the higher the figure, the more there is to measure. If we give a student a score of 0 based on his or her map, that would have to mean the student scored no correct concepts or propositions. Giving numbers to objects requires that we measure things in a meaningful way. Thus, not only must we count the number of concepts in a map, but we must also scrutinize which concepts were recalled. Some concepts and propositions may be more difficult for students to learn or understand, and it is essential that you create a means to score a map before you begin to analyze student maps. As discussed earlier, there are a number of ways to score a map. Consider which you would use in this scenario. Why?

As part of data collection, the authors attempted to gather data for similar groups of students for subsequent comparisons. In this case, based on standardized tests as part of the Finnish National Curriculum, three academically advanced students, three academically average students, and three students who struggled to learn new concepts in the past were identified. By using the data outlined in the original study, it is possible to explore three straightforward examples of hypothesis testing. The first is whether concept maps can be used to demonstrate learning. One way to investigate that question is to test whether the number of concepts and propositions changed between the student's pre- and postmaps. The null hypothesis is that there was no change between the maps. The first step to test this idea involved recording the number of relevant concepts and propositions from the pre-/postmaps, scoring them, and presenting them with relevant demographic data, as in Table 3.3.

Table 3.3 Pre-/Postmap Scores

Number	Education Level	Gender	Premap Concept Score	Postmaps Concept Score	Premap Proposition Score	Postmaps Proposition Score
201	Advanced	Male	6	17	5	17
202	Advanced	Female	8	21	7	20
203	Advanced	Female	11	24	10	23
204	Average	Female	5	24	4	23
205	Average	Male	2	11	1	10
206	Average	Female	9	15	8	14
207	Low	Male	7	8	6	7
208	Low	Male	4	11	3	10
209	Low	Female	3	5	2	4

The second step involved analyzing the data and testing the hypothesis using relevant statistics. In this case a good approach is to use a *dependent samples* t *test*. We use dependent or paired *t* tests when we are comparing data from the same participants and when their chance of being sampled is not independent. If you set up your dependent *t* test properly, you should get a table that provides you with a mean for the two groups, the standard error, and the test statistic. In this case, we will look at mean concept scores first. The mean preunit map concept score was 6.11 (with a standard error of 0.98) and the postunit map concept score was 6.92 (with a standard error of 2.31). The paired or dependent *t* test was 4.7180, with a p value of .00125 (one-tailed).

A *one-tailed test* is one in which we are looking for an increase or decrease in the parameter to see if we can reject the *null hypothesis*. The null hypothesis is that nothing occurred, changed, increased, or decreased. In this case, we wanted to see whether the differences in means between concept counts and propositions in the pre-/postmaps could be due to chance. In general, p values less than .05 are considered significant, which means we would be correct 95 times out of 100 if we rejected the null hypothesis that nothing occurred. In this case we can say the differences between the pre and post mean concept scores were statistically very significant. When we repeated this approach to examine the changes between the pre and post proposition scores, we got a similar result.

Although the first hypothesis suggested that students learned a lot about the atmosphere during the unit, Åhlberg and Ahoranta (2008) also wanted to test whether students had more knowledge of the theme than they were able to represent through the maps they created. Based on their doubts about Edwards and Fraser's (1983, p. 24) claim that concept maps were as accurate as interviews for revealing student comprehension, they tested a second hypothesis by scoring the teacher-made maps and comparing them with the students' postunit concept maps. Table 3.4 presents their data.

By analyzing the data in the same way, we can test the null hypothesis that there was no significant difference between the means in the postmap scores and those in the teacher map scores. Remember that, in this example, the teacher made a map for each student based on his or her answers to an end-of-unit test. Again using a dependent *t* test, Åhlberg and Ahoranta (2008) showed that we could reject the null hypothesis. Again, the p value was less than .05, so we can be confident about the decision to reject the idea that there was no significant difference between the scores.

The third and final hypothesis was that the variations between students' pre-/postmaps and the teacher-made maps could be explained by the past academic performance of the students. This used the data that referred to the three groups of students, identified based on standardized tests. This analysis involved the use of parametric statistical tests. As described above, parametric tests make strict assumptions about distribution and, accordingly, other parameters of population data. In this case, however, the samples were not random but were purposively selected

Table 3.4   Postmap and Teacher Map Comparison

Number	Education Level	Gender	Premap Concept Score	Teacher Map Concept Score	Postmap Proposition Score	Teacher Map Proposition Score
201	Advanced	Male	17	36	17	40
202	Advanced	Female	21	48	20	53
203	Advanced	Female	24	50	23	61
204	Average	Female	24	29	23	31
205	Average	Male	11	21	10	22
206	Average	Female	15	35	14	39
207	Low	Male	8	32	7	33
208	Low	Male	11	31	10	33
209	Low	Female	5	27	4	28

samples of a teacher's own students. Because the sample lacks statistical randomness, it is not possible to generalize these findings to any larger population. However, statistical tests can still be used in describing the purposive samples and to tentatively make theoretical/conceptual generalizations based on data from other purposive samples—in this case national education data (Shadish, Cook, & Campbell, 2002; Yin, 2009).

In this case, the researchers used a one-way ANOVA to analyze the way in which the mean of a variable can be compared between groups. This test can be used to determine whether the variance between the postmaps and teacher maps could be explained based on the academic groupings. The results were compiled by analyzing the three groups of students (low, medium, and high achievers) based on previously taken standardized tests. To set up a one-way ANOVA, the three groups should be seen as the IVs, and the numbers of relevant concepts and propositions as the DVs.

In Table 3.5, two statistically significant results have been bolded. There are statistically significant differences in the number of relevant concepts in the three groups $F(2) = 5.764$, $p < .05$. As presented in the table, the value .657 represents the calculated effect size statistic, known as eta squared. Statistically speaking, this means 65.7% (or 66% rounded) of the variation in number of concepts is explained by the earlier school achievement level of the students in this case.

Table 3.5	Results of One-Way Analysis of Variance in Atmosphere Design Experiment			
Data	F	df	p	eta squared
Premap concept score	1.493	2	.298	.332
Postmap concept score	**5.746**	**2**	**.040***	**.657**
Premap proposition score	1.493	2	.298	.332
Postmap proposition score	**6.326**	**2**	**.033***	**.678**

Note: Boldface type indicates results are statistically significant.

*$p < .05$.

EXERCISE 3.2
Understanding ANOVA

Still confused? Recall the discussion in the Data-Analysis Strategy section, and do some more reading on ANOVA online or in your school's library. Why is it such a useful statistic? To what do the F, the df, the p, and the eta squared refer?

LIMITATIONS OF THE RESEARCH EXAMPLE

A relevant limitation of this study is the fact that the students knew they were part of education research. They were reported by the study's authors to be very attentive and perhaps more interested than they might have otherwise been. The authors suggested that this could have resulted in the *Pygmalion* or *Rosenthal effect* (Åhlberg & Ahoranta, 2008). These terms refer to the phenomenon in which the greater the expectation placed on people such as children or students, the better they perform. This may have the effect of altering the results of a study. Another limitation was the fact that whereas the experiment used a built-in control to assess the role of concept maps in education, it did not include a relevant *control group*. This is a group that is practically identical to the treatment group but that does not receive the intervention, in this case the use of pre-/postmaps. Future research might compare short-answer test results on a specific unit of study between classes that made concept maps and classes that did not.

SUMMARY OF RESEARCH FINDINGS

To summarize this research example, concept maps were used in a variety of ways. They were used to collect pre/post data from students and were used by a teacher to create a map of student answers to a test. Based on these data, three hypotheses were tested. The first explored whether maps were a useful way to demonstrate learning. Based on the data analysis, it was possible to reject the null hypothesis that there was no change between the pre- and the postmaps. It thus appears that maps are a useful way to test student learning. The second hypothesis tested the idea that maps were as good as other means to evaluate student learning. As you may recall, based on a comparison of the postmaps and teacher-made maps, students identified more concepts when prompted by questions than when completing maps on their own. Concept maps, therefore, may not be the best means to assess learning when used by themselves, since in this example, students had more knowledge of the theme than they were able to represent through the maps they created. The final hypothesis tested whether the variations between students' pre/post maps and the teacher-made maps could be explained by the past academic performance of the students. Based on this analysis, it does appear that past knowledge explains some of the variance. In short, the more students had learned in the past, the easier it was for them to learn new ideas, concepts, and connections in the future.

STUDENT ACTIVITY

Some have suggested that learning to make a concept map is very difficult and can take weeks (Novak & Gowin, 1984). We are not so sure. Using a method developed by Åhlberg (1993), many have learned to make concept maps and have taught others in less than 10 minutes. In fact, teaching others is often the best way to learn something yourself. Using the instructions below, teach three people to make a concept map. You should read through the Teaching Others How to Construct a Concept Map section and practice the steps yourself before trying to explain it to others.

Teaching Others How to Construct a Concept Map

1. Pick a topic that you imagine your three participants will know something about. The more meaningful your topic (e.g., university) is to your participants, the better the maps will be.

2. Select six to eight concepts related to the topic you selected. These should be ideas anybody could connect to the topic you selected. Present these concepts in alphabetical order to your participants so that you do not give them any unnecessary

hints, for example, books, dining halls, dorms, exams, gymnasium, professors, term papers, and so forth.

3. Explain to your "students" in basic terms what a concept map looks like, and offer them an exemplar map if possible. To help new mapmakers understand what you mean, it can be useful to begin with an analogy. Concepts can be seen as islands, and linking words are like bridges. These linking words should include arrowheads to show the direction of the relationship between one concept and another. By building concepts, linking words, and drawing arrows, a full proposition or claim about the world can emerge through your map. As you explain the process to your students, remind them that the proposition/claim made in the map has to be at least meaningful, more or less probable, and more or less truthful.

4. Ask the first participant to take any of the concepts in your list and say, "Because everything is connected in one way or another, it is possible to start concept mapping from any concept." When one of the concepts has been selected, use it as a title for the first map.

5. Ask the second student to take another concept island from the list. Allocate it under the first concept. Then ask the third student to say how these two concepts are linked in her or his mind. Remember to offer positive feedback during the activity, and always thank those who are participating. Use terms such as, "OK," "I see what you mean," "very good," or "excellent," depending on the quality of the contribution.

6. Next, draw an arrow from one concept to another, according to which concept was first in the proposition. Write the linking words using just the words the student used, draw an arrow from one concept to the other, and check that a full, meaningful proposition has been created. Explain to everyone that we now have a bridge from one concept to another with the arrowhead demonstrating how they are connected. Ask whether this proposition corresponds to how the participant thinks these two concepts are related in his or her mind. If the participant is not satisfied, modify linking words so it is more in line with his or her perception.

This is the way to teach people the first and most important aspect of a concept map: It has to correspond to key elements of a mapmaker's thinking. This teaches participants to take full responsibility for their concept mapping. This is how participants learn to understand how flexibly concept mapping as a method can be used to transform their thinking from spoken expressions to concept maps and other written expressions.

7. Ask the second student to pick a new concept, and ask the third to express how this concept is linked in his or her mind to either of the two earlier selected concepts. Don't forget to encourage your students. Be sure to check that the proposition corresponds accurately with how the second student thinks these concepts are linked. Continue this way until all the concepts have been used and the full concept map for this group has been created.

Sometimes a student will ask whether another concept that came into his or her mind can be linked within the map. Be sure to express your delight! This is why concept maps can promote active learning among students. Work with the group to figure out where the new concept should go within the map and how it should be linked.

8. Once you have taught three or more people to make maps, think about how you might use a concept map to gather data. Perhaps you could make a map of the three concept maps you gathered from your participants and present it to your class. How could you adapt the above strategy to allow you to make a concept map of three concept maps? If you decide to make a concept map of the gathered maps, be sure to keep the identity of those whose maps you used confidential. For more see Chapters 4 and 6.

CONCLUSION

In this chapter we have explored a number of important aspects of quantitative research and suggested that the concept map is a useful tool for quantitative researchers. Although they offer the benefits of other kinds of maps, concept maps depend on more formal structures, predefined focus areas, related concepts, and clear propositions that establish relationships. Because of this, concept maps are more likely to provide data that allow the measurement and analysis of levels, hierarchies, and relationships. This chapter has suggested quantitative researchers may use concept maps to count and score data presented through created maps using existing scales, models, and methods.

An important aspect of quantitative research is based on the relationships between the assumptions made, language employed, type of data generated, and statistical test used in one's analysis. Both parametric and nonparametric statistics are discussed, but this chapter is intended to introduce key concepts associated with statistics. More study will be needed to fully develop numeric and statistical literacy, and this chapter provides but an overview of what is often a semester-long course. Using concept maps may offer an accessible way to understand how and why "counting" concepts and scoring maps can help give you a sense of the meaning each map demonstrates and how that meaning may change over time. Although concept maps may not provide as much information as other sorts of evaluations, they do offer a more creative and engaging means of quantitative data collection. As we shall see, they have other valuable roles to play in social science research.

REVIEW

1. Define quantitative research, and explain the assumptions about knowledge on which it is based.

2. What are some traditional approaches to data collection in quantitative research? Why might concept maps be a useful addition?

3. Provide three ways that concept maps can be used in quantitative research, and explain one in detail.

4. Compare and contrast mean, median, and mode. Explain the difference between causation and correlation.

5. How might different approaches to scoring concept maps lead to different kinds of data analysis?

SUGGESTED ADDITIONAL READINGS

Åhlberg, M. (2004, September 14–17). Varieties of concept mapping. In A. Cañas, J. Novak, & F. Gonzales (Eds.), *Concept maps: Theory, methodology, technology* (Proceedings of the First International Conference on Concept Mapping, Vol. 2, pp. 25–28). Retrieved from http://cmc.ihmc.us/papers/cmc2004-206.pdf

Bolte, L. A. (1999). Using concept maps and interpretive essays for assessment in mathematics. *School Science & Mathematics, 99*(1), 19–31.

Novak, J. D., & Cañas, A. J. (2008). *The theory underlying concept maps and how to construct and use them.* Pensacola: Florida Institute for Human and Machine Cognition.

Salkind, N. J. (2010). *Statistics for people who (think they) hate statistics.* Thousand Oaks, CA: Sage.

REFERENCES

Åhlberg, M. (1990). *Käsitekarttatekniikka ja muut vastaavat graafiset tiedonesittämistekniikat opettajan ja oppilaiden työvälineinä* [Concept mapping and other graphical knowledge-representation methods as tools for teachers and pupils] (Research Reports of the Faculty of Education No. 30). Joensuu, Finland: University of Joensuu.

Åhlberg, M. (1993, August 1–5). *Concept maps, Vee diagrams and rhetorical argumentation (RA) analysis: Three educational theory-based tools to facilitate meaningful learning.* Paper presented at the Third International Seminar on Misconceptions in Science and Mathematics, Ithaca, NY.

Åhlberg, M. (2004, September 14–17). Varieties of concept mapping. In A. Cañas, J. Novak, & F. Gonzales (Eds.), *Concept maps: Theory, methodology, technology* (Proceedings of the First International Conference on Concept Mapping, Vol. 2, pp. 25–28). Retrieved from http://cmc.ihmc.us/papers/cmc2004-206.pdf

Åhlberg, M. (2008, September 22–25). *Concept mapping as an innovation: Documents, memories and notes from Finland, Sweden, Estonia and Russia 1984–2008.* Paper presented at the Third International Conference on Concept Mapping, Tallinn, Estonia, and Helsinki, Finland.

Åhlberg, M., Äänismaa, P., & Dillon, P. (2005). Education for sustainable living: Integrating theory, practice, design and development. *Scandinavian Journal of Educational Research, 49*(2), 167–186.

Åhlberg, M., & Ahoranta, V. (2008, September 22–25). *Concept maps and short-answer tests: Probing pupils' learning and cognitive structure.* Paper presented at the Third International Conference on Concept Mapping, Tallinn, Estonia, and Helsinki, Finland.

Åhlberg, M., Turja, L., & Robinson, J. (2003). Educational research and development to promote sustainable development in the city of Helsinki: Helping the accessible Helsinki Programme 2001–2011 to achieve its goals. *International Journal of Environment and Sustainable Development, 2*(2), 197–209.

Alkahtani, K. (2009). *Creativity training effects upon concept map complexity of children with ADHD: An experimental study.* Unpublished doctoral dissertation, University of Glasgow, Scotland.

Ausubel, D. (1963). *The psychology of meaningful verbal learning.* New York: Grune & Stratton.

Besterfield-Sacre, M., Gerchak, J., Lyons, M., Shuman, L. J., & Wolfe, H. (2004). Scoring concept maps: An integrated rubric for assessing engineering education. *Journal of Engineering Education, 93,* 105–116.

Bolte, L. A. (1999). Using concept maps and interpretive essays for assessment in mathematics. *School Science & Mathematics, 99*(1), 19–31.

Czuchry, M., & Dansereau, D. F. (1996). Node-link mapping as an alternative to traditional writing assignments in undergraduate psychology courses. *Teaching of Psychology, 23*(2), 91–96.

Daley, B. (2004, September 14–17). *Using concept maps in qualitative research.* Paper presented at the First International Conference on Concept Mapping, Pamplona, Spain.

Edmondson, K. M. (2000). Assessing science understanding through concept maps. In J. J. Mintzes, J. H. Wandersee, & J. D. Novak (Eds.), *Assessing science understanding: A human constructivist view* (pp. 15–40). San Diego, CA: Academic Press.

Edwards, J., & Fraser, K. (1983). Concept maps as reflectors of conceptual understanding. *Research in Science Education, 13,* 19–26.

Field, A. (2009). *Discovering statistics using SPSS* (3rd ed.). Thousand Oaks, CA: Sage.

Goldsmith, T. E., & Davenport, D. M. (1990). Assessing structural similarity in graphs. In R. W. Schvaneveldt (Ed.), *Pathfinder associative networks: Studies in knowledge organization* (pp. 75–87). Norwood, NJ: Ablex.

Gowin, D. B. (1981). *Educating.* Ithaca, NY: Cornell University Press.

Grissom, R., & Kim, J. (2005). *Effect sizes for research: A broad practical approach.* New York: Psychology Press.

Guilford, J. P. (1965). *Fundamental statistics in psychology and education* (4th ed.). New York: McGraw-Hill.

Hall, R. H., & O'Donnell, A. (1996). Cognitive and affective outcomes of learning from knowledge maps. *Contemporary Educational Psychology, 21,* 94–101.

Howitt, D., & Cramer, D. (2008). *Introduction to statistics in psychology* (4th ed.). London: Prentice Hall.

Huerta, P. M., Galan, E., & Granell, R. (2003). *Concept maps in mathematics education: A possible framework for student's assessment.* Valencia, Spain: Department de Didactica de la Matematica, Universitat de Valencia.

Jones, M. G., Carter, G., & Rua, M. J. (2000). Exploring the development of conceptual ecologies: Communities of concepts related to convection and heat. *Journal of Research in Science Teaching, 37*(2), 139–159.

Jones, M. G., Rua, M. J., & Carter, G. (1998). Science teachers' conceptual growth within Vygotsky's zone of proximal development. *Journal of Research in Science Teaching, 35*(9), 967–985.

Kilic, Z., Kaya, O. N., & Dogan, A. (2004, August). *Effects of students' pre- and post-laboratory concept maps on students' attitudes toward chemistry laboratory in university general chemistry.* Paper presented at the 18th International Conference on Chemical Education, Istanbul, Turkey.

Kinnear, P. R., & Gray, C. D. (2010). *PASW Statistics 17 made simple.* New York: Psychology Press.

Kommers, P., & Lanzing, J. (1997). Student's concept mapping for hypermedia design: Navigation through the World Wide Web (www) space and self-assessment. *Journal of Interactive Learning Research, 8*(3/4), 421–455.

Novak, J. (1998). *Learning, creating and using knowledge: Concept Maps™ as facilitative tools in schools and in corporations.* London: Lawrence Erlbaum.

Novak, J. D. (1981). Applying learning psychology and philosophy of science to biology teaching. *American Biology Teacher, 43*(1), 12–20.

Novak, J. D., & Cañas, A. J. (2008). *The theory underlying concept maps and how to construct and use them.* Pensacola: Florida Institute for Human and Machine Cognition.

Novak, J. D., & Gowin, J. B. (1984). *Learning how to learn.* Cambridge, UK: Cambridge University Press.

Novak, J. D., & Msonda, D. (1991). A twelve year longitudinal study of science concept learning. *American Educational Research Journal, 28,* 117–153.

Poole, D., & Davis, T. (2006). Concept mapping to measure outcomes in a study abroad program. *Social Work Education, 25*(1), 61–77.

Ruiz-Primo, M., Shavelson, R. J., Li, M., & Schultz, S. E. (2001). On the validity of cognitive interpretations of scores from alternative concept-mapping techniques. *Educational Assessment, 7*(2), 99–141.

Rye, J. A., & Rubba, P. A. (2002). Scoring concept maps: An expert map-based scheme weighted for relationships. *School Science and Mathematics, 102*(1), 33–44.

Salkind, N. J. (2010). *Statistics for people who (think they) hate statistics.* Thousand Oaks, CA: Sage.

Shadish, W., Cook, T., & Campbell, D. (2002). *Experimental and quasi-experimental designs for generalized causal inference.* Boston: Houghton Mifflin.

Siegel, S., & Castellan, N. J. (1988). *Nonparametric statistics for the behavioral sciences* (2nd ed.). New York: McGraw-Hill.

Srinivasan, M., McElvany, M., Shay, J., Shavelson, R., & West, D. (2008). Measuring knowledge structure: Reliability of concept mapping assessment in medical education. *Academic Medicine, 83*(12), 1196–1203.

Stoddart, T., Abrams, R., Gasper, E., & Canaday, D. (2000). Concept maps as assessment in science inquiry learning—A report of methodology. *International Journal of Science Education, 22*(12), 1221–1246.

Teddlie, C. B., & Tashakkori, A. (2009). *Foundations of mixed methods research: Integrating quantitative and qualitative approaches in the social and behavioral sciences.* Thousand Oaks, CA: Sage.

Thompson, T., & Mintzes, J. (2002). Cognitive structure and the affective domain: On knowing and feeling in biology. *International Journal of Science Education, 24*(6), 645–660.

Turns, J., Atman, C., & Adams, R. (2000). Concept maps for engineering education: A cognitively motivated tool supporting varied assessment functions. *IEEE Transactions on Education, 43,* 164–173.

West, D. C., Park, J. K., Pomeroy, J. R., & Sandoval, J. (2002). Concept mapping assessment in medical education: A comparison of two scoring systems. *Medical Education, 36,* 820–826.

Wheeldon, J. (2010). Mapping mixed methods research: Methods, measures, and meaning. *Journal of Mixed Methods Research, 4*(2), 87–102.

Wheeldon, J. P., & Faubert, J. (2009). Framing experience: Concept maps, mind maps, and data collection in qualitative research. *International Journal of Qualitative Methods, 8*(3), 68–83.

Yin, R. K. (2009). *Case study research: Design and methods* (4th ed.). Thousand Oaks, CA: Sage.

4

From the Ground Up

Using Mind Maps in Qualitative Research

CHAPTER OVERVIEW AND OBJECTIVES

In Chapter 3, we explored how concept maps can be used in quantitative research to gather, analyze, interpret, and present quantities or numeric information. Although some of the language of quantitative research remains relevant in Chapter 4, the focus on qualitative research is quite different. Instead of trying to generalize findings based on assumptions about data, qualitative researchers often focus on exploring the meaning individuals assign to a particular event or phenomenon. Through inductive approaches, qualitative researchers often focus on the gathering, analysis, interpretation, and presentation of *narrative* information. Traditional qualitative data-collection techniques include surveys, interviews, or other more detailed ethnographic approaches. This chapter presents mind maps as another useful technique for qualitative researchers.

Mind maps may be of interest to qualitative researchers because they are more user generated than other data-collection techniques and can be designed to be unsolicited, open ended, and individualistic or personal. In this chapter, we will discuss how mind maps can be used to gather qualitative data based on the ideas represented within the map and the structure of the map itself. As we discussed in Chapter 2 maps can be seen as data. In this chapter we will also explore how they can be used alongside more traditional data-collection techniques to prime the pump of participant reflection and can be used by the researchers themselves to reflect on their research and assist in their interpretation of gathered data. In this chapter, readers will be encouraged to gather mind maps from friends, family members, or colleagues and come up with an analysis strategy they can present to their class. By the end of this chapter, readers should be able to do the following:

- explain some of the assumptions and characteristics of qualitative research;
- outline the theoretical basis for the use of mind maps in qualitative research;
- list some of the ways mind maps can be used for qualitative research;
- consider how participant-created mind maps can assist researchers to develop interview questions; and
- understand how to make mind maps and how to use them to gather data.

THEORETICAL JUSTIFICATION

As we saw in Chapter 3, quantitative research focuses on postpositivist assumptions about meaning. Concept maps may be especially useful for research problems that are based on certain and quantifiable assumptions about knowledge. The acceptance of assumptions about what knowledge is and how it is constructed in maps is also relevant for some traditional approaches to qualitative research. Indeed, qualitative concept map researchers have used concept maps to organize research projects, reduce data, analyze themes, and present findings (Daley, 2004). In principle, whereas concept maps can be used for either research tradition, it is important to understand that the process of teaching one how to make a map often involves the researcher in a direct and unambiguous way. This is at odds with emergent approaches to qualitative research.

As discussed in Chapter 1, qualitative researchers are often associated with constructivist accounts of knowledge. Meaning is assumed to be personal and subjective and to be best understood through social interaction, personal histories, and experiences (Creswell & Plano Clark, 2007). As a result, knowledge is inherently localized. A number of approaches to research grew out of this recognition. In sociology, Garfinkel (1967) suggested understanding a culture required that one determine the unspoken rules that guide the actions of its members. In anthropology, Geertz (1973) provided a means to understand how to make "thick" descriptions of events, rituals, and customs. These observations in turn influenced subsequent developments in qualitative research as discussed in more detail below. The idea that knowledge is subjective may also be relevant in understanding some of the possible complications inherent in employing visual techniques in qualitative social science research.

One problem, according to Johanna Drucker (2009), is that many visualization techniques were originally developed for "empirical sciences and quantitative analytics." Thus, these techniques can be easily tangled up with quantitative assumptions about knowledge, meaning, and definitions of data. The use of visual data requires a greater focus on epistemological questions about how one might situate human experience within visual and graphical forms. Mind maps may offer one solution to this concern. In some ways, they are just the latest means to develop data-collection tools that are more explicitly user generated and unsolicited. As discussed in Chapter 2, the use of vignette- or scenario-based responses, subject-operated cameras/videos/sound recordings, focus groups, journaling, and visual life history interviews have become more popular within qualitative research (Wheeldon & Faubert, 2009).

Mind maps can be seen as an extension of this more general trend. Unlike concept maps, they are often less structured and hierarchical and more easily constructed by participants themselves without the interference of the researcher. Drawing on other kinds of skills that are more artistic, interrelational, and free form, the way mind maps are constructed may make them less useful when one is trying to assess the logic and correctness of propositions and connections. For qualitative researchers, however, mind maps offer a distinct way for researchers to "search for codes, concepts and categories within the data . . . based on how the participant(s) frame(d) their experience" (Wheeldon & Faubert, 2009, p. 72–73).

Mind maps are most often associated with Tony Buzan. A prolific writer, Buzan has published multiple books on mind maps and their uses in a variety of settings. He argues that mind maps promote creativity through *radiant thinking*—a process that mimics your brain's natural thinking process. By focusing on a creative process like mind mapping, one can enhance associative, nonlinear thought processes; assist brainstorming; and strengthen one's memory (Buzan & Buzan, 1996, p. 53–57). The focus on creativity in radiant thinking appears to be based in some ways on the split-brain research of Robert Sperry (1966). This and subsequent research suggests that the two hemispheres of the brain operate distinct executive functions. The right hemisphere of the brain is dominant in intellectual functions such as spatial awareness, imaginative thought, daydreaming, dimension, color separation, and analysis, whereas the left is considered dominant in intellectual functions such as words, logic, numbers, sequence, linearity, analysis, and lists.

The idea of a rigid right/left split in the brain is simplistic. However, it is an area of research that continues to be investigated (Gazzaniga, 2005). Although it might be more accurate to speak of areas that are more often associated with the right or the left side of the brain, it does appear that maximizing creativity involves finding ways to allow both hemispheres to operate together (Torrance & Rokenstein, 1987). The value of mind mapping, according to Buzan, is that it can combine left and right brain functions by focusing on how individuals create associations that branch or radiate out from a central word or theme. Instead of focusing on hierarchical structures or the quality of mapped propositions, mind maps allow researchers to focus on how respondents represent different associations. Using maps can also provide a means to engage the artistic and imaginative abilities of participants and thereby unlock creative intelligence. Buzan suggested the use of pictures, graphics, and colors within mind maps to maximize this potential (Buzan & Buzan, 1996).

The value of mind mapping might also be seen in the light of *gestalt theory*. As discussed in Chapter 2, this approach emphasizes perception, insight, and meaning as the key elements of learning. Indeed it is how an individual organizes, interprets, and gives meaning to the events in his or her life that is of most interest and value. The formality of concept maps may suit some individuals; others may prefer a more creative process, with fewer rules and more flexibility. Based on the theory of multiple intelligences developed in 1983 by Dr. Howard Gardner, these representations should also be considered valuable. Gardner, a professor of education at Harvard University, suggested that the traditional notion of intelligence, based on linguistic competence in reading and writing or logical intelligence in math, is limited (Gardner, 1983). He proposed that many other kinds of intelligence are valuable and that supporting students in educational environments required an understanding of these other intelligences and an integration of multiple methods in the classroom (Gardner, 1993). The recognition that people, groups, and personalities learn and understand things in different sorts of ways (Rohm, 1994) provides a justification for the use of flexible and personalized mind maps. It also appears connected to assumptions in qualitative research as discussed in Chapter 1.

KEY CHARACTERISTICS OF QUALITATIVE RESEARCH

Qualitative researchers often focus on the gathering, analysis, interpretation, and presentation of *narrative* information. The focus on this type of information is based on a desire to describe real life as credibly as possible. Of importance to qualitative researchers is the attempt to engage in a more holistic examination of data based on the acknowledgment that multidirectional relationships can, and often do, influence each other simultaneously. Qualitative researchers prefer gathering information from human beings in natural and/or real-life situations and aim to reveal otherwise unknown or unexpected understandings by analyzing data in depth and on multiple levels. Patton (2002, pp. 40–41) provided a detailed overview of key characteristics of qualitative research in the design, data-collection, and analysis stages of research. As presented in Figure 4.1, key issues in the design stage, according to Patton, are connected to the nature of the inquiry, the flexibility of the design, and the approach to sampling.

Figure 4.1   Design Stage Considerations in Qualitative Research

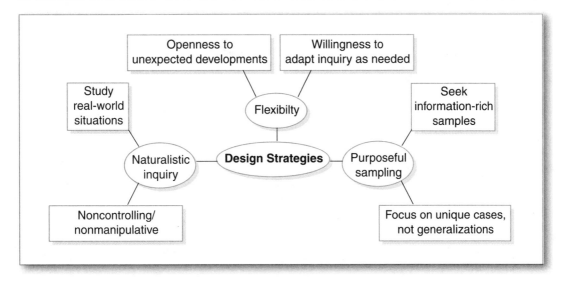

Unlike quantitative researchers' focus on gathering data from random samples where possible, qualitative researchers seek information from selected individuals, groups, and cultures and about events, incidences, and occurrences. The focus on finding and describing unique cases and participant perceptions takes precedence over trying to discover generalizable findings that can be applied from a sample to a population. Other elements of interest are how and what kinds of data should be collected. This includes understanding the nature of qualitative data and the importance of gathering data on the ground. As Figure 4.2 suggests, it also requires a commitment to flexibility, an absence of judgment, and an awareness of the broader realities and dynamics of the research process and phenomenon under investigation (Patton, 2002).

Finally, Patton (2002) outlined five characteristics associated with qualitative analysis strategies. Present in Figure 4.3, these include the importance of treating each case as unique, relying on inductive approaches to discover patterns and themes, the need to remain context sensitive, and focusing on the voice, perspective, and role of the researcher. The last element, connected to the acknowledgment of the difficulty faced by researchers in distancing themselves from their own voices, values, and perspectives, cannot be overstated. The recognition that the approach chosen by the researcher will shape any interaction between the phenomena studied and the data collected is profound (Feyerbend, 1978), though perhaps not new. In sociology *verstehen* is associated with Max Weber and has come to mean a systematic interpretive process in

Figure 4.2 Data-Collection-Stage Considerations in Qualitative Research

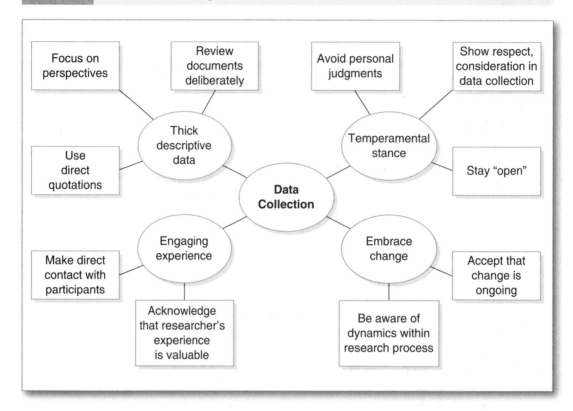

which people try to understand others by recognizing that we each have our own point of view shaped by culture and societal forces (Burger, 1977). This suggests important challenges to traditional notions of objectivity, neutrality, and the separateness of the "knower and the known" (Teddlie & Tasakkori, 2009, p. 90). Garfinkel (1967) also considered the importance of understanding how people within social situations guide and are guided by the nature of these interactions. This understanding has led qualitative researchers to acknowledge the importance of the role they themselves play within their own research (Guba & Lincoln, 1989).

In recent years, there has been a move to integrate and address this limitation through *reflexivity* (Willig, 2001). Reflexivity requires an awareness of the improbability of the researcher's remaining neutral, impartial, and unconnected to his or her subject (Nightingale & Cromby, 1999, p. 228) and a willingness to undergo a process of internal reflection. It may also both entail that researchers acknowledge the reasons for their selection of a phenomenon to study and be extremely transparent about the process they use to interpret their data (Charmaz, 2006). Wheeldon and

Figure 4.3   Data-Analysis-Stage Considerations in Qualitative Research

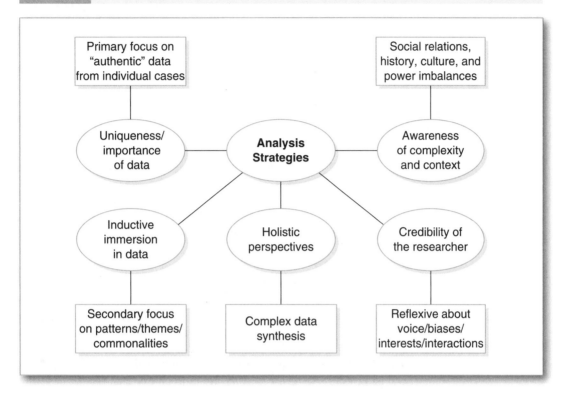

Faubert (2009) have suggested mind maps may offer a unique visual means to ground research in participants' knowledge and demonstrate clearly how themes within the data are developed. In this way, maps can promote more transparency in the research process and show how qualitative researchers identify themes, connections, and findings. For now, let's examine in general terms how mind maps can be used within qualitative research.

MIND MAPS AND QUALITATIVE STUDY: EXISTING STUDIES AND ENGAGING PARTICIPANTS

There are a number of characteristics of qualitative research. A common starting point is a focus on the gathering, analysis, interpretation, and presentation of narrative information (Teddlie & Tashakkori, 2009, p. 6). This has often resulted in data collection that is structured through interviews. Kvale (1996, p. 88) described seven stages of interview investigations, shown in Figure 4.4.

Figure 4.4 Seven Stages of Interview Investigation

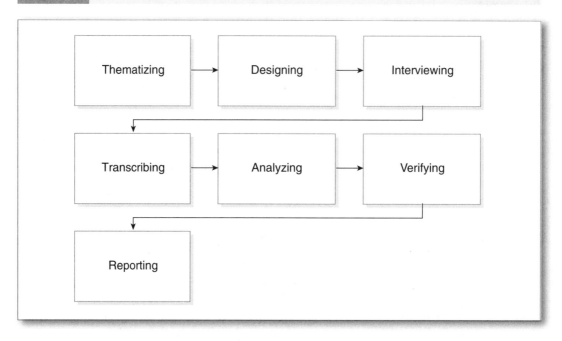

"Thematizing" refers to formulating the purpose of the investigation of the topic(s) to be investigated, and "designing" refers to how to plan the design of the study. Kvale (1996) suggested the researcher should consider the seven stages before the interview starts. "Interviewing," of course, refers to the actual process of conducting the interviews. Kvale suggested that interviews be based—however loosely—on a plan or guide but that researchers ought to keep an open mind and use reflective approaches to information gathering, being mindful of their own role in the interview. "Transcribing" refers to the process of preparing the interview material for analysis. Commonly this involves transcribing oral speech to written text. "Analyzing" is how researchers decide on and engage in a process of interpretation. This may be based on past approaches to qualitative analysis, or it may emerge in a unique way based on an interaction between the researchers and the material.

Another important stage is "verifying." Traditionally this is the process of considering the validity of the study by investigating whether your study addresses what it purports to and investigating the reliability of findings and/or the credibility of your results. Golafshani (2003) suggested we expand these ideas and redefine these concepts to reflect that there are multiple ways of establishing truth. Thus, instead of importing traditional understandings based on quantitative research assumptions, *reliability* and *validity* should be seen in the context of the qualitative paradigm. We will discuss this in more detail in Chapter 7. Some important actions in verifying and validating qualitative research are connected to the researcher's reflexivity, the acknowledgment of relevant limitations, and a consideration of how and why complementary data support or contest the findings. The final step is "reporting." This refers to how you present the findings of your study, the methodological plan you used, and the specific methods on which you relied. The most important goal here is to communicate key elements of the study through the creation of an accessible product. We will discuss some strategies for compiling and presenting research in Chapter 6.

It is not difficult to see how maps might fit within the seven steps described above. Maps can help researchers brainstorm and plan research. They can be used before, in the place of, or even after an interview to provide additional data. In addition, comparing interviews with mind maps from the same participant may offer a useful means to validate the data collected. Maps can also be used to demonstrate an analysis strategy or to present findings of interviews in a visually appealing and accessible way. Finally, of specific interest is the use of maps to probe the back stage of participants' experiences and perceptions. Used in this way, maps represent a new strategy to go beyond soliciting "a rehearsed form of narrative that precludes more spontaneous answers" (Hathaway & Atkinson, 2003, p. 162).

However promising mind maps appear, a challenge for their broader use in qualitative research is the comparative lack of useful models and methods. The use of pictorial data is common in other disciplines. One way to understand the value of maps is to consider similar techniques used in other disciplines. A *genogram* is a pictorial display of a person's family relationships and medical history and may include visualized hereditary patterns and psychological factors that inform relationships. Genograms are often used in psychotherapy and use lines to indicate relationships within families. Often the thickness of the lines indicates the importance of the relationships within the visual displays (McGoldrick, Gerson, & Schellenberger, 1999). Another approach increasingly used in business and marketing applies the import of visual images to understanding both conscious and unconscious thoughts about consumer products (Zaltman, 1997). The Zaltman Metaphor Elicitation Technique involves the combination of interviews with images chosen by research study participants. Through this technique participants collect a set of pictures that represent their thoughts and feelings about a topic of interest. The combination of the participant-created collage of meaningful images and interviews can provide a deeper window into the motivations, beliefs, and choices made by individuals (Zaltman & Zaltman, 2008).

As we will see in Chapter 7, these are not the only models and approaches that have been used. Of immediate interest, however, are the ways in which mind maps combine the visual potential of the Zaltman Metaphor Elicitation Technique with the relational aspects of genograms. The use of mind maps in qualitative social science research is in its early stages, but as a data-collection technique it has been used in tourism studies (Witsel, 2008), as a classroom exercise in education (Budd, 2004), and to teach social problems in community college coursework (Peterson & Snyder, 1998).

As Tattersall, Watts, and Vernon (2007) pointed out, mind maps have been used with the most regularity in nursing and health studies. This includes references to mind maps as part of nursing education (Rooda, 1994), in care planning (Kern, Bush, & McCleish, 2006; Mueller, Johnston, & Bligh, 2001), and for reflection and evaluation (Jenkins, 2005). For example, research by Farrand, Hussain, and Hennessy (2002) explores mind mapping as a memory aid among medical students. Students who used mind maps saw a 10% increase in recall over baseline versus students who used their preferred study methods, who had only a 6% increase over baseline.

Despite some important uses to date, there is plenty of potential for increasing the use of maps in qualitative research. A useful starting place builds on Patton's (2002) discussion of design, data collection, and analysis in qualitative research. One novel idea is to use maps to plan your project and update them as you go. Another is to use maps to assist a participant's recall of an event or interaction (Wheeldon, 2011). Finally, mind maps can also be used to assist researchers to transcribe additional data, such as nonverbal cues or other sorts of reactions (Tattersall et al., 2007). In general, as Figure 4.5 demonstrates, there are a number of ways mind maps can assist researchers in qualitative research. Let's consider some of these uses in detail.

Because mind maps are easy to construct and can provide an outline of one's understanding about a topic, they offer a creative and user-generated means of engagement. For now let's focus on using mind maps to identify and plan steps in

Figure 4.5   Uses of Mind Maps in Qualitative Research

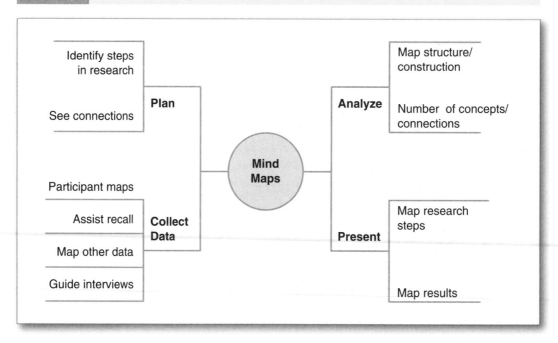

a research project, as a means of data collection, and as part of data-analysis and -interpretation strategies. A little later in this chapter, we will examine how maps can also be used to design additional data collection.

Using Maps to Plan and Identify Steps in Qualitative Research

As we saw in Chapter 2, maps can be used to help explain, outline, and represent the steps in qualitative research. To understand how, it may be useful to revisit the idea that qualitative analysis through inductive reasoning aims to build theory by focusing in more depth on individual cases and context-specific realities. This sort of approach to theory building can be subdivided into two types. As discussed in Chapter 1, *classical theory building* is similar to deductive reasoning because it establishes a concept or proposition and then conducts analysis to explore it through the research, as Figure 4.6 presents.

In contrast, *grounded theory building* is a process by which one first collects and analyzes data and then, based on the concepts of themes that emerge from that data, attempts to formulate concepts about these relationships. The chief difference between these approaches is how and at what stage researchers identify themes. In traditional approaches, the identification of themes often occurs before data collection. In grounded approaches, themes are identified only after data collection to ensure the researcher keeps an open mind and does not seek to "fit" data into past findings. A visual representation of this approach is presented in Figure 4.7.

Whichever approach to qualitative research you employ, visualizing the steps involved is often a useful place to start. Once you have decided on a plan, maps can also be used to collect data.

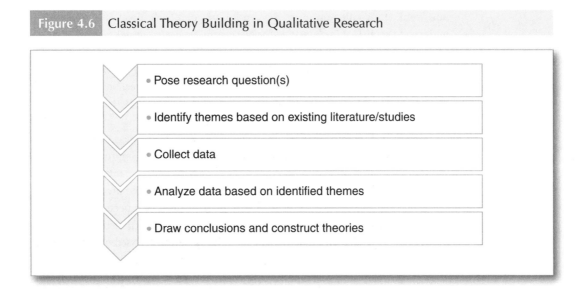

Figure 4.6   Classical Theory Building in Qualitative Research

- Pose research question(s)
- Identify themes based on existing literature/studies
- Collect data
- Analyze data based on identified themes
- Draw conclusions and construct theories

Figure 4.7   Grounded Theory Building in Qualitative Research

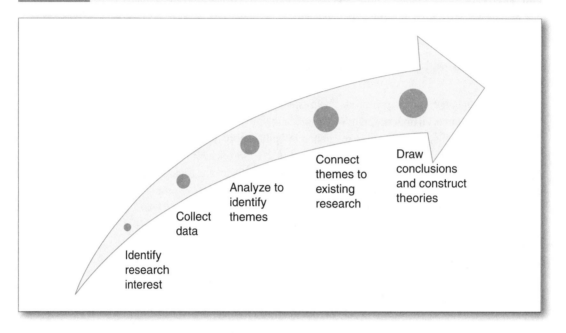

Using Maps to Collect and/or Assist in Data Collection

One of the most useful features of mind maps is how easy they are for people to make. To make one, take a blank piece of paper, and turn it on its side so that it is wider than it is high. Starting in the middle of the page, make a central image or write an important word. Draw a line out from the central image in each direction, and write an important theme that is connected to your central image or word. Write other words or draw other images that are connected to this theme, and continue to build your map outward (Buzan & Buzan, 1996). Buzan suggested focusing on one and only one word for each association and using color, the thickness of lines, boxes, or pictures and graphics to make one's map unique and expressive (Buzan, 1991).

Other approaches are also valid. In 1996, Tony Buzan's coauthor and brother Barry described his version of a mind map as one that focuses less on graphics and colors and more on free-from associations. He argued this approach was more suitable to his academic work and that it had assisted him to organize his thoughts; connect his past, present, and future research; and become more productive (Buzan & Buzan, 1996, pp. 13–14). For us, there are perhaps two key aspects to mind maps that make them valuable for qualitative research. The first is that they focus on a central theme or idea and radiate associated ideas outward, based on related ideas and examples. The second is that they should be as much as possible free form, creative, and developed by participants with minimal instruction by the researcher. This can allow the participant's individual creative process to emerge. Figure 4.8 provides an example of a mind map.

Mind maps can be used alone to gather data from research participants; they can also be seen as a complementary approach used in conjunction with traditional data-gathering techniques. These include participant observation, interviews, and focus groups (Wolcott, 1990). For example, to augment data collected through written transcription or interviews, the researcher can use mind maps to document or capture nonverbal communication such as eye contact, posture, facial expression, personal space, and touch. Although mind mapping and transcribing verbal interactions simultaneously would be difficult, a mind-mapping research assistant could observe the interaction and add important, relevant data (Tattersall et al., 2007). An important consideration here is how to assign meaning(s) associated with nonverbal interactions without verifying what these mean to the actor him- or herself.

Another way to view the utility of mind maps in qualitative data collection is to see them as a means to "prime the pump" of participant reflection (Wheeldon, 2011). By requiring research participants to first frame their experience, maps may help researchers

Figure 4.8   Constructing a Mind Map

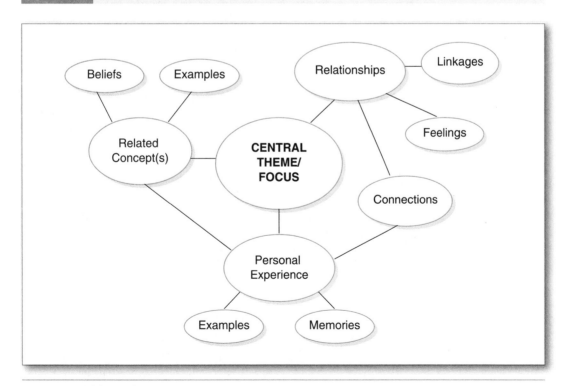

Source: Wheeldon (2010b, p. 91).

in the refinement of other data-collection strategies. In a study based in Latvia among development project participants, data were collected from participants in two stages. In the first, participants were asked to draw mind maps of their experience during the project. In the second, the same general and open-ended interview questions were asked of all participants. The group was divided into two subgroups, the first containing 14 participants who completed both stages of the data collection and the second containing 5 participants who completed only the interviews. The results of the two groups' interviews were compared based on the number of individual concepts identified through the interviews and the length, detail, and number of specific examples provided in the participants' responses. In this study, the group that had completed the maps before the interviews identified, on average, seven more individual concepts than the group that did not first complete maps, as presented in Table 4.1 (Wheeldon, 2011).

Table 4.1	Average Number of Concepts Identified by Map and Nonmap Groups

Map Status	Average Number of Concepts
Map	16.57
Non Map	9

Source: Wheeldon (2011, p. 517)

In addition, participants who completed maps provided more depth when recounting their experience during the interviews. This included a greater number of specific examples, memories, and suggestions. When asked to reflect on the experience of creating a concept map, virtually all participants in the map group identified maps as a "useful way to see experience." Some suggested this was because making a map "helped them to remember events from years ago" and "organize their thoughts about the experience systematically." Others suggested that as a visual aid, the map helped put the experience in "context" and provided a "clearer view" when they looked at events again, helped them realize how much had happened, and helped them "focus on the key experiences, concepts and connections" (Wheeldon, 2011, p. 518).

Data Analysis, Organization, and Designing Additional Data Collection

Another way mind maps could be useful in qualitative research is in the analysis of collected data. Instead of simply reading transcriptions, researchers might read, map, read, and add to their original map or might decide to create another. This can allow for more flexibility to draw out different sorts of connections, relationships, or themes (Tattersall et al., 2007). It may also assist researchers to break out of their own cycles of assumption or expectation by forcing them to graphically represent what they are reading. This approach to data analysis is in line with more traditional strategies derived from Pope, Ziebland, and Mays (2000). The suggestion that researchers immerse themselves in the data, identify key themes, connect these themes to concepts in the data set, and then rearrange the data based on the themes is often much easier to enact graphically than textually. One approach uses mind maps to show the research process from the researcher's point of view (Wheeldon, 2007). This may have the added benefit of serving as a reflexive demonstration of how themes emerge from the data. This process is represented in Figure 4.9.

Figure 4.9   Analyzing Maps and Interviews

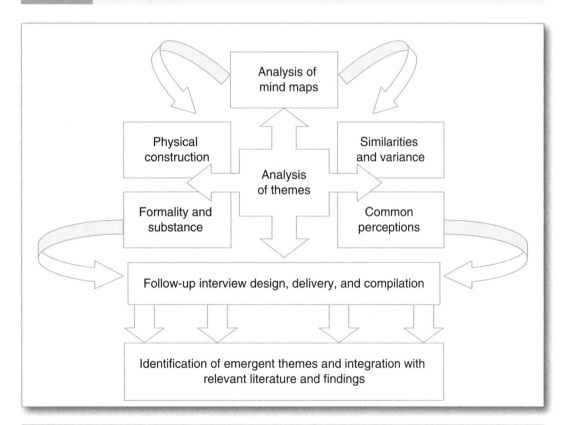

Source: Wheeldon (2007).

Another approach would be to use the construction of mind maps as a means to guide subsequent data-collection techniques. Consider Figure 4.3 once again. Can you imagine how the analysis of different maps could help a researcher to design interviews? Outlined in the research example below, this approach is connected to a debate within qualitative research about the role of analysis strategies in grounded theory. As discussed in Chapter 1, whereas more traditional approaches to qualitative research specifically frame a research question before collecting data, grounded theory favors collecting data before identifying themes through analysis. It has emerged as a major approach because it offers a means for data to emerge and as the best way to develop new theories instead of testing old ones. Before we turn to the example, let's consider some of the major types of qualitative research.

MAPPING QUALITATIVE APPROACHES AND METHODOLOGICAL CHOICES

As we have discussed, research in the social sciences involves a number of choices, decisions, and assumptions. There are many qualitative approaches and methods to consider. The philosophical basis and characteristics underlying the above approaches are useful in understanding most qualitative methodologies; however, there are subtle but important differences between and among approaches such as *ethnography, phenomenology,* and *grounded theory.* You may recall that in Chapter 3 we outlined a series of steps within quantitative research designs. Although qualitative research can also involve different steps and stages, the credibility of the research findings is often informed by the broader methodological choices made by the researcher. A full understanding of these approaches and their similarities, differences, and applicability to various research areas and questions will require more reading, study, and reflection. However, the unique contribution of these approaches to our understanding of the social world compels us to try to consider each of these distinctive types in brief below.

A useful starting place is ethnography. This approach sees research as both a process and a product of participant observations of a culture (Spradley, 1979). As discussed above, the roots of ethnography lie in sociology (Garfinkel, 1967) and cultural anthropology (Geertz, 1973), and as an approach it remains focused in many ways on the nature, construction, and maintenance of cultures and subcultures. A key question for this type of research is, What are the cultural characteristics of this group of people, culture, or subculture? Ethnographers set out to understand lifestyles as a function of the context within which they are lived. To do so, ethnographic researchers may engage in extended observational work in particular settings. According to Hammersley and Atkinson (1983, p. 2), this involves research in which the ethnographer participates overtly or covertly in people's daily lives for extended periods of time watching what happens, listening to what is said, asking questions. In fact collecting whatever data are available to throw light on issues with which he or she is concerned.

Ethnographers may use direct observation, questionnaires, and interviews to obtain data for ethnographic analysis, and once data are gathered they are subjected to a process of systematic inquiry to give both form and content to social processes while inviting researchers to recognize their own role within the research and the social world. This personal and direct approach to research can show how people reflect, order, interpret, and give meaning to events in terms of their existing culturally available beliefs. The focus on the broad role of culture as the system of shared beliefs, values, practices, language, norms, and rituals allows ethnographers to study micro cultures, in a classroom or workplace, or macro cultures, such as the culture(s) of a state, region, or country.

Of importance is developing a portrait of people's lives by studying their behavior in everyday contexts, rather than under experimental conditions created by the researcher. Data may be gathered from a range of sources, but direct observation and/or relatively informal conversations are usually preferred. There are three elements within ethnographies to consider. The first is related to participants, or as ethnographers sometimes refer to them, "informants." This is generally a small number of people or groups and requires some consideration about selection and whether the information collected is representative of the experiences and cultural perspectives of the group as a whole. The approach to data collection is unstructured in the sense that it does not necessarily involve developing an initial plan. Data analysis does not involve creating categories to interpret what people do and say beforehand. In short, data should be collected, analyzed, and presented in such a way as to keep the data in as raw a form as is feasible (Agar, 1996).

As an approach to qualitative research, ethnography has both strengths and weaknesses. Given the subjective nature of this approach, it acknowledges the criticism that all observers are also participants, and thus research findings cannot be easily untangled from the researchers themselves. Other challenges are related to the nature of the attempt to derive intensive observations from a small component of a total community. The focus on a single location also may limit the extent to which the researcher can recognize significant influences that are present on wider regional or national levels. As with other qualitative approaches, a challenge for ethnography is how to connect it to traditional understandings of scientific enquiry. By embracing the notion of subjective realities as opposed to an objective reality, it can appear to some as a form of journalism disguised as academic inquiry. These critiques appear not to appreciate the credibility attached to the reflexive requirements of rigorous qualitative methods nor consider the value of investigating social interactions, cultural patterns, and the relationship between the two.

Another approach is phenomenology. Developed and described first by Husserl (1962) and Heidegger (1962), it can be seen both as a philosophy and as a methodological approach (Schutz, 1967). As a philosophic stance, phenomenology is a framework for describing and classifying subjective experiences of what Husserl termed "the life world" (Langenbach, 1995). As a methodological approach, Schutz (1967) developed phenomenology to incorporate details of everyday experiences often considered mundane, commonplace, or otherwise unimportant. Through a detailed and descriptive study of how individuals experience a phenomenon, ethnographers seek more complete, accurate, and accessible descriptions of a particular human experience to draw out the deeper meaning(s) associated with an experiential moment. A foundational question for phenomenology is, What is the meaning, structure, and essence of lived experiences of a phenomenon by selected individual(s)?

Various phenomena are of interest including memories of specific events, perceptions of individuals or relationships, and descriptions of social activities and/or interactions. Through the discovery of "social realities," phenomenology attempts to provide specific meanings and references for the ways in which human beings live, act, and think (Schutz, 1967, p. 59). This is less about identifying facts and more about understanding lived experience. According to Van Manen (1990, p. 10),

> from a phenomenological point of view, we are less interested in the factual status of particular instances: whether something happened, how often it tends to happen, or how the occurrence of an experience is related to the prevalence of other conditions and events. For example, phenomenology does not ask, "How do these children learn this particular material?" but it asks, "What is the nature or essence of the experience of learning (so that I can now better understand what this learning experience is like for these children)?

Of additional importance are the specialized methods that guide a researcher's approach, participant selection, information gathering, data analysis, and compilation and presentation of findings. Moustakas (1994) emphasized two broad aspects of the phenomenological method: (a) bracketing and phenomenological reduction and (b) an emphasis on intuition, imagination, and universal structures in analysis. The first stage involves a researcher's identifying and acknowledging his or her own subjective beliefs and assumptions and then deliberately setting those aside (Creswell, 1998). The next stage, data collection, often involves in-depth interviews with participants (Patton, 2002) designed to ensure the researcher can more fully understand the experience from the participant's point of view. During data analysis, researchers often search for commonalities across different individuals' experience, and like ethnography, phenomenological approaches attempt to ensure that findings emerge on their own from within the data themselves. Listing and evaluating significant statements can be part of the process, and there is often a tendency to resist the urge to delete from, add to, change, or distort anything originally presented by participants.

The focus on exploring meaning based on the descriptions of specific events and/ or experiences provides a way to understand the world from another's point of view. However, phenomenology is not without its own drawbacks. For example, to present conclusions from data as they were originally collected, researchers must depend a great deal on the ability of research participants to say what they mean in articulate, clear, and compelling ways. In addition, the focus on individual moments or experiences may result in research that misses the forest for the trees and focuses on specific descriptive events without understanding the broader contextual, historical, and temporal elements that may be related. Nevertheless, phenomenology offers a means to critically reflect on the details of conscious lived experience rather than trying to untangle the complications inherent in subconscious motivation (Jopling, 1996).

As we have seen, ethnography focuses on participant-based observations to understand cultures, and phenomenology concentrates on in-depth interviews that uncover the details of daily life to describe a lived experience. In contrast, grounded theory offers perhaps the most complete and compelling set of strategies for conducting qualitative research (Glaser & Strauss, 1967). Unlike in some traditional approaches, the researcher begins with no preexisting theory, hypothesis, or expectation of findings. Generally, interviews and observations are used to collect data, and as with phenomenology, the findings are permitted to emerge directly from the data. Unlike phenomenology, however, grounded theory aims not only to describe the topic of study but also to develop an adequate theoretical conceptualization of the findings (Silverman, 2005). Since grounded theory emerged, it has played an important role in specifying how a qualitative approach to data analysis can privilege localized understanding in theory creation (Wheeldon & Faubert, 2009). A core question in grounded theory is, What theory or explanation emerges from an analysis of the data collected about this phenomenon?

As a systematic methodology, grounded theory offers a means by which researchers can build on traditional ethnographic descriptions and develop theories explicitly based on gathered data. In general, grounded theory consists of four stages that can be seen as overlapping in the sense that they can be used to constantly compare data, intuitions, and assumptions in the creation of a theory. Through data collection, researchers observe people or situations, conduct interviews, or engage in both, perhaps alongside other appropriate data-collection approaches. Following this process, the researcher immediately captures key sentences for each type of data collection conducted. Next the researcher writes in the margin of the notes the "categories" and "properties" contained in or implied by each sentence of the notes and develops these "codes" into theoretical hypotheses to be further tested and considered (Glaser & Strauss, 1967).

Based on the work of Glaser and Strauss (1967), Silverman (2005) suggested analysis in grounded theory involves an initial attempt to develop categories from the data, efforts to locate the data within these categories to demonstrate relevance, and a means to develop these categories into a more useful framework for general understanding (Silverman, 2005, p. 179). The strength of this method is that it provides rigorous, systematic, and specific procedures for researchers to check, refine, and develop their intuitions about findings as the data are collected. However, as Brand and Anderson (1999) pointed out, most grounded theory research has failed to produce substantive, formal theories from which specific hypotheses can be developed. Nevertheless, it can offer a unique way to ensure research findings are credible by ensuring they remain very close to the collected qualitative data.

It is important to note that despite the general agreement between Glaser and Strauss about how to analyze data from the ground up, differences have emerged about the value of different analysis strategies (Kelle, 2005). Should researchers focus on structured coding schemes developed by others and/or tested in the past, or should they remain more flexible, providing a means to build ad hoc coding schemes based on the collected data? Of course, both approaches may be appropriate based on the research area under investigation and the kind of data you collect. We will turn to the practical meaning of this debate below; for now let's review how different types of qualitative research may be valuable to different sorts of research questions. Figure 4.10 offers an introductory visual means to consider the kinds of questions, approach to data collection, and analysis strategies that could be appropriate for ethnography, phenomenology, and grounded theory.

The map below (Figure 4.10) is a useful way to think about ethnography, phenomenology, and grounded theory, but there are a variety of qualitative approaches and additional ways maps might also be relevant. As we will see in Chapter 7, ethnographic approaches can benefit from visual representations of time and place, and mind maps might be used alongside other techniques to assist communities to explore their own perceptions around culture and place (McIntyre, 2003). Likewise, for researchers interested in phenomenological approaches and the value of presenting "raw" data, mind maps can be seen as unique artifacts of individual understanding (Wheeldon, 2010b). As part of qualitative data collection, they can be reproduced easily and presented within reports to clearly show the connection between data and findings.

Finally, for those interested in grounded theory and the debate between Glaser and Strauss, mind maps may provide a means to find middle ground between the two approaches (Wheeldon & Faubert, 2009). Despite their general agreement about how to analyze data from the ground up, specific differences exist between Glaser and Strauss about how the analysis should unfold and the role and relevance of structured versus more ad hoc coding (Kelle, 2005). Mind maps may be useful because instead of looking to the researcher to develop themes, concepts, and categories based on the data, these themes can be identified from the front-end construction of a participant's mind map. Thus, ad hoc approaches can be based on the structures created by participants themselves. This allows researchers to design subsequent stages of data collection using participant-generated subject areas. These subject areas can be grouped into themes, can guide more data collection and analysis, and can test initial themes through additional processes. It may be useful to see how this might operate in a real research situation.

Figure 4.10   Decisions, Data, and Analysis in Qualitative Research

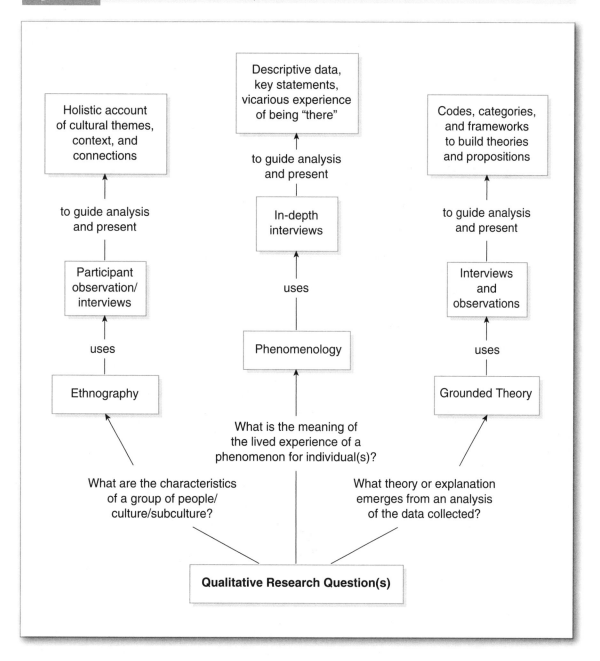

A RESEARCH EXAMPLE

Based on research by Wheeldon and Faubert (2009), this example is interesting for a couple of reasons. It shows how literature reviews can guide the analysis process, and it shows how maps might be used to design subsequent interview questions. Perhaps the most useful aspect of this example is that it provides some of the real-world research challenges that exist in data collection. Research often requires flexibility.

This project began as a pilot study examining the perceptions of legal technical assistance trainers who worked in Latvia from 2002 through 2004 (Wheeldon & Faubert, 2009). The study first examined the dichotomy that exists in the literature about the role of formal or informal training approaches (Rogers, 2005). Although formal organizational tools are a general feature of many legal technical assistance projects (Shaw & Dandurand, 2006), including training tools such as assessments, reports, laws, and policies as well as the development of procedures, project success is also related to more individual elements, such as the role of intercultural competence and relationship building within development (Kealey, Protheroe, MacDonald, & Vulpe, 2005). Of interest in our study example, given the debate identified in the literature, was how project participants would view their experience as trainers.

In this small study, 4 participants were invited to complete maps on their role as trainers during their time in Latvia on the Latvian Legal Reform Project. Respondents were selected based on convenience, their proximity to the researcher, and the fact that each came from a different institution and covered a variety of training topics while in Latvia. In agreeing to be part of the study, all participants signed informed consent documents that outlined the nature of the research and the means of data collection. An exemplar map was provided that demonstrated a variety of ways the concept of St. Nicholas was understood. It was selected because it included different names, physical features, activities, linking words, and additional characteristics. It is reproduced as Figure 4.11. In addition to the concept map example, the following instructions were provided to participants:

- Concept maps can demonstrate how people visualize relationships between various concepts.
- Concept maps do not require complete comprehensiveness; however, the map should reflect key experiences and perceptions related to your role as trainer.
- You are encouraged to include both challenges and successes (where applicable) in the creation of your concept maps.
- Please limit your concept map to one page (8.5 × 11").

Following the completion of the maps, the participants were asked to return them by fax or e-mail, and themes were identified based on the completed concept maps. Based on these themes, follow-up telephone interviews were designed. These interviews focused on content mining, or asking participants questions "designed to explore the detail which lies within each dimension, to access meaning it holds for the interviewee, and to generate an in-depth understanding from the interviewee's

| Figure 4.11 | Exemplar Concept Map of St. Nicholas |

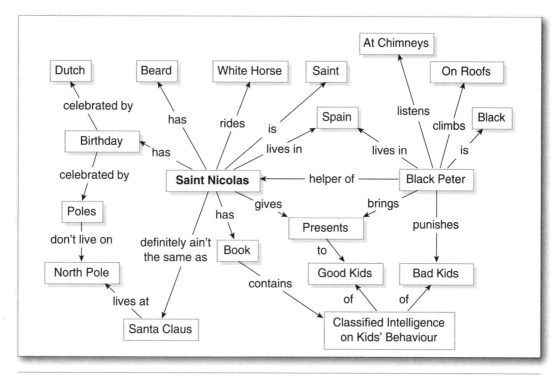

Source: Lanzing (1996).

point of view" (Legard, Keegan, & Ward, 2003, p. 148). The original plan was for the participants to return concept maps. However, the maps that were returned differed both from the provided exemplar map and from each other in style, substance, and focus. Although the information contained within the maps was important, the maps did not conform to the structure above. This served as an important lesson for novice researchers about the importance of clearly defining one's terms.

The research was initially based on data gathering using concept maps. However, the maps that were returned were far closer to mind maps (Wheeldon & Faubert, 2009). In hindsight, because the type of map was not specifically defined, it might have been expected that different map styles and formats would be returned. Instead of abandoning the study, another approach was employed. Instead of attempting to score the maps using one of the approaches discussed in Chapter 3, additional questions were designed based on the construction of the maps and the literature review. Based on this revised methodology, the returned maps were divided by style and substance, and subsequent interview questions were developed based on larger themes within the overall maps. This more flexible approach allows that the challenges of real research situations should not be held hostage by idealized research designs (Wheeldon, 2011). Figures 4.12 and 4.13 provide two examples of the sorts of maps returned.

Figure 4.12 Group A Participant's Example

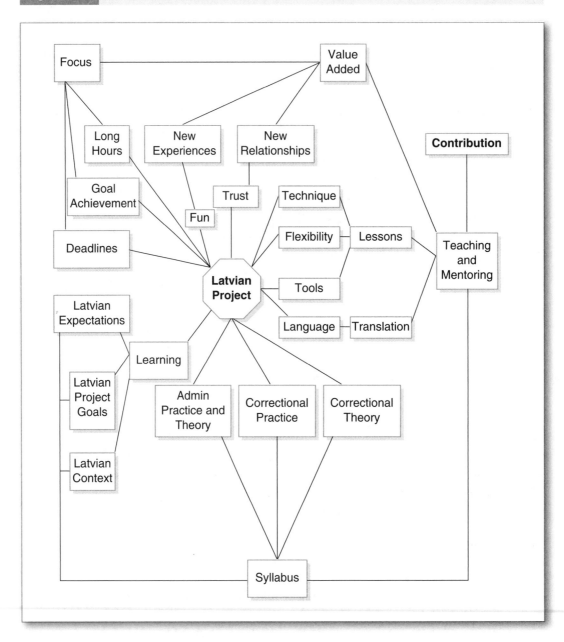

Figure 4.13   Group B Participant's Example

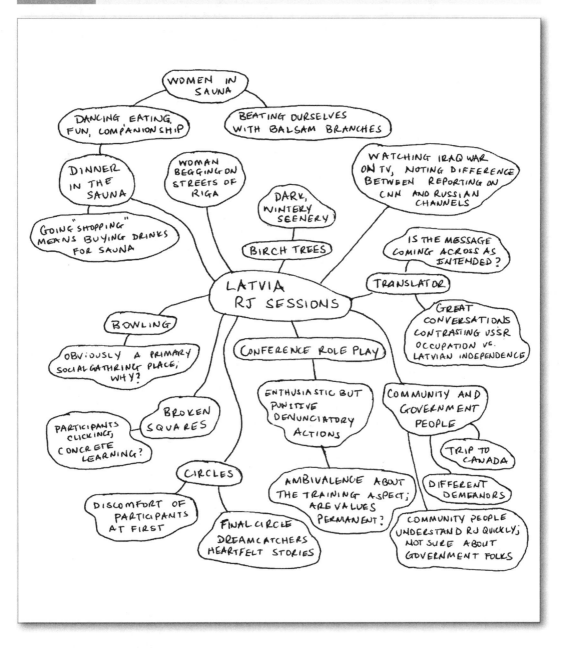

EXERCISE 4.1
Mapping a Map Comparison

Look at the mind maps in Figures 4.12 and 4.13. Without skipping ahead, make a map that includes your own observations about the style of the maps, their contents, and anything else you think might be relevant.

Map Analysis Strategy

So how does one approach the differences between the two maps above? As we have seen, there are a variety of ways a researcher might use concepts or constructions within participant-created mind maps in qualitative research. Some of these approaches can be borrowed from existent quantitative studies of concept maps. One might simply rely on "concept counting" to identify which (and how often) concepts were identified by participants within the maps (Turns, Atman, & Adams, 2000). Another option would be to focus on the placement of the concept or idea within the map or the connection between and among different levels of concepts (Bayram, 1995).

In this study, the maps in Figure 4.12 and 4.13 were analyzed by the researchers based on an observation of their physical construction, the degree of formality involved in the mapping, and analysis of the concepts identified in the maps. Despite differences in the maps' construction among participants, some common themes emerged. These included common issues around language, the importance of translation, the development of relationships, and the Latvian context. Despite these commonalities, the maps were constructed in very different ways. Figure 4.12 is quite formal, created using a word processor, and includes one-word concepts or ideas that are linked in a variety of ways. Figure 4.13, on the other hand, is less formal, was created by hand, and refers in more detail to personal experiences, events, and insights. Neither approach is definitively right or definitively wrong, and the way in which they were constructed and the concepts they included were used in the development of a subsequent data-collection strategy—telephone interviews.

Through the initial division of the maps into two groups, based on style and substance, general interview questions were designed to explore common themes, and more specific questions were designed to explore specific details in individual maps, based on the literature review. Those who completed more formal maps and included specific references to project tools and outcomes (Group A) were asked two additional questions about the role of relationships and informal networks between Latvian participants from the government and community. Those who returned less formal maps, including specific references to the role of relationships and informal networks (Group B) were asked specific questions about project tools and outcomes delivered by the trainers (Wheeldon & Faubert, 2009). In this way, both common themes and individual reflections could be explored, and each group was given a chance to explore themes identified by the other.

As described by Wheeldon and Faubert (2009), 10 structured but deliberately open-ended questions designed to "open up the research territory and to identify the dimensions or issues that are relevant to the participant" (Legard et al., 2003, p. 148) were presented to the participants through telephone interviews. Although 8 were common questions to all participants, 2 specific questions were developed, based on the constructed maps and subsequent analysis of the two groups as detailed previously. These questions are highlighted in bold in Table 4.2 below.

In this study, the maps initially suggested that the dichotomy in the literature between formal and informal was also a feature of the trainers' real-world experience. However, through subsequent data collection it became clear that for all of the participants in this study, being a trainer was "all about relationships" (Wheeldon & Faubert, 2009). Common reflections focused on associations formed both through the formal delivery of project activities and through the social exchanges and events that

Table 4.2   Follow-Up Questions

Question	Question Set 1—More Formal Maps	Question Set 2—Less Formal Maps
1	Most positive experience	Most positive experience
2	Most negative/challenging experience	Most negative/challenging experience
3	Most memorable	Most memorable
4	Are you still in touch with the Latvians	Are you still in touch with the Latvians
5	What if anything did you learn through the concept map exercise	What if anything did you learn through the concept map exercise
6	Role of the translator	Role of the translator
7	Role of formal relationships	Biggest project result
8	Role of informal networks	Biggest training outcomes
9	Role of the government and community in reform process	Role of the government and community in reform process

Source: Wheeldon and Faubert (2009, p. 77).

are an important part of Latvian culture. Through the development of "personal networks" between the Canadian trainers and Latvian participants, training sessions included "meaningful participation, networking, and collective problem solving" (Wheeldon, 2010a, pp. 523–524). The maps provided one interpretation, but additional data collection provided more nuance. Based in the literature and suggested in the construction of the maps, the dichotomy between formal tools and informal processes appeared less important within this sample. By combining the themes in the maps with the themes that emerged through the interviews, a broader picture emerged of the overall participant experience.

Limitations of the Research Example

A number of limitations are relevant in this study. One can be based on the number of participants, the geographic location, and the lack of previous studies on which to base the methodology. The exploratory character of the research was also tested by the style of the maps that were returned. As discussed above, one important question that emerged was what one should do when completed maps do not meet the strict criteria of traditional concept maps. In this example, the researchers changed the focus of the exploration based on the data that were returned by using the maps to develop interview questions to explore the themes identified both in the maps and through the literature review. Although this procedure is defensible, this choice might be seen as a limitation. Instead of using the data as they were provided, the researchers might have decided to try to collect data again and tried to ensure the maps conformed to a traditional structure. A final limitation was the decision not to treat the absence of detail in the maps as a finding in and of itself. Instead, another strategy would have been to design follow-up questions based more on the relevant literature than on the maps themselves.

Summary of Research Example

To summarize this research example, participants were asked to complete concept maps based on their experience as international criminal justice trainers. Participants returned maps that were not expected; however, the research evolved by using additional data-collection techniques based on the maps that were returned. This strategy allowed for data collection that, in some ways, challenged past literature. It also forced the researchers to consider other kinds of maps and their utility for different types of research problems. As a result, the potential for mind maps in qualitative research later emerged. Unlike some traditional requests for data in qualitative research, their use can provide a visual means for people to share their experiences and perspectives in new and unique ways. Indeed, "by offering a clear graphic snapshot of individual perception, researchers can ground any theoretical contributions in the visual representations of experience that participants create" (Wheeldon & Faubert, 2009, p. 78).

STUDENT ACTIVITY

There are a number of formidable people who and experiences that shape who we are. Understanding our past can help us appreciate our present circumstances and may help us think about our future. In this activity, you will ask a friend or family member to create a mind map by reflecting on a central person or experience in his or her life. Please follow the guidelines below in addition to any other instructions provided by your professor.

Guidelines for Data Gathering With a Mind Map

1. Obtain permission and consent from the individual who has agreed to complete a mind map for this assignment—the person should know why you are asking for his or her assistance. You must inform the individual that you will not refer to him or her by name, but you may share the map or interview responses with your professor or your class. Your professor may have a specific template that you should use to obtain consent, so be sure to check with him or her before you begin. An example template is included in Appendix B.

2. After obtaining consent, ask your participant to complete a mind map of a central person or experience in his or her life. You may use Figure 4.1 as an example or draw your own. Be sure to give him or her as much time as needed (within reason), and provide the participant with the following instructions:

    a) Starting in the middle of the page, write the experience or person you think has been important to your life.

    b) Draw a line out from the central image in each direction, and write an important theme that is connected to your central word.

    c) Write other words or images that are connected to this theme, and continue to build your map outward.

    d) Use color, the thickness of lines, boxes, or pictures and graphics to make your map unique and expressive.

3. Once your participant has completed the map, review it. What do you notice? Was it constructed based on the guidelines? Is it different in some ways? What are the main features, themes, concepts, or ideas? Does the map make you curious about one area or another identified in the map?

4. Using the mind map, develop some interview questions based on the construction of the map. Start with journalistic questions such as who, what, when, and why, but then use the map to probe how this person or event was important to your participant. For example, how has this person or experience changed your participant? Can he or she provide a concrete example of how this person or event influenced a decision the person has made? Be sure to allow him or her to reflect on the map and add anything else before drawing the interview to a close.

5. Prepare to present your mini research project to the class. Be sure that there are no identifying features within the map to protect the confidentiality of your research participant. Scan your participant's mind map so you can present it using a computer or through PowerPoint. If you don't have access to computers in your classroom, you can make a transparency of the map. The idea is that the class or group should be able to see the map as you present your project. It will be important for you to be able to explain and even justify how you decided on your interview questions based on the map. During your presentation, talk about what you saw in the map and how your interview questions validated, brought into doubt, or further augmented your initial interpretation of the map. What did you learn about your participant through this exercise?

CONCLUSION

The focus on capturing detailed narrative information in qualitative research may initially appear to be a limitation in the use of mind maps. However, maps do provide a means to explore the meaning research participants assign to a particular event or phenomenon. Mind maps can be used in a number of ways to assist researchers in general within social science research, and they offer a complementary strategy for data collection in qualitative research because they are designed to be user generated, unsolicited, and flexible. This chapter has demonstrated how mind maps can be used to gather qualitative data and can be used to help participants prime the pump for later interviews. Researchers can use mind maps in advance of interviews to facilitate more detailed and in-depth recollection by participants and alongside other, more traditional, qualitative data-collection techniques. Finally, within grounded research, mind maps may also provide a useful means to guide subsequent data collection by allowing researchers to see how participants connect various concepts, experiences, and propositions.

REVIEW

1. Define qualitative research, and explain the assumptions about knowledge on which it is based. How is it different from quantitative research?

2. What are some traditional approaches to data collection in qualitative research? Why might mind maps be a useful addition?

3. Provide three ways that mind maps can be used in qualitative research, and explain one in detail.

4. What might be some of the limitations in using mind maps? Can these be overcome?

5. How can the structure of mind maps lead researchers to ask more meaningful questions within ethnographic, phenomenological, and grounded theory approaches?

SUGGESTED ADDITIONAL READINGS

Budd, J. (2004). Mind maps as classroom exercises. *Journal of Economic Education, 35*(1), 35–46.

Tattersall, C., Watts, A., & Vernon, S. (2007). Mind mapping as a tool in qualitative research. *Nursing Times, 103*(26), 32–33.

Wheeldon, J. P., & Faubert, J. (2009). Framing experience: Concept maps, mind maps, and data collection in qualitative research. *International Journal of Qualitative Methods, 8*(3), 68–83.

REFERENCES

Agar, M. (1996). *The professional stranger: An informal introduction to ethnography.* San Diego, CA: Academic Press.

Bayram, S. (1995). *The effectiveness of concept and software mapping for representing student data and process schema in science.* Unpublished masters thesis, University of Pittsburgh, PA.

Brand, W., & Anderson, R. (1999). *Transpersonal research methods for the social sciences.* Sage: London.

Budd, J. (2004). Mind maps as classroom exercises. *Journal of Economic Education, 35*(1), 35–46.

Burger, T. (1977). Max Weber, interpretive sociology, and the sense of historical science: A positivistic conception of verstehen. *Sociological Quarterly, 18,* 165–176.

Buzan, B., & Buzan, T. (1996). *The mind map book: How to use radiant thinking to maximize your brain's untapped potential.* New York: Plume.

Buzan, T. (1991). *Use both sides of your brain.* New York: Plume.

Charmaz, K. (2006). *Constructing grounded theory.* London: Sage.

Creswell, J. W. (1998). *Qualitative inquiry and research design: Choosing among five traditions.* Thousand Oaks, CA: Sage.

Creswell, J. W., & Plano Clark, V. L. (2007). *Designing and conducting mixed methods research.* Thousand Oaks, CA: Sage.

Daley, B. (2004, September 14–17). *Using concept maps in qualitative research.* Paper presented at the First International Conference on Concept Mapping, Pamplona, Spain.

Drucker, J. (2009). *SpecLab: Digital aesthetics and speculative computing.* Chicago: University of Chicago Press.

Farrand, P., Hussain, F., & Hennessy, E. (2002). The efficacy of the mind map study technique. *Medical Education, 36*(5), 426–431.

Feyerbend, P. (1978). *Science in a free society.* London: New Left Press.

Gardner, H. (1983). *Frames of mind: The theory of multiple intelligences.* New York: Basic Books.

Gardner, H. (1993). *Multiple intelligences: The theory in practice.* New York: Basic Books.

Garfinkel, H. (1967). *Studies in ethnomethodology.* Englewood Cliffs, NJ: Prentice Hall.

Gazzaniga, M. S. (2005). Forty-five years of split-brain research and still going strong [Review]. *Nature Reviews Neuroscience, 6*(8), 653–659.

Geertz, C. (1973). *The interpretation of other cultures: Selected essays.* New York: Basic Books.

Glaser, B. G., & Strauss, A. (1967). *Discovery of grounded theory: Strategies for qualitative research.* Chicago: Aldine.

Golafshani, N. (2003). Understanding reliability and validity in qualitative research. *Qualitative Report, 8*(4), 597–607.

Guba, E., & Lincoln, Y. (1989). *Fourth generation evaluation.* Newbury Park, CA: Sage.

Hammersley, M., & Atkinson, P. (1983). *Ethnography: Principles in practice.* New York: Tavistock.

Hathaway, A. D., & Atkinson, M. (2003). Active interview tactics in research on public deviants: Exploring the two-cop personas. *Field Methods, 15,* 161–185.

Heidegger, M. (1962). *Being and time.* New York: Harper & Row.

Husserl, E. (1962). *Ideas: General introduction to pure phenomenology* (W. R. Boyce Gibson, Trans.). New York: Collier.

Jenkins, A. (2005). Mind mapping. *Nursing Standard, 20*(7), 85.

Jopling, D. (1996). Sub-phenomenology. *Human Studies, 19*(2), 153–173.

Kealey, D., Protheroe, D., MacDonald, D., & Vulpe, T. (2005). Re-examining the role of training in contributing to international project success: A literature review and an outline of a new model training program. *International Journal of Intercultural Relations, 29,* 289.

Kelle, U. (2005). Emergence vs. forcing of empirical data? A crucial problem of grounded theory reconsidered. *Qualitative Social Research, 6*(2), Article 27.

Kern, C. S., Bush, K. L., & McCleish, J. M. (2006). Mind-mapped care plans: Integrating an innovative educational tool as an alternative to traditional care plans. *Journal of Nursing Education, 45,* 112–119.

Kvale, S. (1996). *Interviews—An introduction to qualitative research interviewing.* London: Sage.

Langenbach, M. (1995). Phenomenology, intentionality, and mental experiences. *History of Psychiatry, 5,* 209–224.

Lanzing J. W. A. (1996). *Everything you always wanted to know about . . . concept mapping.* Unpublished manuscript, University of Twente, the Netherlands.

Legard, R., Keegan, J., & Ward, K. (2003). In-depth interviews. In J. Ritchie & J. Lewis (Eds.), *Qualitative research practice: A guide for social research students and researchers* (pp. 138–169). Thousand Oaks, CA: Sage.

McIntyre, A. (2003). Through the eyes of women: Photovoice and participatory research as tools for reimagining place. *Gender, Place, and Culture, 10*(1), 47–66.

McGoldrick, M., Gerson, R., & Schellenberger, S. (1999). *Genograms: Assessment and intervention* (2nd ed.). New York: Norton.

Moustakas, C. (1994). *Phenomenological research methods.* Thousand Oaks, CA: Sage.

Mueller, A., Johnston, M., & Bligh, D. (2001). Mind-mapped care plans: A remarkable alternative to traditional nursing care plans. *Nurse Educator, 26*(2), 75–80.

Nightingale, D. J., & Cromby, J. (Eds.). (1999). *Social constructionist psychology: A critical analysis of theory and practice.* Buckingham, UK: Open University Press.

Patton, M. Q. (2002). *Qualitative research & evaluation methods* (3rd ed.). Thousand Oaks, CA: Sage.

Peterson, A. R., & Snyder, P. J. (1998, August 20–22). *Using mind maps to teach social problems analysis.* Paper presented at the annual meeting of the Society for the Study of Social Problems, San Francisco, CA.

Pope, C., Ziebland, S., & Mays, N. (2000). Qualitative research in health care: Analysing qualitative data. *British Medical Journal, 320,* 114–116.

Rogers, E. M. (2005). *Diffusion of innovations* (5th ed.). New York: Free Press.

Rohm, R. (1994). *Positive personality profiles.* Atlanta, GA: Personality Insights.

Rooda, L. (1994). Effects of mind mapping on student achievement in a nursing research course. *Nurse Educator, 19*(6), 25–27.

Schutz, A. (1967). *The phenomenology of the social world.* Evanston, IL: Northwestern University Press.

Shaw, M., & Dandurand, Y. (2006). Maximizing the effectiveness of technical assistance provided by member states in crime prevention and criminal justice. In M. Shaw & Y. Dandurand (Eds.), *Maximizing the effectiveness of the technical assistance provided in the fields of crime prevention and criminal justice* (pp. 19–34), Helsinki, Finland: HEUNI.

Silverman, D. (2005). *Doing qualitative research.* Thousand Oaks, CA: Sage.

Sperry, R. W. (1966). Brain bisection and mechanisms of consciousness. In J. C. Eccles (Ed.), *Brain and conscious experience* (pp. 298–313). Heidelberg, Germany: Springer-Verlag.

Spradley, J. P. (1979). *The ethnographic interview.* New York: Holt, Rinehart & Winston.

Tattersall, C., Watts, A., & Vernon, S. (2007). Mind mapping as a tool in qualitative research. *Nursing Times, 103*(26), 32–33.

Teddlie, C. B., & Tashakkori, A. (2009). *Foundations of mixed methods research: Integrating quantitative and qualitative approaches in the social and behavioral sciences.* Thousand Oaks, CA: Sage.

Torrance, E., & Rokenstein, Z. (1987). Styles of thinking and creativity. *Gifted International, 4*(1), 37–49.

Turns, J., Atman, C., & Adams, R. (2000). Concept maps for engineering education: A cognitively motivated tool supporting varied assessment functions. *IEEE Transactions on Education, 43,* 164–173.

Van Manen, M. (1990). *Research lived experience: Human science for an action sensitive pedagogy.* New York: State University of New York Press.

Wheeldon, J. (2007). *Bringing British Columbia to Latvia: Canadians reflect on expert designation in an international criminal justice project.* Burnaby, Canada: School of Criminology, Simon Fraser University.

Wheeldon, J. (2010a). Learning from Latvia: Adoption, adaptation, and evidence based justice reform. *Journal of Baltic Studies, 41*(4), 507–530.

Wheeldon, J. (2010b). Mapping mixed methods research: Methods, measures, and meaning. *Journal of Mixed Methods Research, 4*(2), 87–102.

Wheeldon, J. P. (2011). Is a picture worth a thousand words? Using mind maps to facilitate participant recall in qualitative research. *Qualitative Report, 16*(2), 509–522. Retrieved March 1, 2011, from http://www.nova.edu/ssss/QR/QR16-2/wheeldon.pdf

Wheeldon, J. P., & Faubert, J. (2009). Framing experience: Concept maps, mind maps, and data collection in qualitative research. *International Journal of Qualitative Methods, 8*(3), 68–83.

Willig, C. (2001). *Introducing qualitative research in psychology: Adventures in theory and method.* Buckingham, UK: Open University Press.

Witsel, M. (2008, May 29). *Mind mapping as a qualitative research tool.* Paper presented at School of Tourism & Hospitality Management's Seminar Series, Southern Cross University, Lismore, New South Wales, Australia.

Wolcott, H. F. (1990). *Writing up qualitative research.* Newbury Park, CA: Sage.

Zaltman, G. (1997). Rethinking market research: Putting people back in. *Journal of Marketing Research, 34*(4), 424–437.

Zaltman, G., & Zaltman, L. (2008). *Marketing metaphoria: What deep metaphors reveal about the minds of consumers.* Cambridge, MA: Harvard Business School Press.

5

Mapping Mixed-Methods Research

Theories, Models, and Measures

CHAPTER OVERVIEW AND OBJECTIVES

As we saw in Chapters 3 and 4, quantitative and qualitative researchers pursue different approaches to gathering and analyzing data. For many years, these differences have underscored broader political disagreements (Jick, 1979). For a new generation of researchers, the either/or approaches of the past are incomplete and outdated. Instead, the complexity of today's research problems requires more comprehensive and nuanced efforts (Wheeldon, 2010b). Indeed, past divisions among researchers often failed to consider that, in many ways, qualitative and quantitative data are inherently related. All quantitative data are based on qualitative judgments; all qualitative data can be described numerically. As presented in Chapter 1, all research is a series of decisions (Palys, 1992). Mixed-methods research provides more choices, options, and approaches to consider. For this reason, it has emerged as the "third methodological movement" (Creswell & Plano Clark, 2007, p.13). As an important new research community, it involves research in which both qualitative and quantitative approaches to data gathering, analysis, interpretation, and presentation are used (Teddlie & Tashakkori, 2009, p. 7).

Both concept maps and mind maps can be used as part of mixed-methods research. This chapter will provide examples of how concept maps can be used as part of pre/post mixed-methods designs and will offer a new mixed-methods measure based on the use of mind maps. To understand these examples, it is important to understand the theoretical basis for this sort of integration and to know how different data-collection procedures can be used together. Finally, through the use of a research example, readers will be encouraged to consider how the use of mixed methods offers another means to address activities presented in Chapters 2, 3, and 4. By the end of this chapter, readers should be able to do the following:

- describe the potential of mixed-methods research and one theoretical basis often associated with it;
- explain the different ways data, methods, and approaches can be mixed;
- provide examples of research designs to which different maps are best suited; and
- define the salience score and explain its potential.

THEORETICAL JUSTIFICATION

As we have seen in previous chapters, the existing theoretical bases for quantitative and qualitative research are rooted in postpositivism and constructivism. To understand how mixed-methods research provides a different sort of theoretical understanding of research, it may be useful to recall that earlier discussion. Postpositivists see human knowledge as speculative and, therefore, not based on unchallengeable, rock-solid foundations. They argue that the external world exists independently of an individual's experience of it, and thus knowledge is not hypothetical and foundation-less. They acknowledge that all research will be incomplete in one way or another, and they hold that approaches that can be tested and explored through the scientific method should be favored. This often results in the application of deductive approaches that rely on a series of steps to reach specific conclusions based on general premises.

In general, quantitative research seeks generalizability through controlled, value-free (or value-neutral) processes that can test and validate theories through a process of falsification. The emphasis on falsification often leads quantitative researchers to focus on sample size and statistics to showcase broad generalizability. At its most shortsighted, some quantitative research considers the role of setting and context either irrelevant or unmanageable. A central critique is that some quantitative research models are statistics dependent, inflate the importance of mathematical averages, and cannot capture the complexity associated with human behavior (Goertzel & Fashing, 1981). By focusing solely on numeric information, some approaches miss the depth and detail that are assigned to phenomena by participants themselves.

Another view is one promoted by constructivists. Skeptical of the idea of one universalistic notion of truth, they view meaningful understanding as contingent on human practices and thus different people's ability to socially construct reality in different ways. Although many qualitative researchers acknowledge the limitations inherent in reporting individual understandings of complex ideas and concepts, in their view research must do a better job in telling the stories of individuals. This often results in inductive approaches to research that rely on a series of steps to reach general conclusions based on specific premises. Qualitative research seeks to understand or make sense of the world based on how individuals experience and perceive it. Framed through social interaction and personal histories and narrative experiences (Creswell & Plano Clark, 2007), knowledge is inherently localized, and the notion of generalizability overly mythologized.

Unlike quantitative researchers, qualitative researchers focus on the development of theories based on an interpretive or individualized process. Because there are many possible interpretations of the same data, however, qualitative researchers refuse to assign value to one interpretation of meaning without acknowledging the role they themselves play within this construction (Guba & Lincoln, 1989). This requires that researchers study the experiences, influences, and activities of research participants while explicitly and reflexively acknowledging their own personal biases. Yet the acceptance within qualitative research of the inherent bias of any researcher challenges the tradition of objectivity and threatens the potential for nonpartisan research. In addition, while privileging localized understanding through the inclusion of depth and detail, qualitative research sometimes proudly presents findings that would benefit from more rigorous analysis.

An emergent tradition based on a more pragmatic approach rejects either/or approaches to understanding reality and developing knowledge. Through multiple stages and methods of data collection and/or analysis, researchers can get a better understanding of a phenomenon by combining the reliability of empirical counts with the validity of lived experience. As discussed in Chapter 1, mixed-methods research is understood as an *abductive* process that values the expertise, experience, and intuition of researchers themselves. To understand the value of pragmatism and its connection to abductive reasoning, it may be useful to recount our discussion of key issues in social science research and reexamine a table presented in Chapter 1. Table 5.1 provides an important reminder about some of the key issues in social science research.

As we saw in Chapter 3, deductive reasoning is associated with quantitative research and uses a top-down process that tests general premises though a series of steps to reach specific conclusions. Researchers seek to be objective through the research process and strive for generalizable findings by testing hypotheses through a deliberate series of steps. In contrast, inductive reasoning is associated with qualitative research and develops general conclusions based on the exploration of how individuals experience and perceive the world around them. Presented in Chapter 1, Figure 5.1 provides some differences between deductive and inductive reasoning.

Table 5.1	Key Issues in Social Science Research		
	Quantitative Approach	**Qualitative Approach**	**Pragmatic Approach**
Connection of Theory and Data	Deductive	Inductive	Abductive
Relationship to Research Process	Objectivity	Subjectivity	Intersubjectivity
Inference From Data	Generality	Context	Transferability

Source: Morgan (2007, p. 71).

Figure 5.1	Comparing Deductive and Inductive Reasoning

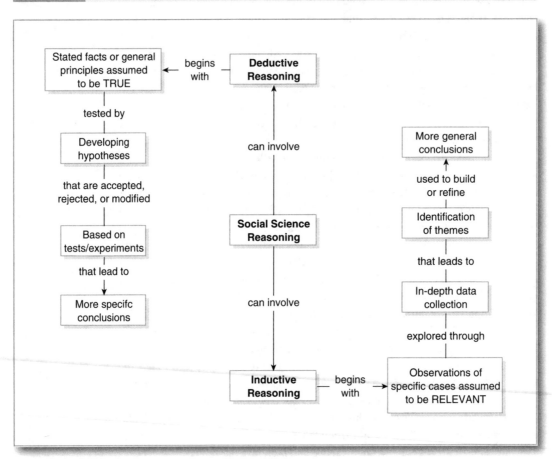

Mixed-methods research represents an important departure from the either/or assumptions of quantitative or qualitative approaches because it allows that both methods may be valuable depending on the type of research question under investigation. A central assumption in mixed-methods research is that there are many social science issues that can be better explored through the combination of different methods and techniques. *Abductive reasoning* can be understood as a process that values both deductive and inductive approaches but relies principally on the expertise, experience, and intuition of researchers (see Figure 5.2). Associated with mixed-methods research, through the *intersubjectivity* of researchers and their understanding based on shared meaning, this approach to reasoning encourages testing intuitions theoretically and empirically. Based on the best information at hand, tentative explanations and hypotheses emerge through the research process and can be developed and/or tested using methods that are either quantitative, qualitative, or a mix of both.

By relying on abductive reasoning, mixed-methods research offers an important new way to conceive of research and can produce more robust measures of association while allowing that multiple paths to meaning exist (Wheeldon, 2010b). In addition to escaping the trap of seeing research as an either/or choice between quantitative or qualitative designs, mixed methods provide practical benefits as well.

Figure 5.2   One View of Abductive Reasoning

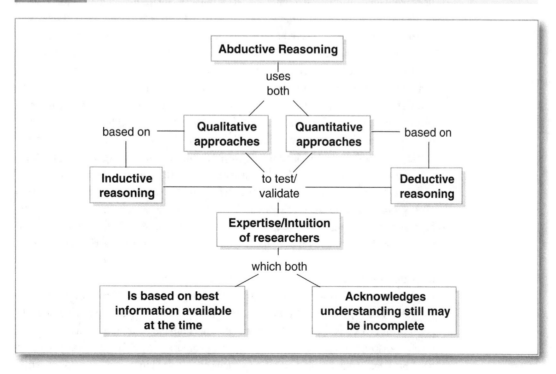

For example, students are often overcome by the nature of quantitative information collected within some data sets and the view that, to be valid, quantitative research requires a large number of cases to analyze. As discussed in Chapter 3, this is because of the assumptions required by certain statistical tests often used in the analysis of numeric information. On the other hand, whereas qualitative research can require smaller samples and thus may be easier for students to engage in, many are uncertain about how to identify a good group from which to gather data or are unclear about the interview process and how to prepare. Mixed methods may require more work, multiple analyses, and nuanced thinking; however, they also can provide flexibility for researchers. Miles and Huberman (2002) urge all researchers to entertain mixed models. By avoiding polarization, polemics, and life at the extremes, they suggested that

> both quantitative and qualitative inquiry can support and inform each other in important ways. Narratives and variable-driven analyses need to interpenetrate and inform each other. Realists, idealists and critical theorists can do better by incorporating other ideas than remaining pure. (Miles & Huberman, 2002, p. 396)

Beyond these practical benefits, conceptually mixed-methods research and the associated methodological concerns that may emerge can perhaps be addressed by pragmatism (Morgan, 2007). John Dewey has been associated with both postpositivism and constructivism, but he is perhaps best understood as a pragmatic philosopher who has influenced contemporary thinkers, including Richard Rorty. As a philosophical movement, *pragmatism* holds that claims about the truth of one view or another must be connected to the practical consequences of accepting that view. Although Rorty rejects the idea of one truth, he does consider the value of consensus or intersubjective agreement about various beliefs as a means to understanding provisional or conditional truths. One means to obtain what he called "reflective equilibrium" is through research that can provide both realistic and socially useful outcomes (Rorty, 1999). In this way, mixed-methods approaches may be valuable to new social science research procedures because they provide "new ways to think about the world—new questions to ask and new ways to pursue them" (Morgan, 2007, p. 73).

This kind of flexibility arises because instead of starting from theories or conceptual frameworks and testing them through deductive approaches or starting from observations or facts, researchers can view both of these processes as part of the broader research cycle (Teddlie & Tashakkori, 2009, pp. 87–89). For example, quantitative approaches can be used to identify groups or individuals to interview and/or relevant issues that make these people unique or interesting based on the analysis of numeric data. In addition, qualitative techniques can lead researchers to discover existing data sets, develop survey questions, and/or weight data in different ways based on narrative data (Wheeldon, 2010b). Maps may be especially valuable from a pragmatist's point of view because visualizing and imagining connections and relationships can be creative, distinctive, and thus productive in ways other kinds of data collection may not be. A broader understanding about how maps can be used in mixed-methods research requires an understanding of current models, approaches, and techniques.

UNDERSTANDING, PLANNING, AND DESCRIBING MIXED-METHODS RESEARCH

Mixed-methods research has been defined by Creswell and Plano Clark (2007, p. 5) as a research design based on assumptions that guide the collection and analysis of data and the mixture of qualitative and quantitative approaches. A central premise is that the use of quantitative and qualitative approaches together can provide a better understanding of research problems. Mixed methodologies can provide a useful and novel way to communicate meaning and knowledge (Johnson & Onwuegbuzie, 2004) because they can combine the reliability of counts with the validity of lived experience and perception. Mixed approaches to social science research are increasingly popular. Tashakkori and Teddlie (1998) included 152 references in their exploration of the growth of mixed methods in research areas such as evaluation, health science and nursing, psychology, sociology, and education, among others.

As mixed-methods research has grown during the past two decades, different approaches to mixed-methods designs have been developed (Greene, Caracelli, & Graham, 1989), revised (Creswell & Plano Clark, 2007), and reorganized (Teddlie & Tashakkori, 2009). As discussed in Chapter 1, a variety of types and approaches of mixed-methods research have been defined (Creswell & Plano Clark, 2007). One approach is to use qualitative techniques to develop a theory that can then be tested by establishing a conceptually connected hypothesis and quantitative means. Figure 5.3 provides an example.

Figure 5.3 Quantitatively Testing Qualitative Findings

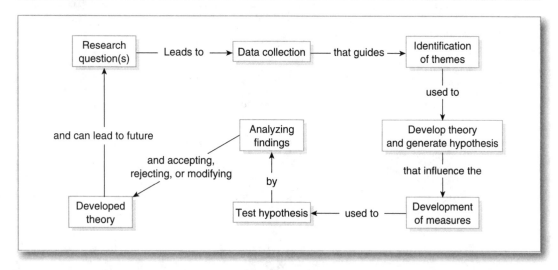

Another approach is to develop a quantifiable means that can test a generated hypothesis and then explore these findings using more qualitative techniques, as presented in Figure 5.4.

With the use of these mixed approaches, research problems can benefit from both qualitative and quantitative approaches to data analysis and the measurement of meaning. There are a number of issues and considerations in both of the approaches above, but for the sake of simplicity we describe three considerations based on the useful overview provided by Creswell and Plano Clark (2007, pp. 79–85). These include timing, weighting, and mixing.

The first surrounds the *timing* and *ordering* of methods within your study. Sometimes these terms refer to when the data were collected and whether they were collected at the same time (simultaneously) or during different periods (sequentially). Some researchers interested in comparing how different tools capture perceptions collect both qualitative and quantitative data at the same time (Gogolin & Swartz, 1992; Jenkins, 2001). Others have collected and analyzed data sequentially and at different times. For example, in a study on cross-national differences in classroom learning environments in Taiwan and Australia by Aldridge, Fraser, and Huang (1999), qualitative data were used to explain, in more detail, quantitative results. The authors used two separate data-collection phases. The first was a quantitative instrument with multiple subscales to assess aspects of the classroom environment. Some months later, they used classroom observations and qualitative interviews with students and teachers to get a more detailed picture of the differences in classroom environments in each country.

Figure 5.4 Qualitatively Validating Quantitative Findings

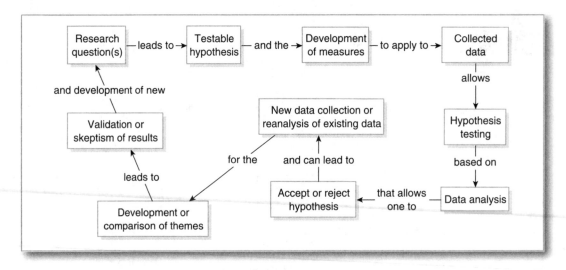

Another example of interest is a study by Myers and Oetzel (2003) that used qualitative data to create and validate a quantitative instrument. This study was also organized through two phases of data collection. Based on qualitative interviews, the authors first gathered data through field notes and transcripts. Later they engaged in analysis using techniques drawn from qualitative data including coding, theme identification, and connection to existing literature. Based on this analysis, the authors developed an instrument that could provide quantitative measures based on the qualitative interviews. They then administered this instrument, and the quantitative data were analyzed to test correlations from the qualitative interviews.

However, data collection and data analysis may not always be so closely intertwined. There may be times that data collected simultaneously are analyzed separately, in different ways, and at various times. Other studies might collect data through multiple data-collection phases over longer time periods. Although collecting data in multiple settings may be useful, there may be research designs in which data can be usefully compiled and analyzed together and at the same time. Thus, there is an important difference between descriptive and analytic timing/ordering considerations (Creswell & Plano Clark, 2007). Descriptive considerations focus on whether data were collected at the same time or over a longer period of time. Analytic considerations focus on whether the data were analyzed together, at the same time, or separately, one after another. Whereas both may require some justification, they ought not be confused. Figure 5.5 provides a visual overview of some of these considerations.

The second question is related to how you *weight* different methods in your study, or the relative importance of each approach. This is often indicated using capital letters for the dominant approach (QUAN or QUAL) and lowercase letters for the secondary, less dominant methodological approach (qual or quan). Of course, you may choose to give equal weight to both traditions, in which case both would be capitalized (QUAL/QUAN). More often one tradition is selected as dominant. Whether your approach is primarily quantitative or qualitative in nature depends to a large degree on the type of research question you are interested in. Both approaches have strengths and weaknesses, of course, but thinking about how and why some methods might work together better than others is important. Some researchers have gathered data through quantitative surveys and qualitative interviews (Baumann, 1999; Way, Stauber, Nakkula, & London, 1994). This allows researchers to define beforehand the kind of data they seek by utilizing specific data-collection tools. In essence this question boils down to whether you will assign equal or unequal weight to the different sorts of data you have collected and whether your analysis emphasizes quantitative or qualitative assumptions about meaning. Your decision about how to weight data may also be related to the

Figure 5.5 Timing and Ordering of Data Collection/Analysis in Mixed Methods

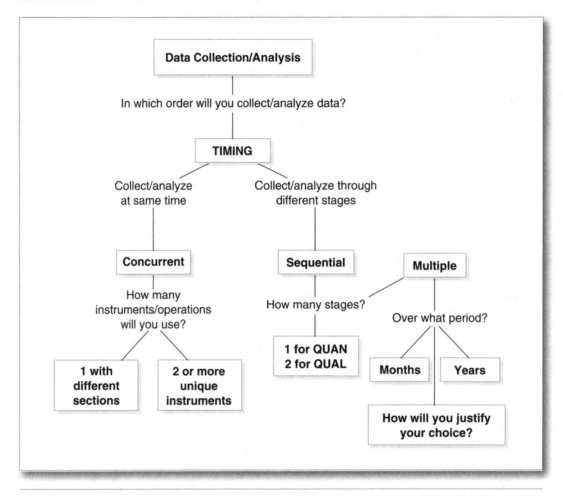

Note: QUAN = primarily quantitative; QUAL = primarily qualitative.

research question, your epistemological view, practical issues surrounding access to data, data types, and additional issues associated with research—such as deadlines and due dates.

To assist researchers in clearly presenting how they mixed methods within a study, a series of useful notations has been developed. These can indicate not only which approach was more dominant in a mixed-methods design but also whether data collection and/or analysis was simultaneous or sequential (Morse, 2003, p. 198). Table 5.2 provides some notation examples.

Table 5.2   Notions in Mixed-Methods Research

Symbol	Meaning
QUAN	Primarily a quantitative mixed-methods project
QUAL	Primarily a qualitative mixed-methods project
Plus sign (+)	Data collection/analysis conducted at the same time
Arrow ($\rightarrow$)	The sequence of data collection/analysis in mixed-methods projects
quan	Secondarily a quantitative mixed-methods project
qual	Secondarily a qualitative mixed-methods project

EXERCISE 5.1
Think You Get It?

What kind of mixed-methods projects do the following notations indicate?

QUAN + qual _____

QUAL $\rightarrow$ quan _____

quan + QUAL _____

QUAL $\rightarrow$ qual _____

These notations can help researchers present their approaches and think about their designs. However, simply noting which design they have chosen, whether a quantitative or qualitative approach will be dominant, or how their data will be mixed is not enough. Central to any research, and perhaps especially to mixed-methods research, is how researchers justify their approach. This is especially important with regard to the question of *mixing*. There are at least three options available when deciding how and why to mix your data. Data can be merged by transforming and/or integrating two data types together, one data type can be embedded within another, or they can be presented separately and then connected to answer different aspects of the same or a similar research question. Creswell and Plano Clark (2007, p. 80) have compiled a useful decision tree that provides an overview of a number of relevant mixed-methods concerns. Building on their work, Figure 5.6 provides some examples of how data might be mixed.

Figure 5.6 Mixing Strategies in Mixed-Methods Research

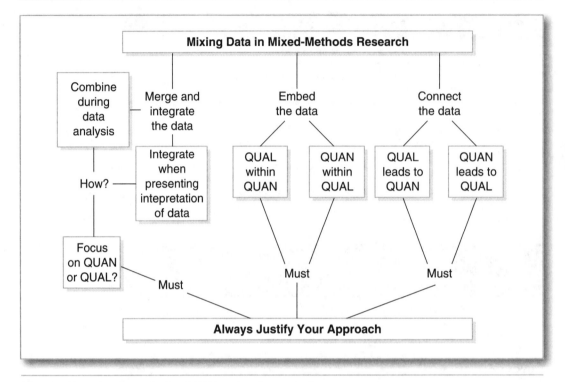

Note: QUAL = primarily qualitative; QUAN = primarily quantitative.

But what about mixed-methods approaches that seek to integrate data analysis in a more interactive way? Teddlie and Tashakkori (2009, pp. 280–281) presented a study by Jang, McDougall, Pollon, Herbert, and Russell (2008) that analyzed both QUAN and QUAL data independently and then attempted more integrative analysis by presenting both QUAN and QUAL to participants for feedback. By transforming QUAN factors into QUAL themes, and vice versa (for comparison), they consolidated the themes and factors that emerged through both analyses and used QUAL data to provide nuance to the consolidated themes/factors. This is perhaps more complex than is practical to consider at this point; however, that example points to one of the major strengths of mixed-methods data. By providing multiple options, researchers can experiment with different analysis strategies and, provided they justify their approach, can offer valuable new approaches, methods, and even measures. The mind map research example in this chapter provides perhaps a more simplistic example of how different sorts of data can be integrated and combined in a novel and potentially useful way.

MAPS, DATA, AND INTEGRITY IN MIXED-METHODS RESEARCH

Before we turn to a couple of mixed-methods research examples, it may be useful to reflect on our discussion in Chapter 2 about maps as data. Although mixed-methods research has emerged as an important approach to social science research, it still relies on data collection often associated with either quantitative or qualitative research. As discussed in Chapter 2, quantitative data are often based on instruments that measure individual performance and attitudes, based on clearly predefined categories. By contrast, qualitative data are generally based on themes that emerge through open-ended interviews, observations, or the review of various documents. As we have seen in Chapters 3 and 4, whereas both concept maps and perhaps mind maps can be used to generate social science data, the kind of data elicited by each approach to mapping requires some discussion.

This book presents the idea that knowledge and understanding are based on patterns (Kaplan, 1964) and these patterns can be represented and analyzed in a variety of ways. As Chapter 2 argued, and Chapters 3 and 4 explained, these patterns might be better identified, recognized, and understood through more graphic representations of knowledge, experience, and perception (Wheeldon, 2010b). We have presented a number of examples of quantitative and qualitative research using concept maps and mind maps; however, it may be that the mapping process is best suited to mixed-methods researchers because as a data-collection technique, it can offer both numeric and narrative data, provide a means to showcase analysis procedures, or even be a means to present research findings. This flexibility is in line with mixed methods as a pragmatic approach to research (Johnson & Onwuegbuzie, 2004), and whereas researchers may choose to rely on traditional data-collection means and ordering, combining, or embedding findings through existent models, other approaches exist and should be explored.

Another issue is how to consider reliability and validity in mixed-methods research. As you may recall, in Chapter 3 we discussed the idea that in quantitative research, *reliability* is concerned with questions of stability and consistency and whether the same measurement tool can yield stable and consistent results over time. In contrast, *validity* considers how well we were able to design methods or measures to investigate the broader constructs under investigation. In qualitative research, the focus on these concepts is slightly different. As discussed in Chapter 4, these same concepts mean different things within the context of the qualitative paradigm. This requires that researchers focus on how they justify their approach, whether they consider alternate explanations and approaches, and whether they address the researcher's reflexivity. We will return to these issues in Chapter 7. It is important to acknowledge that depending on the mixed-methods design, each of these approaches must be considered, either separately or together.

It is important to recognize that the quality of mixed-methods research is based on the integrity of the process used to integrate or combine different methods within one project. For mixed-methods projects that emphasize quantitative research, key questions surround the hypothesis under investigation, the size and justification for the gathering of data from the samples selected, and the appropriateness of the statistical tests and operations employed. For mixed-methods projects that emphasize qualitative research, key questions surround the nature of data collection, the analytic process used to discover themes and commonalities and differences, and how the data are presented. Although mixed methods involve both quantitative and qualitative components that consider the elements described above, they must do more than simply report the results of two separate projects (Teddlie & Tashakkori, 2009). Meaningful mixed-methods research combines the quantitative and qualitative results to offer more than the sum of each part. Qualitative approaches might be used to contextualize numeric findings, or quantitative methods might be used to assist readers to understand the generalizability of narrative findings. New approaches to mixed methods can build on past designs that aim to explore topics from more than one angle and use maps to collect data in a variety of ways and for a variety of purposes. It may be useful to explore in practical terms how concept maps and mind maps can be used through two mixed-methods research examples.

RESEARCH EXAMPLES USING CONCEPT MAPS AND MIND MAPS

Based on research by Wheeldon (2010b), this example shows how maps can offer a unique way for research participants to represent their experiences while assisting researchers to make better sense of gathered data. Maps can be used both in established pre/post designs and in the construction of unique and novel mixed-methods measures constructed by assigning weights to different data-collection stages. Do you agree with the notion that data can be weighted in this way? On what assumptions is it based?

Pre/Post Concept Maps and Validation in Mixed-Methods Research

As discussed in Chapters 2 and 3, concept maps are most commonly used in quantitative research. This may be because earlier versions of concept maps were used to explore science education (Stewart, Van Kirk, & Rowell, 1979) and were often quantitatively scored by an expert to assess how understanding was demonstrated through the structure of the map itself. A focus on structure remains an integral feature for many concept map researchers (Novak & Cañas, 2008) because structured maps can be consistently assessed, scored, and/or compared to assess an individual's understanding of a topic. Novak and Gowin (1984) described the utility of maps to assess understanding in education. They argued that by having students complete concept maps on certain topics, structured interview questions can be posed to a student to explore areas of misunderstanding or confusion based on the student's map. To score a concept map, Novak and Gowin suggested that maps be assessed by a subject matter expert based on the number of valid propositions, levels of hierarchy, and number of branchings, cross-links, and specific examples provided in the maps. As presented in Chapter 2, there are a number of ways to score a map, including based on the map's structure.

By using concept maps as a pre/post data-collection tool, we can quantitatively test if understanding, views, and/or perceptions change over time (Kilic, Kaya, & Dogan, 2004). In mixed-methods designs, scoring pre/post concept maps can also be used to test hypotheses that emerge from qualitative data analysis. Based on a pilot study to assess different teaching strategies for internship students related to values and ethics in criminal justice (Wheeldon, 2008), the example below provides one way that concept maps might be used to test qualitative findings. As you read this example, consider which qualitative findings were validated by the analysis of the pre/post concept maps. Which questions remain?

Overview and Mixed Design

Forty-five students enrolled in the Administration of Justice internship program at George Mason University were assigned unique identifier codes and tracked during 16 months between 2007 and 2009. This program involved the completion of a preinternship course and a subsequent 4-month internship at a criminal justice agency. Of interest was which methods of ethical instruction used in the preinternship class students would identify as most useful. Based on a debate within the literature about the best means to guide instruction on values and ethics (Cederblom & Spohn, 1991), a variety of approaches were used. Through nine scenarios students were presented with dilemmas and had to work together to identify the best course of action. An equal number of scenarios were drawn from texts that used a more general philosophic approach, a more practical criminal justice–focused approach, and a hybrid approach that involved criminal justice examples and step-by-step deliberation. Student perceptions were based on data collected in a variety of ways. Quantitative data about personal ethics and their origins were collected before and after the pre-internship class through concept maps. Some time later, qualitative data through surveys and focus groups were collected before and after students' criminal justice internships.

As described above there are three central concerns related to mixed-methods design. These include the timing, weighting, and mixing of data. In this example, the timing aspect of the mixed-methods design might be described as multistage and sequential. First, the quantitative data were collected through the pre/post concept maps, and later, qualitative data were collected through surveys and focus groups. Descriptively, this might be represented by the notation quan → QUAL. However, in this case, the pre/post data were used to test whether the change in views suggested by qualitative data collection through a survey and focus groups could be quantitatively validated. Thus, in analytic terms, it may be useful to describe the project as QUAL → quan. The important thing to remember is that this was principally a qualitative project (QUAL). Quantitative data were collected first; however, they were analyzed only later. The mixing strategy involved connecting some of the qualitative findings to the quantitative pre/post analysis to corroborate key themes identified.

Collecting and Analyzing Qualitative Data

Data were collected during a 16-month interval from a student's first preinternship class to his or her final class following a criminal justice internship. The first stage of data analysis was based on the qualitative data collected through the surveys and focus groups. The open-ended survey and focus groups allowed students to provide their views on the importance of ethics to their placements and the value of the different approaches, exercises, and scenarios used to teach ethical decision making during the preinternship course (Wheeldon, 2008). This provided more nuance and context to the quantified differences expressed in the maps. The survey questions of interest are outlined in Table 5.3.

Table 5.3 Mapping Values Survey Questions

Number	Question
1	How important are one's ethics and values to a career in criminal justice?
2	How well did ADJ 479 assist you to consider where your values and ethics come from?
3	How useful were the exercises and discussions to assist you to identify and address ethical dilemmas?
4	List any scenarios you recall from class that were useful in exploring values, ethics, and criminal justice.
5	Anything you would like to add?

Note: ADJ = Administration of Justice.

Following the conclusion of their internships, these same students participated in focus groups on values, ethics, and the criminal justice system in their last class, Administration of Justice 480. Following these discussions, students were encouraged to write to the researcher privately and/or anonymously to share their views about their experiences.

The qualitative analysis strategy built on past approaches (Wheeldon & Faubert, 2009) and involved mapping the survey responses to identify common perceptions. This included combining the presence and frequency of unique individual concepts into a color-coded Excel spreadsheet. Perhaps simplistic, this concept-counting approach (Wheeldon, 2011) offered a useful way to present common sentiments expressed by students. Another approach was to connect common sentiments to illustrative quotations from the students. These quotations provided a means to identify thematic findings while rooting any conclusions in the language of those surveyed. This approach was repeated in the focus groups held within class after students had completed their internships. Wide-open discussion ensued, and students offered insights into perceived strengths and weaknesses of the preinternship course, teaching strategies, and the internship program overall. Both common concepts and sentiments were again captured to provide additional and reflective data. The qualitative findings provided key insights into student perceptions.

Based on the survey results, virtually all students identified values and ethics as important or very important to a career in criminal justice, and most identified the course and the exercises as important or very important to their ability to identify and address ethical dilemmas. One theme that emerged was the belief that the course helped "students to understand their own values, and identify and address ethical dilemmas." When asked which scenarios were most useful, the majority of students identified examples drawn from a text that combined specific real-work situations with a step-by-step approach to identifying the dilemmas and possible solutions. Another important theme was that teaching ethics required that real-life scenarios be used to "help students to evaluate how ethics are connected to the criminal justice system." These should not be "too easy," because they can provide a false sense of security and a limited understanding of the "real-world complexity of ethics."

The focus group results offered another view of the role of ethics. Although many students acknowledged that the class "helped them identify ethical dilemmas in their placements," many more students saw ethics as "situational" and varied "depending on the type of agency." Some students wished that the course had "taught [them] what the ethics in the criminal justice system were" and focused on the specific guidelines required at the agencies where they did their internships. Other students shared more personal accounts of their internship experience and some of the challenging or traumatic incidences they faced during their placements. These included seeing a dead body, interviewing a victim of domestic violence, and accompanying a sheriff to a home where a youth was to be taken to a juvenile facility jail. For these students the value of ethics instruction was very personal. They suggested the experience of thinking through the ethical dilemmas prepared them because they said they "knew themselves a bit better" as a result.

Testing the Findings: Quantitative Pre/Post Concept Map Analysis Strategy

To test the extent to which the preinternship class assisted students to consider and reflect on their values, the pre/post concept maps were quantitatively assessed. As you may recall, students were asked to complete concept maps during the first preinternship class based on the general instructions to identify both important values and ethics and their origin(s). These maps demonstrated how, beginning with themselves, participants could provide what they believed to be core values and connect them with lines to where they believed these values originated. They were provided an exemplar map for how their maps should be constructed as well as basic instructions about which sorts of concepts might be included (e.g., honest, hardworking) and where these concepts may have originated (e.g., parents, religion, school). Each student was asked to complete another concept map using the same instructions and exemplars near the end of the course.

If the qualitative data are to be believed, we ought to be able to see a change in student concept maps before and after the course. To test this idea the premaps and postmaps were quantitatively assessed, and values and ethics identified in the maps and their perceived origins before and after the preinternship class were compared. In this case, the null hypothesis is that there would be no difference between the means of the premaps and postmaps. The research hypothesis was that the maps completed after the course would contain more concepts and would be constructed in more complex ways. To test this hypothesis, all relevant data for each student were compiled into an Excel table. Based on this process, a descriptive analysis was made possible that included the values in the maps and data about from whom, or from where, students suggested they had originated. Values in the premaps and postmaps were first compared in a table, as presented in Figures 5.7 and 5.8 below.

As you can see, truth and loyalty remained important for these students throughout the course, but compassion was identified more often in the postmaps, with open-mindedness identified for the first time in the postmaps. The use of traditional tables is common, but another approach is based on a computer program called Wordle (Feinberg, 2010). This online program is free for all, is easy to use, and provides another means to visualize which values were important. To create Figures 5.5 and 5.6, one can simply copy the text into the Create box at www.wordle.net. The more

Figure 5.7   Most Common Premap Values

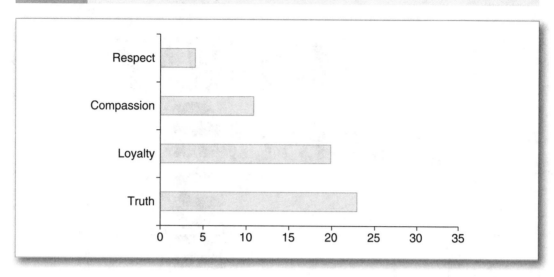

Figure 5.8   Most Common Postmap Values

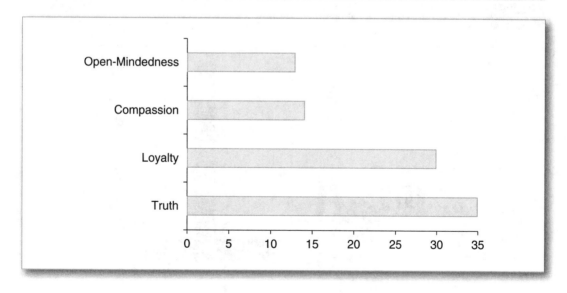

words you type, the more placement of the text changes, and the size of an individual word depends on the number of times you enter the word into the Create box. The resultant "wordle" is another way to visualize data. Figures 5.9 and 5.10 show the most common values in the student pre- and postmaps.

Figure 5.9   Premap Values in Wordle

Figure 5.10   Postmap Values in Wordle

In addition, the student maps provided data about where these values originated. As Figure 5.11 presents, these changed pre- and postcourse.

As discussed above the value of using maps is that they can provide both narrative and numeric data. Through a comparison of the pre- and postmaps, a number of interesting narrative observations can be made. The values of honesty and loyalty remained important for students both before and after the course; compassion as a value of importance was identified more often postcourse, and open-mindedness was identified for the first time postcourse. In terms of value origins, family, friends, school, and religion all remain core sites of value origin. Postcourse, however, school was identified more often. In addition to this descriptive information, the pre- and postmaps also provided numeric data. The maps were scored based on the number of concepts and the maps' complexity, as outlined in Figures 5.12 and 5.13. In this study, a complexity score was calculated based on one point for each unique concept and five points for maps that included two or more connections between values and origins.

To assess the significance of the changes in the pre- and postmaps, we can return to our familiar friend: the dependent t test. As discussed in Chapter 3, this is a very useful tool when we are comparing pre/post data from the same people. By compiling the mean number of concepts in the premaps and the postmaps, and the mean complexity of the pre- and postmaps, you might get something that looks like Table 5.4.

Figure 5.11   Pre/Post Comparison of Value Origins

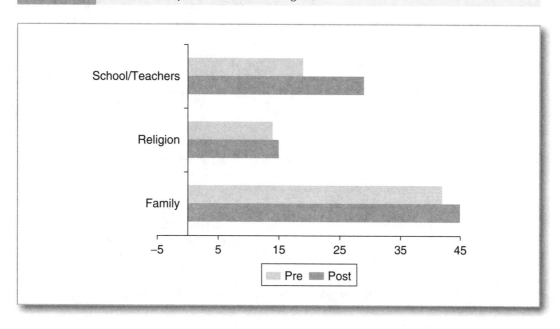

Figure 5.12 Scoring Complexity in Pre- and Postmaps, Example 1

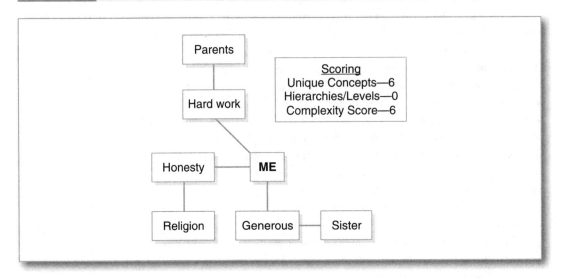

Figure 5.13 Scoring Complexity in Pre- and Postmaps, Example 2

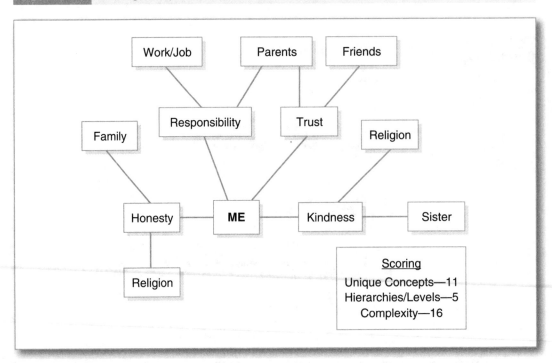

Table 5.4	Pre-/Postmap Concept and Complexity Comparison				
Gender	n	Mean Pre Concepts	Mean Post Concepts	Mean Pre Complexity	Mean Post Complexity
Male	18	8.05	13.87	9.72	17.94
Female	27	9.83	15.88	11.85	20.59

By using a one-tailed dependent *t* test, the mean difference on the number of concepts is reported as 5.49 (with a standard error of .42) and a *p* value of less than .001. The mean difference on the complexity score is reported as 8.53 (with a standard error of .68) and a *p* value again less than .001. As you will recall, a *p* value less than .05 is considered significant enough that we can reject the null hypothesis that there were no differences between the pre and post means. Based on the scoring of pre- and postmaps, maps completed postcourse contained more concepts and were constructed in more complex ways. The differences were statistically significant and suggested that the course assisted students to provide a more detailed account and understanding of their values.

Discussion and Limitations

In this example, of interest were the types of ethical instruction identified by students based on the three approaches to this training provided during the preinternship class. This involved a qualitative analysis of student surveys and focus groups that suggested that approaches to ethical instruction should not be "too easy" and not shy away from the "real-world complexity of ethics." Some common themes were that ethical instruction needed to provide (a) a means for students to understand their own values and (b) opportunities to identify and address ethical dilemmas. Examples drawn from a text that combined specific real-work situations with a step-by-step approach to identifying the dilemmas and possible solutions were identified as useful by students (Wheeldon, 2008). Yet not all students saw the preinternship course as valuable, and as some suggested in the focus groups, ethics in the classroom and ethics in the real world were two different things.

These qualitative findings led to the second, more general research question designed to better understand the role of the preinternship class. The pre/post concept maps were used to validate the hypothesis that exposure to ethical dilemmas would influence how students represented their ethics and values and understood their origins. Overall, the qualitative data suggested that students saw ethical decision making as very important in the justice system and that the instruction was most useful when it provided them with an opportunity to work in groups to identify ethical dilemmas and analyze different approaches to resolving them. Although the pre/post concept maps could not be used to corroborate all the qualitative data, they did validate the general notion that the course was useful in assisting students to reflect on their values and ethics and provided some additional hypotheses that could be tested in subsequent studies. This analysis strategy is represented in Figure 5.14.

Although this pilot study has since been built on and more data have been collected and analyzed from the sample, it provides a useful example to consider how maps can be used in mixed-methods designs and how to think about the timing, weighting, and mixing of the data. Nevertheless, a number of limitations should be noted. These include the size of the sample, the limited geographic location of the students, and the failure to capture other kinds of demographic data such as ethnicity, income level, and previous criminal justice employment. Another issue refers to how the data from the maps and data drawn from surveys were combined and compiled. In this example the qualitative findings were tested quantitatively. Yet the quantitative analysis did not consider all of the qualitative data that emerged from the surveys

Figure 5.14   Validating Qualitative Data on the Value of Ethical Instruction

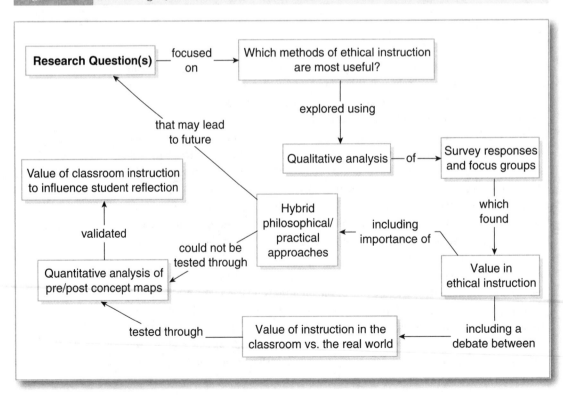

and focus groups. Thus, we can say the pre-/postmaps suggested the course assisted students to provide a more detailed account and understanding of their values; however, they did not (and could not) validate the survey data that suggested which types of ethical instruction were best. The choice to focus principally on qualitative data collection might be seen as a limitation.

Another approach might have tried to find new ways to combine the map data and survey results by individual students. In addition, by having students complete yet another concept map on how best to teach ethics, these data might have suggested how changes in values orientation were specifically connected to the style of ethical instruction favored by each student. Another concern in this example might be the assumption that concept count/complexity measures are useful proxies for knowledge transfer. This has not yet been fully demonstrated. Although there is research on the value of concept maps in education, science, and nursing, their application and the validity of different approaches in criminal justice is still emerging (Wheeldon, 2010b).

Mind Maps and Constructing a Mixed-Methods Measure

Another approach to the use of maps in mixed-methods research attempts to locate the strength of mind maps with the kind of research being undertaken. Using pre/post concept maps as in the example above may be a useful way to measure how views change over time, but quantitative comparisons may be less important than the ways participants represent their individual understanding. Using less formal mind maps to collect data may provide an important window into how participants understand issues, events, or approaches. This technique was used in a study to assess training approaches in the development of the first probation service in Latvia (Wheeldon, 2010a). Although this example also relied on sequential multistage data collection, the ways in which the data were weighted and mixed is quite different from the pre/ the ways in which the data were weighted and mixed is quite different from the pre/ post concept map example presented above. Instead of comparing pre- and post-maps, in this example the identification of themes within the maps led to another, more complex analysis process that combined and quantified the frequency of individual variables identified during a variety of data-collection stages.

Overview and Mixed Design

Through an innovative, exploratory mixed methodology involving a multistage data-collection process, mind maps were used to gather evidence, capture experience, and frame additional interviews among 14 research participants who during a 2-year period were exposed to a variety of training methods. This project considered which training approaches were of most value to participants based on a dichotomy within the organizational change literature between sharing specific organizational training tools and the development of individual capacity to pursue reform through local innovation (Wheeldon, 2010a). Building on past research, this study contributed to emerging knowledge-transfer scholarship and considered the potential of legal technical assistance projects to model democratic values in the former Soviet Union. In terms of the timing, weighting, and mixing of data, this example provides yet another approach to thinking about mixed-methods research. The timing once again involved sequential data collection as the mind maps were collected first and the themes contained within them informed the development of subsequent interviews. However, once the interview data were collected, both the maps and the interviews were reanalyzed concurrently. During this reanalysis concepts that emerged through more unsolicited data-collection techniques were weighted higher than concepts identified in other stages. This allowed for the construction of a novel mixed-methods measure, the salience score that was used to identify the most common elements that emerged through data collection but that explicitly privileged those captured in more unsolicited ways.

Once again, in this example, the sequence of data collection was less important than the process by which the data were weighted and analyzed. As described below, the salience score emerged from concurrent analyses that could be represented by the notation QUAL + quan. On the other hand, although the sample was small, one could argue that the quantitative measure developed through a series of numeric operations is equally important as the qualitative assumptions from which it is drawn. If this view is correct, the notation could also be described as QUAL + QUAN. As you read the example, consider which notation you think is more appropriate. As we will see the mixing strategy involved merging and integrating the data to develop a mixed measure and then embedding the qualitative findings within the numeric salience score.

Data Collection and the Quantitative Salience Score

Like in the example above, the process of data collection and analysis here also involved a number of steps and stages. In the first stage of data collection, participants were asked to complete mind maps about their experience of a legal technical assistance project. Participants were provided with an exemplar map and encouraged to make their own as reflective of their experiences during the project as possible. One map adapted from the maps that were returned is presented in Figure 5.15.

In the second stage of data collection, participants were asked general interview questions. Listed in Table 5.5, these general questions were open ended and probed positive and negative experiences, perceived results and challenges, and previously indentified concepts, gathered through a literature review.

In addition to the general questions, conclusionary and more reflective open-ended questions followed the more directive data-collection stages. By providing participants an opportunity to identify areas not previously addressed, the researcher

Figure 5.15   Example of Latvian Mind Map

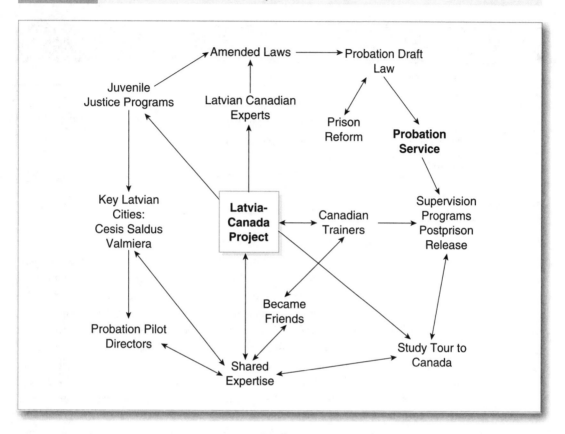

Table 5.5   General Interview Questions

Question Number	Question Text
1	Describe your most positive or memorable experience with Canadian trainers.
2	Describe your most negative or challenging experience with Canadian trainers.
3	What if anything did you learn through the mind map exercise?
4	How important was the role of the translator/translation within the training sessions?
5	Have you remained in touch with any of the Canadian trainers?

(Continued)

Table 5.5 (Continued)

Question Number	Question Text
6	What would you say was the biggest result of Latvian-Canadian cooperation?
7	What would you say was the biggest challenge of Latvian-Canadian cooperation?
8	Was working with Canadians different than working with other international experts?
9	If you could change one thing about Canada's involvement with Latvia, what would it be?
10	Anything else you'd like to add?

Source: Wheeldon, 2010b.

hoped they would reflect on their experience as whole, restating aspects of particular significance, or provide additional clarifying commentary. By combining the maps with the different stages of follow-up interviews, the frequency with which individual variables were identified through the multiple data-collection stages was recorded.

To analyze the interview data in a more meaningful way, a mixed-methods measure called a "salience score" was developed (Wheeldon, 2010b). The construction of a mixed-methods salience score may involve a number of separate yet rather simple operations. In the first step, unique, individual concepts, elements, and activities identified by participants in different stages of data collection can be recorded as variables. Individual variables might be identified in mind maps, through general or specific interviews, or in summative and reflective statements. They also may be identified in one, multiple, or all stages of data collection. These variables can then be quantified through the use of a concept-counting technique that records the frequency or presence of individual variables throughout data collection. Table 5.6 lists some of the variables identified through the study.

The number of times a variable was identified in total across the data-collection stages and the number of times each participant identified a variable across multiple data-collection stages were interesting, but these sorts of frequency measures can provide only a sense of whether, and how often, these variables were identified. An important assumption in this study was that the way in which the variables were identified might more usefully demonstrate the relevance or legitimacy of a proposed association (Cash et al., 2002).

For each variable identified in multiple stages of data collection, a salience score or weighted measure was developed using a weighted count system (Stillwell, Winterfeldt, & John, 1987). This strategy allows the researcher to assign participants a score for each individual variable they identify depending on the stage(s) at which these variables were recorded. For example, individual variables that emerge from

Table 5.6   Individual Variables Identified

Variables Identified	Variables Identified
Presentence Report	Job Shadowing
Risk/Needs Assessment	Role-Plays
Prison Intake Assessment	Working Groups
Reintegration Plan	Canada Site Visits
Case Management	Regional Coordination Councils
Canadian Program Manuals	Networking
Probation Draft	Personalities
Legislative Reform	Pilot Projects
Police Reform	Restorative Justice Exercises

user-generated, open-ended, and unsolicited data-collection procedures can be treated as more valuable and given more weight in the overall measure. In this example, user-generated concepts gathered through the maps were deemed worth four points, and the responses to general, nonspecific questions were worth three. Concepts identified following conclusionary questions asked at the end of both the general question sets were worth two points. Given that participants came back to these concepts after several other data-collection stages, they were felt to be less valuable than concepts generated without the priming of earlier data collection.

This approach to data transformation allowed a score to be tabulated for each individual variable, the common unique variables identified in each mind map (Turns, Atman, & Adams, 2000), and those that emerged through the qualitative interviews (Sandelowski, 2001). These were combined for each individual by adding the points assigned through each stage of the data-collection process. Salience scores for identified variables can produce values ranging from 0 (*not salient*) to 9 (*extremely salient*). Table 5.7 presents an example of how a salience score of 5 might be tabulated for a concept identified in two out of four stages of data collection.

By repeating this process, a mixed-methods salience score was tabulated for each variable. The individual variable salience scores (IVSSs) for each individual were then combined to get an overall variable salience score (OVSS) for the total sample. All participants' IVSSs were added together, and the result was divided by the total number of people in the sample (n). This operation is represented by the formula $OVSS = [(IVSS1 + IVSS2 \ldots IVSSn) / n]$. This weighted scoring scheme can incorporate both overall variable frequencies while accounting for variables identified throughout multiple data-collection stages. When combined with the more nuanced qualitative data gathered through interviews, this approach may provide a strengthened means to clarify and build on the results of one method with the perspective of another (Greene & Caracelli, 1997). Top OVSSs are reported in Table 5.8.

Table 5.7 Example of Salience Scoring Procedure

Data-Collection Stage	Frequency	Weighted Measure	Percentage
Mind map	1	4	50.0
General Interview	0	3	0.0
Reflective Statement	1	2	50.0
Total	2		100.0
Salience Score		**6**	

Table 5.8 Top Overall Variable Salience Score for Sample

Individual Variable	Salience Score
Personalities	5.64
Site Visits	4.86
Networking	4.71
Role-Plays	3.93
Probation Draft	3.64
Pilot Projects	3.42

A final step involved validating the salience score by considering whether differences between groups within the sample had skewed the findings. Differences between groups can mean that what you thought were generalizable findings are instead the results of strongly held views within one or more groups. In this example there were three groupings of interest. These included male and female, participants from Riga and outside Riga, and headquarters staff and probation officers. There were mean differences between the groups within the sample; through *t* tests (adjusted for undertaking multiple tests), these differences were found to be statistically insignificant in all instances. This means that the findings that made up the salience score can be attributed to the group as a whole.

Qualitative Nuance and Embedding Data

As we saw above, the data were collected sequentially and weighted in such a way as to privilege data collected through the mind maps and open-ended interview questions. Although the quantification of qualitative data (Sandelowski, 2001) provided a means to develop a unique "mixed methods measure" (Wheeldon, 2010b), this study relied on qualitative data gathered from the interviews to provide another means to understand the value of the project from the participant's point of view. These data were mixed in such a way that compiled interview data were embedded within the numeric findings to provide a more detailed means to understand "why the concepts were identified as important, and how they might be interrelated" (Wheeldon, 2010a, p. 519). Using this approach allowed the qualitative data drawn from the interviews to provide some context to the numeric salience scores.

As depicted above, personalities were identified as the single most important feature of the project. As such, interview results that spoke to the nature of the relationships should be presented first. These included statements about the trust participants had in the "experience and expertise" of the trainers and how they saw them as "friends and role models" who were willing to share both their successes and their failures and "took time to learn about Latvia." Embedding qualitative data based on numeric salience also lends itself to the inclusion of interview data that considered site visits to Canada. These were described as integral in allowing the participants a chance to "see a variety of programs and services" and learn about "pre-sentence reports, risk needs assessments, mediation programs, and post-penitentiary assistance." By seeing the "work in action" the tour provided important "practical experience." Finally, the third most "salient" aspect of the training was networking. Participants suggested project activities had assisted "team building between Latvians" and helped to create a "common strategy" for Latvia (Wheeldon, 2010a).

Discussion and Limitations

This study developed an approach that allowed for the numeric salience score to help present and organize qualitative findings about which elements of the training methods and approaches were most useful. By mixing methods in this way, the research not only presented a sense of what worked but provided some context and nuance about why and how. The participants also noted the utility of the maps. Virtually all participants identified the maps as a "useful way to see experience." Some suggested this was because making a map "helped them to remember events from years ago" and "organize their thoughts about the experience systematically." Others suggested that as visual aids, maps helped put the experience in "context," provided a "clearer view" by allowing them to look at events again and realize how much had happened, and helped them to "focus on the key experiences, concepts and connections." For these participants, there was value in visualizing their experiences and organizing their thoughts through maps. Although the data collected in this study have been analyzed in a variety of ways (Wheeldon, 2010a, 2011), they also provide a useful example to consider another way maps can be used in terms of the timing, weighting, and mixing of data. Using mind maps in this way allows researchers to embrace quantitative measures that use qualitative assumptions about which sorts of data are valuable and how they might be privileged. The mixed measure should be built on and revised, but it represents a unique way to combine quantitative and qualitative data as presented in Figure 5.16.

Some limitations with this study include the sample size and the choices made within the method and analysis strategy. The development of a mixed-methods measure called the salience score usefully combines elements from both the quantitative and the qualitative traditions; however, it remains untested and only a first draft of sorts. By privileging more user-generated data-collection stages by assigning more weight to the variables that emerge through these stages, the mixed-methods measure combined the "clarity of counts, with the nuance qualitative reflection can provide" (Wheeldon, 2010b, p. 87). Yet its novelty is an inherent limitation. There are few studies that have attempted to weight data in this way, and more study is needed to understand the value of a mixed-methods measure. One useful approach for others testing this measure would be to develop an additional validation process in which focus groups made up of a study's participants could validate the main findings. In this way, one could test whether the main findings that emerged through the score

Figure 5.16 One View of a Mixed-Methods Measure

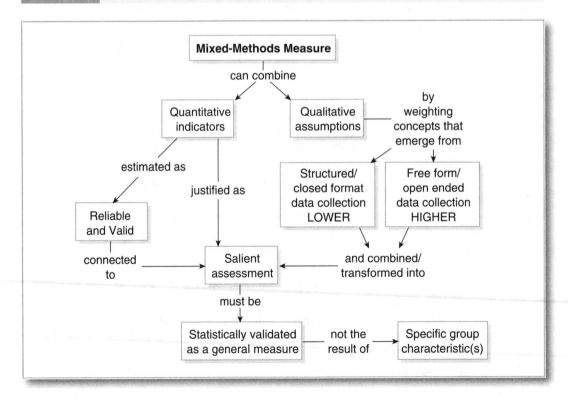

were seen as important by focus groups representative of the total sample. These sorts of validation exercises can allow the findings to be reviewed by the participants themselves through a more participatory approach toward the research process itself.

STUDENT ACTIVITY

Review the student activities in Chapters 2, 3, and 4. Consider how adding another method to either of these activities can assist you to better understand the issue under investigation. In Chapter 2, your class might have considered students' ability to recall key concepts and their relationships based on a lecture using concept maps. In contrast, your class might have used mind maps to consider student perceptions of the value of the material presented on that day. How might a mixed approach give you more data from which to draw conclusions? Imagine each person in your class completed a mind map about the perceived value of that week's lesson at the beginning of class, based on that week's readings. Now imagine that following the lesson, each person completed a concept map in which he or she was to connect concepts and propositions based on the lesson. Generate some hypotheses about what you might see if you were to compare an individual's prelesson interest level with his or her postlesson understanding. What might this approach to student comparison miss? How might you address this limitation?

Based on Chapter 2's activity and the analysis presented in Chapter 3, how could concept maps be used to explore how students learned concepts presented in a weekly lesson? What additional information might be useful to gather? How could questions to students about the most difficult concepts, propositions, or connections assist them to reflect on their own learning and allow for teachers to better understand student difficulties? How might you combine different sorts of data based on the timing, weighting, and mixing considerations described above? Based on Chapter 4's activity and the analysis presented in Chapter 5, how could mind maps and interviews be scored to assess their description of key people or events in their lives? How might the different approaches to data gathering influence how you might score the data collected in each? Are there common ideas that continually emerge? What additional information might be useful to gather? How does this attempt to quantify qualitative data assist your understanding, and to what extent do the numbers in your scoring system connect to your experience interviewing your participant?

CONCLUSION

As mixed-methods research continues to grow, the use of maps as an alternative form of data collection can be seen as part of a more pragmatic understanding of intuitive and abductive connections between theory and data. Indeed by combining quantitative and qualitative approaches alongside their associated data analysis strategies, mixed methods provide a means to gain a better understanding of phenomena under investigation. As visual records of understanding, concept maps and mind maps may be important tools in this regard because the data that are represented through their construction can be assessed both quantitatively and qualitatively.

This chapter has provided both a theoretical justification for the use of concept maps and mind maps in mixed-methods research and some examples of how maps might be used in this way. Pre/post concept maps offer one way to investigate how views have quantitatively changed over time and suggest a means to explore in more detail some of the reasons why using qualitative techniques makes sense. The mixed-methods measure is a unique way to consider how data gathered through multiple stages of data collection can be compiled. This single measure explicitly values data collected through more unsolicited means while at the same time ensuring the reliability of counts is respected.

REVIEW

1. Define mixed-methods research, and explain the assumptions about knowledge on which it is based. How is it different from quantitative and qualitative research?

2. What are three ways mixed-methods studies have been undertaken in the past?

3. Why might concept maps and mind maps be useful for mixed-methods research?

4. How can pre/post concept maps be used with other kinds of methods?

5. What is a mixed-methods measure? How was it first constructed, and how might it be improved?

SUGGESTED ADDITIONAL READINGS

Creswell, J., & Plano Clark, V. (2007). *Designing and conducting mixed methods research.* London: Sage.

Morgan, D. L. (2007). Paradigms lost and pragmatism regained: Methodological implications of combining qualitative and quantitative methods. *Journal of Mixed Methods Research, 1*(1), 48–76.

Teddlie, C. B., & Tashakkori, A. (2009). *Foundations of mixed methods research: Integrating quantitative and qualitative approaches in the social and behavioral sciences.* Thousand Oaks, CA: Sage.

Wheeldon, J. P. (2010). Mapping mixed methods research: Methods, measures, and meaning. *Journal of Mixed Methods Research, 4*(2), 87–102.

REFERENCES

Aldridge, J. M., Fraser, B. J., & Huang, T. (1999). Investigating classroom environments in Taiwan and Australia with multiple research methods. *Journal of Educational Research, 93,* 48–57.

Baumann, C. (1999). Adoptive fathers and birthfathers: A study of attitudes. *Child and Adolescent Social Work Journal, 5*(16), 373–391.

Cash, D., Clark, W. C., Alcock, F., Dickson, N., Eckley, N., & Jäger, J. (2002). *Credibility, legitimacy and boundaries: Linking, assessment and decision making.* Cambridge, MA: Kennedy School of Government.

Cederblom, J., & Spohn, C. (1991). A model for teaching criminal justice ethics. *Journal of Criminal Justice Education, 2,* 201–218.

Creswell, J., & Plano Clark, V. (2007). *Designing and conducting mixed methods research.* London: Sage.

Feinberg, J. (2010). *Wordle.* Retrieved July 28, 2010, from http://www.wordle.net/

Goertzel, T., & Fashing, J. (1981). The myth of the normal curve: A theoretical critique and examination of its role in teaching and research. *Humanity and Society, 5,* 14–31.

Gogolin, L., & Swartz, F. (1992). A quantitative and qualitative inquiry into the attitudes toward science of nonscience college students. *Journal of Research in Science Teaching, 29,* 487–504.

Greene, J. C., & Caracelli, V. J. (1997). Defining and describing the paradigm issue in mixed-method evaluation. In J. C. Greene & V. J. Caracelli (Eds.), *Advances in mixed-method evaluation: The challenges and benefits of integrating diverse paradigms* (New Directions for Program Evaluation, No. 74, pp. 5–17). San Francisco: Jossey-Bass.

Greene, J. C., Caracelli, V. J., & Graham, W. F. (1989). Toward a conceptual framework for mixed-method evaluation design. *Educational Evaluation and Policy Analysis, 11*(3), 255–274.

Guba, E., & Lincoln, Y. (1989). *Fourth generation evaluation.* Newbury Park, CA: Sage.

Jang, E. E., McDougall, D. E., Pollon, D., Herbert, M., & Russell, P. (2008). Integrative mixed methods data analysis strategies in research on school success in challenging circumstances. *Journal of Mixed Methods Research, 2*(3), 221–247.

Jenkins, J. E. (2001). Rural adolescent perceptions of alcohol and other drug resistance. *Child Study Journal, 31*(4), 211–224.

Jick, T. D. (1979). Mixing qualitative and quantitative methods: Triangulation in action. *Administrative Science Quarterly, 24,* 602–611.

Johnson, R. B., & Onwuegbuzie, A. (2004). Mixed methods research: A research paradigm whose time has come. *Educational Researcher, 33*(7), 14–26.

Kaplan, A. (1964). *The conduct of inquiry: Methodology for behavioral science.* San Francisco: Chandler Press.

Kilic, Z., Kaya, O. N., & Dogan, A. (2004, August 3–8). *Effects of students' pre- and post-laboratory concept maps on students' attitudes toward chemistry laboratory in university general chemistry.* Paper presented at the International Conference on Chemical Education, Istanbul, Turkey.

Miles, M., & Huberman, M. (2002). Reflections and advice. In M. Huberman & M. Miles (Eds.), *The qualitative researcher's companion* (pp. 393–397). Thousand Oaks, CA: Sage.

Morgan, D. L. (2007). Paradigms lost and pragmatism regained: Methodological implications of combining qualitative and quantitative methods. *Journal of Mixed Methods Research, 1*(1), 48–76.

Morse, J. M. (2003). Principles of mixed methods and multi-method research design. In A. Tashakkori & C. Teddlie (Eds.), *Handbook of mixed methods in social and behavioral research* (pp. 189-208). Thousand Oaks, CA: Sage.

Myers, K., & Oetzel, J. (2003). Exploring the dimensions of organizational assimilation: Creating and validating a communication measure. *Communication Quarterly, 51,* 436–455.

Novak, J. D., & Cañas, A. J. (2008). *The theory underlying concept maps and how to construct and use them.* Pensacola: Florida Institute for Human and Machine Cognition.

Novak, J. D., & Gowin, J. B. (1984). *Learning how to learn.* Cambridge, UK: Cambridge University Press.

Palys, T. (1992). *Research decisions: Quantitative and qualitative perspectives* (3rd ed.). Toronto: Thompson Canada.

Rorty, R. (1999). *Philosophy and social hope.* London: Penguin.

Sandelowski, M. (2001). Real qualitative researchers do not count: The use of numbers in qualitative research. *Research in Nursing and Health, 24*(3), 230–240.

Stewart, J., Van Kirk, J., & Rowell, R. (1979). Concept maps: A tool for use in biology teaching. *American Biology Teacher, 41*(3), 171–175.

Stillwell, W., Winterfeldt, D. V., & John, R. S. (1987). Comparing hierarchical and nonhierarchical weighting methods for eliciting multiattribute value models. *Management Science, 33*(4), 937–943.

Tashakkori, A., & Teddlie, C. (1998). *Mixed methodology: Combining qualitative and quantitative approaches.* Thousand Oaks, CA: Sage.

Teddlie, C. B., & Tashakkori, A. (2009). *Foundations of mixed methods research: Integrating quantitative and qualitative approaches in the social and behavioral sciences.* Thousand Oaks, CA: Sage.

Turns, J., Atman, C., & Adams, R. (2000). Concept maps for engineering education: A cognitively motivated tool supporting varied assessment functions. *IEEE Transactions on Education, 43,* 164–173.

Way, N., Stauber, H. Y., Nakkula, M. J., & London, P. (1994). Depression and substance use in two divergent high school cultures: A quantitative and qualitative analysis. *Journal of Youth and Adolescence, 23*(3), 331–335.

Wheeldon, J. P. (2008, November 12–15). *Mapping ethics, values and problem solving among criminal justice students.* Paper presented at the American Society of Criminology Annual Meeting, St. Louis, MO.

Wheeldon, J. P. (2010a). Learning from Latvia: Adoption, adaptation, and evidence based justice reform. *Journal of Baltic Studies, 41*(4), 507–530.

Wheeldon, J. P. (2010b). Mapping mixed methods research: Methods, measures, and meaning. *Journal of Mixed Methods Research, 4*(2), 87–102.

Wheeldon, J. P. (2011). Is a picture worth a thousand words? Using mind maps to facilitate participant recall in qualitative research. *Qualitative Report, 16*(2), 509–522. Retrieved March 2, 2011, from http://www.nova.edu/ssss/QR/QR16-2/wheeldon.pdf

Wheeldon, J. P., & Faubert, J. (2009). Framing experience: Concept maps, mind maps, and data collection in qualitative research. *International Journal of Qualitative Methods, 8*(3), 68–83.

6

Putting It All Together

Using Maps and Diagrams to Organize, Write, and Reflect on Research

CHAPTER OVERVIEW AND OBJECTIVES

Throughout the book we have explored ways concept maps and mind maps can be used in the research process. These include using maps to gather data, to describe one's methodology, and to analyze findings. Maps can also be used when writing up a paper and can help one to brainstorm ideas and review the sections within it. Several important aspects of writing up a project include finding good sources and finding an individual writing style and voice. One of the most challenging aspects of writing is figuring out how to structure a paper so that it addresses the requirements outlined in a course or by a professor. Maps can be used throughout the writing process, and often within the research paper itself, to provide greater insight into what was discovered, how it was discovered, and what you learned throughout the process.

This chapter explores how to construct a research paper and how the use of maps and other types of diagrams can help you to organize thoughts, format projects, and reflect on the research journey. Finally, through a practical activity, you will be encouraged to use maps to engage in a mini content analysis of a peer-reviewed article in your field. Using this article, you will develop a Vee heuristic diagram to provide an example of how to reflect on the research process. This chapter is designed to assist you in writing up a research project, so you must first consider what your assignment is and what your professor is expecting. By the end of this chapter, you should be able to do the following:

- understand the major sections of a research paper;
- explain the elements within each section of the paper;
- define plagiarism and provide two strategies to avoid it in your writing;
- provide an example of how maps can be used to organize, structure, and present different aspects of writing a research paper; and
- consider the value of the Vee heuristic diagram for reflecting on the research process.

GETTING STARTED

The first thing to do is review the requirements of the paper or project. It is not necessary to focus on every little detail at this stage; however, getting a broad overview is essential. Once you have a clear understanding of the expectations, a useful first step is to brainstorm. One approach is to use maps to visually represent different aspects of an issue and to draw connections between and among them. Alvarez and Gowin (2009) provided a variety of other approaches. One key issue is to understand how you might develop your own research strategy. Figure 6.1 provides one example.

After some initial brainstorming, do some reading on your topic. Start with four to five recent *peer-reviewed studies* that address the issue of interest. Peer-reviewed studies are those published in academic journals through a blind peer-review process. This blind process ensures that when academics read the work of other academics, neither knows who the other is. Through this process, a higher standard of scholarship can be achieved than is found elsewhere. One thing to consider is the rise of mixed-methods studies in recent years. It may be useful to vary your reading by finding a mix of quantitative, qualitative, and mixed-methods research papers to see how different scholars approach a similar issue. In addition to research studies, it may be useful to use other credible academic sources, found in academic journals or quarterlies, in academic nonfiction books, or in chapters from those books. Don't forget to check Google Scholar for relevant academic articles as you prepare your project or paper. In addition, it can be very helpful to make use of databases that compile articles from a variety of journals. These databases have greatly assisted the

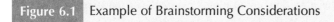

Figure 6.1   Example of Brainstorming Considerations

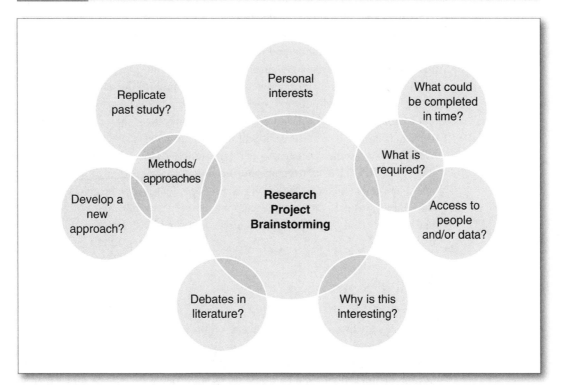

literature review process and allow searches by keyword, subject, or author. Examples are EBSCO, JSTOR, ProQuest, and Project Muse, among others. Check with your library—it is there to help!

As you compile academic sources through your research, remember to keep track of the author, title, journal, publication data, and page number. A great online tool is called Zotero (www.zotero.org). It is an easy-to-use research tool that helps you gather, organize, and analyze sources as you surf the web. It automatically keeps track of sources and allows you to export the list as a Word document. Whatever your strategy, you will be tempted to use other, nonacademic sources. These might include newspaper or magazine articles, fiction, or nonacademic websites. Although these sources may be useful to help make a point and can be used in moderation, they should not be used in place of academic sources. Instead they should be used to add color or context to a discussion or debate. Try to avoid sensationalized, unsourced discussions and politicized, one-sided polemics. Instead, focus on sources that offer balanced views and that cite their own sources. Some professors reject the idea that nonacademic sources can be used in academic papers. Be sure to check. A good approach is to use three academic sources for every nonacademic source you include.

Remember that all sources used must be properly cited, and in the format specified in your discipline and by your professor. There are a variety of online resources that can assist you in properly formatting your paper and citations. Try not to leave citations and references to the last minute. Be extra careful when citing material found online. Copying and pasting materials from Wikipedia is not a winning strategy. A declining number of students see this approach as problematic (Blum, 2009); however, it still amounts to *plagiarism* or academic theft. We will discuss some strategies to avoid this practice later in the chapter as it can have profound consequences on your academic career. Although the wealth of online material can make life much easier for us all, it is still necessary to review the sources, validate online material, and combine, compile, and synthesize the material you find in unique ways. Sources and the ideas of others must always be cited.

ORGANIZING YOUR RESEARCH PAPER

Papers should always be organized based on the instructions provided in the syllabus and/or in class. In general, however, a research paper includes the following: title page, introduction, literature review, research questions, methodology and data collection, findings, discussion and limitations, and conclusions. Don't forget that all academic papers must include references, a bibliography, or a works cited page, where all the books, articles, and other sources used in the paper are listed. Why do we focus so much on structure? Structuring your writing requires that you first structure your thinking, and this analytic process can assist you in not only understanding what you need to do but helping you organize how to do it. By developing a narrative through line, your paper can be shaped to provide a road map for your reader (Germano, 2005). A practical reason for focusing on the structure of a paper is that it requires that each section be completed and thus ensures coverage of all the major elements of the paper. It can be very useful to organize your paper using headings and subheadings. Recall the outline presented in Chapter 1, which is reintroduced in Figure 6.2.

Title Page (1 Page)

Be sure to include the title of the paper, your name, your student number, and the date. Your professor's name and the course name should be there as well. Avoid the use of a running head unless otherwise directed.

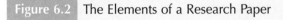

Figure 6.2   The Elements of a Research Paper

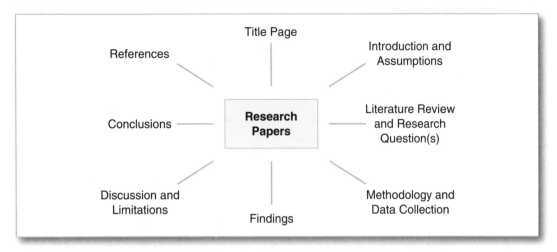

Title Page Tips (Portillo, Wheeldon, & Williams, 2008)

1. Scan the titles of published articles from journals in your library database or in your textbook. Try to emulate the tone and formatting but not the ideas of one that you find effective.

2. After you have crafted a title, ask yourself these questions: Does my title establish an academic tone? Does my title introduce my paper in a unique way? If I were thumbing through a journal, would this title interest me?

Introduction and Assumptions (1–2 Pages)

Introduce the paper's topic in this section. A good introduction creates a good impression and sets the stage for the rest of the paper. Tell the reader why the topic is of interest, and summarize the main approaches, arguments, or agreements that exist (Cryer, 1996). This section might also briefly describe the assumptions made in the paper or project, explain the methodology, and outline the main findings of your study. It may also be useful to provide an outline of how the remainder of the paper is organized so the reader can follow your train of thought. By introducing each section, authors can help readers understand how the work will be presented, and where the paper is ultimately going. An integral component of this section is defining the terms you use. In the social sciences, there are clear differences between terms, words, and concepts. Everyday language may not capture the specific definitions and meanings; people may use the same words to mean very different concepts. It is important to be

Figure 6.3 Elements of an Introduction

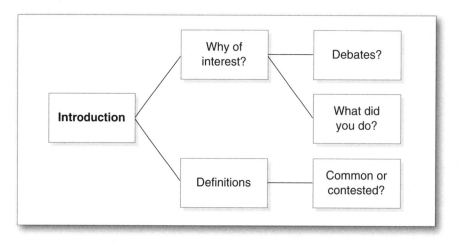

clear about the meaning of the specific terms being used (see Figure 6.3). In academic work, it is advisable to focus on accepted definitions of terms or concepts as cited in academic sources and as part of scientific theories (Germano, 2005).

Setting the Stage With a Strong Introduction (Portillo et al., 2008)

1. Introduce your topic—Avoid grand-sounding phrases such as "throughout history" or "people have always been. . . ." These statements are incomplete and don't inform the reader about your topic. Keep in mind that you should try to teach your reader something new—vague generalizations don't allow you to do that.

2. Define your terms—Be sure to use academic sources, not the dictionary. One aim of academic writing is to move beyond simple definitions and engage in a conversation that addresses complexities; using dictionary definitions doesn't allow you to do this. Find an academic definition, and try to build onto it by adding your own perspective.

3. Take your time—One strategy is to write your introduction after you have written your paper. If you have a first draft written and aren't happy with the introduction, see if your conclusion works better as the introduction. You can revise what you already have and write a new conclusion at the end.

Literature Review and Research Question(s) (2–4 Pages)

Literature reviews should provide some context about the area that you have explored; the major debates, approaches, or past findings; and which questions remain. It should assist you and your readers in understanding how you have formulized the research problem to be investigated (Alvarez & Gowin, 2009). This section establishes your command of a subject area and fosters an understanding of the main problem, issue, or debate that you seek to explore. Integral in this section is the use of *academic sources* that are credible, relevant, and in most cases, recent. In addition, it may be useful to consider how current definitions, debates, and disagreements are themselves based on the unique history of your specific discipline. We hope our readers will consider that a deeper and more profound understanding is possible by learning the history of ideas and philosophy of practices within their own fields.

Although it is not possible to cover all the literature related to an issue area, it is important that you address the main findings of the selected literature. A good strategy is to look for review articles that include a number of references and that will give you a good overview of past research (Hart, 1998). A good literature review provides the reader with relevant definitions, considerations, and debates. It also provides the basis for the overall research question(s), explains the methodology you chose to employ for your project, and highlights what is known about an issue and what is contested. This section typically concludes with a research question that informs the rest of the paper. The research question is the main question, issue, or argument that will be explored in your study and serves as a focal point for the rest of your paper (see Figure 6.4).

Figure 6.4   Organizing Literature Reviews

LITERATURE REVIEWS

Provide informational overview

Highlight leading studies

Note past limitations

Provide justification for your approach

Informed Literature Reviews (Portillo et al., 2008)

1. A literature review should provide an organized and informational overview of an area of focus. Your review needs to demonstrate your ability to scan the literature efficiently and identify a set of useful articles and books.

2. Another important aspect of a literature review is that it shows you can critically review the literature and identify studies that have strong research designs and/or those that are free from potential biases.

3. Once you establish some good studies to reference, you need to synthesize the results into a summary of what is known and what is not. Of specific interest are areas of disagreement or controversy within the reviewed literature.

4. A final step is using this synthesis to formulate additional questions that need further research. In some cases this may be applying a methodology to a new population to see whether existing findings remain relevant for different groups. In other cases, it may be useful to replicate a study to validate the findings of previous research and address unanswered questions.

Methodology and Data Collection (2–4 Pages)

In simplistic terms, the *methodology* section outlines the research plan. It spells out the theoretical assumptions made in detail and describes clearly what was done. Transparency in this stage of a paper is essential—it is better to be too detailed than not detailed enough (Silverman, 2005). The methodology should outline the theoretical approach you employed, how your research plan was connected to this approach, and how your data-collection strategy connects to both. For example, some research might be based on a literature review that led to a researcher's asking specific interview questions of a specific population. In this case the methodology section would need to provide reasons why the interview questions helped to answer your overall research question and a justification for the selection of the participants. Another methodology might attempt to replicate a past study and rely on revised survey questions presented to a specific group of people. In this case, this section would need to provide justification for any revisions to the past approach and reasons why it was useful to replicate the past study in the first place. Again, the key aspect here is justifying why a quantitative, qualitative, or mixed methodological approach is appropriate to the research question you are seeking to address (Teddlie & Tashakkori, 2009).

In addition to a description of your methodology, it is important to include some discussion of your approach to data collection. This requires that a connection be made between the overall methodological plan you have chosen, your approach to data collection, and the practical methods used. Remember, the method is the nuts and bolts of how data will be collected, and the methodology provides the justification for the overall approach (see Figure 6.5). These are related but distinct concepts. In this section, it may also be useful to describe how relevant variables were defined and, if relevant, outline the dependent, independent, and control variables. If needed, this section can first outline how analysis was planned and then note any differences from the original plan that emerged as you carried out your research (McShane & Williams, 2008).

Another central issue is whether you use human participants in your research. The use of human participants (aka people) in research has a long and complicated history. Marred by unethical practices in the past, all research involving people is today governed by federal regulations. An important responsibility of research in the social sciences is to understand the various protections that exist. We suggest you investigate low-cost and reputable online courses run through universities. Increasingly required to conduct research, these courses can provide the groundwork into a more substantive discussion. Exemptions do exist for some kinds of research, but in general any "systematic investigation, including research development, testing and evaluation, designed to develop or contribute to generalizable knowledge" using human participants must always be handled with care and respect (Office for Human Research Protections, 2011). This must include respect for those you interview and care for the integrity of the research process. For specific guidelines, consult the *institutional review board* (also called the human subjects research board) at your university.

Figure 6.5 Methodological Considerations

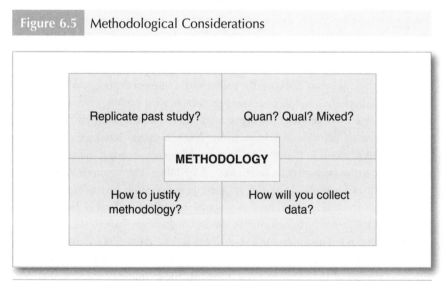

Note: Quan = quantitative; Qual = qualitative.

Different kinds of research projects will involve different procedures. It is imperative that you liaise with your professor, review the institutional review board website for more information, and ask questions about anything about which you are unclear. It may be useful to complete a checklist like the one in Appendix A. If you do use human participants, ensure they sign an informed consent document like the one included in Appendix B. Remember that it is your responsibility to keep these consent forms per the requirements at your university. You must ensure your participants' personal information is always kept confidential.

Methodological Tools of the Trade

1. Be sure to have your instructor or supervisor review your interview questions and any newly developed or revised surveys, questionnaires, or other data-collection instruments.

2. Take the requirements of informed consent seriously. Your instructor or supervisor will be a great resource here, but ultimately it is your responsibility to ensure that all people who provide you with data sign informed consent documents. You must keep identifying material safe and ensure you maintain participants' confidentiality. Never refer to individuals by their names unless specifically authorized by your participant(s) and instructor or supervisor.

3. It is useful to include a copy of the questions or survey instrument in your project. Some instructors may ask you to include this information within the methodology section itself; others may request that it be attached as an appendix.

Findings (1–3 Pages)

The findings section should provide the reader with a sense of the results of the project. This section should be a simple and clear recitation of what was discovered. This could include a narrative account of the approach to data analysis based on the methodological approach outlined earlier in the paper. Was it statistical, interpretative, or both? Another consideration is how the findings should be presented. If the research was quantitative in nature it may be useful to develop tables, maps, graphs, or figures to present findings. These should have clear titles and be accessible for readers. Even if you create a graph or table, you still need to describe its content in the text. Never assume that readers will know the topic as well as the author does (McShane & Williams, 2008).

If the research is qualitative in nature, it can be useful to include quotations from participants to help in the identification of themes or provide nuance and context to the presentation of the data. The way mixed-methods findings are presented will depend, to a large extent, on the type of mixed-methods design that was used and/or how the data were mixed (Teddlie & Tashakkori, 2009). No matter what kind of data is presented, it is important that this section be limited to what was found through the research. Be descriptive here, and be aware when describing what you found that it may be hard for those reading your work to understand what it is you found. Focus on describing findings in clear and simplistic terms. Interpretation of the findings and how they can be connected to the broader literature is important, and this account should come later, in the discussion section.

Presenting Your Findings

1. Keep it simple—which approach did you take to data analysis? Was it based on quantitative, qualitative, or mixed methodological assumptions? What did you find?

2. Think of visual ways to present key findings, and consider the use of graphs, charts, maps, or tables to summarize what you found.

3. Resist the urge to discuss implications, draw inferences, or develop inter-pretations in this section. To quote an old television program, a "just the facts" approach is useful here.

Discussion and Limitations (2–4 Pages)

In this section, the findings of the paper or project are connected to relevant findings from other studies or to the literature reviewed earlier in the paper. Do the findings support the literature? Do they differ? How and why? When writing this section, it is important to consider how the project builds on, validates, or challenges past find-ings. Does the research have policy implications? Can it be used to pursue new research in the future? Although hyperbole should be avoided, considering how your research connects to broader themes identified in the literature is a good idea. In this section, interpretation of the data as well as the kind of inferences that can be drawn from the research are important. We will consider some of the challenges and consid-erations related to drawing inferences again in Chapter 7.

Another important aspect of this section is how the limitations of the study are acknowledged. They might be general and/or specific in nature. All research is limited in one way or another. Some ways might appear obvious. For example, the literature review is almost never completely comprehensive. The sample used in data gathering might be small or nonrandom; thus, the results may not be quantitatively generaliz-able. Likewise, if the study relied on data sets collected in the past or general data from diverse sources, it may not be possible to provide qualitative nuance or in-depth descriptions of experiences, understanding, or perceptions (see Figure 6.6).

Figure 6.6 Locating Limitations

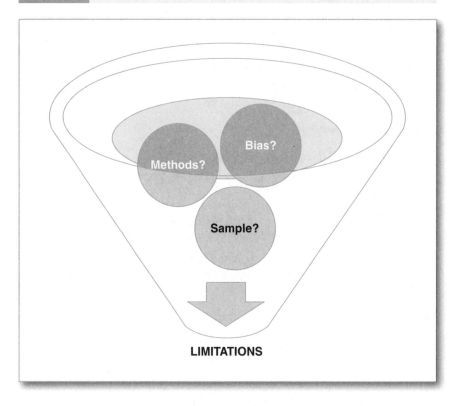

Other limitations may be more difficult to identify. As discussed throughout this book, the methodological approach taken is itself based on certain assumptions. A core part of responsible social science research is acknowledging why and how these assumptions limit the applicability of the research. It might be useful in this section to think about what could be done the same way or differently the next time around. A final consideration is the researcher's own role in the study. A feature common to reflexive approaches in qualitative designs, researchers should acknowledge and take responsibility for their biases, interests, or assumptions and explain how these may have played a role in their findings (Nightingale & Cromby, 1999). To be credible, the research process should be transparent. Latour (2005) contended that to move closer to objectivity we must become more reflexive of our interpretive practices rather than try to hide the place of the researcher within research. This sort of acknowledgment is not always a part of traditional quantitative designs, but it should be considered an aspect of ethical research practice. Even for those not swayed by the value of greater transparency in social science research, it seems only fair to acknowledge that try as we might, each of our experiences before, during, and after a research project may be relevant.

Conclusion (1–2 Pages)

This section concludes the paper or project. It can be useful to remind readers of the points raised in the introduction, including why the topic is of interest, how past studies informed the approach taken, and what the main findings were. It may be useful to consider some of the remaining questions that future studies or researchers might consider.

References (1–3 Pages)

Don't forget that every academic paper must include a bibliography, references, or a works cited page. Check with your professor for the required format in your discipline or class. Many use slightly different styles and formats; all include the author, the date of publication, the title of the work, and either the journal name and publication details or the book's publisher and its location.

WRITING AND REVISING TOWARD A STRONG RESEARCH PAPER

Citing Sources

Citation is the process of explaining to readers where they can find the information used in a paper. We must always give credit to the original writers and researchers whose work has been studied. Remember, to borrow ideas, phrases, or other material without giving the source is *plagiarism*. There are two types of plagiarism:

a) using ideas, information, or language without crediting the source and

b) documenting the source but paraphrasing the language too closely without using quotation marks to indicate which words or phrases have been borrowed.

To avoid plagiarizing, always document sources properly. This includes citing author and date for summaries (e.g., Wheeldon, 2007) and author, date, and page numbers for paraphrases and direct quotes (e.g., Åhlberg, 2009, p. 45). When in doubt, document! An emergent challenge in the Internet age is that many students do not know and have not been taught how to cite online materials. Just because an online article does not have a clear author does not mean it should not be cited. Styles will vary between different disciplines, but it is useful to cite not only the URL but also the date retrieved for inclusion within your references section. Be sure to check with your professor and ask questions if you are unclear.

Quotes, Summaries, and Paraphrases

There are three common ways to cite the work of another. Direct quotations are when someone else's words are reproduced exactly as they were first presented. Direct quotations should be used sparingly and, when used, must include the author, date, and page number so the quotation can be located. If the quoted text is longer than three lines, it should be single spaced and indented. This is not required if you use quotations from any interviews conducted during your research process. Although direct quotations are useful at times, it is better to put the work of others in your own words and cite the source. This can be done in two ways: summaries and paraphrases.

Summaries are the most common form of citation. They require that you put into your own words material gathered from other sources. You do not need to cite your own ideas, common knowledge, or information you have seen in multiple sources, unless it is controversial in some way. Summarizing other sources is a good way to demonstrate that you can use academic sources to help you present your thesis or argument in your own words. Summaries require that you provide the author and date of the original source. Your summary should be in your own words and acknowledge the contribution of others. In many cases you can cite the work of others at the end of the summarized sentence (e.g., Wheeldon, 2009). When summarizing more than one author, separate the citations with a semicolon (;), for example, "Some researchers disagree (Buzan & Buzan, 2010; Novak & Cañas, 2008)." You can also mix it up. One approach is to use language such as "As Wheeldon and Åhlberg (2011) argued . . ."; "Another approach to concept maps (Åhlberg, 2008) is to . . ."; "Mind maps can be used in a variety of ways (Wheeldon & Faubert, 2009)."

Sometimes it is useful to paraphrase the work of another. This may be because the author has said something better than you can (!) or because you think it may be useful to restate another person's specific ideas using your own sentence construction. Like direct quotes, paraphrases must include the author, date, and page numbers of the original source but must be in your own words unless you use quotation marks. Just restating another's original idea using different words does not make it your own. Close paraphrases are the most common form of plagiarism. This is usually done unintentionally, such as when you change the structure of the sentence or use synonyms. To avoid this, one strategy is to read your source, put it away, and take notes from memory or make a quick map. Then reopen your source material and check your notes (or map) for accuracy.

One of the most difficult parts of becoming a strong writer is making drafting, editing, and revising part of your scholarly ritual. Portillo et al. (2008) suggested you complete your first draft early. Take a break for a couple of days, and then come back to it. Revise and edit it, and then send it to a friend you trust. You can often make an appointment at your school's writing center for free or seek online resources such as the excellent Online Writing Lab. Remember to reread the assignment as it is listed in the syllabus before you start your draft, and review any notes or hints your professor has provided in class. These might include requested or required approaches, the number of academic sources required, and any formatting or citation suggestions. Take notes to compare with your draft. Once you get your draft back from your reviewer, read his or her comments with an open mind. Make any corrections, and reread again with your notes close by—does your paper do what is required? Good writing is rigorous work and a continuous process. It takes practice and a willingness to read, write, revise, and repeat, and it should never be left to the night before an assignment is due (Alasuutari, 1995).

PARAGRAPH STRUCTURE AND FINDING YOUR VOICE

Sources, citations, and paper structure are perhaps of most importance for young writers; however, good writing also consists of well-organized paragraphs. Paragraphs comprise complete, correct, and concise sentences that flow together, and each paragraph should focus on one subject, theme, or central idea. Although this format will not always be relevant, it may be useful to consider the structure listed below:

1. a topic sentence—captures readers by introducing an idea in an interesting way;

2. the first main point—proves, backs up, or explains the topic sentence;

3. the second main point—usually provides a reason for the first point made;

4. the third main point—can help prove the topic sentence or back up the first or second main point of the paragraph; and

5. the conclusion—sums up the main points or ideas. It usually completes the topic and provides a transition to the next paragraph.

EXERCISE 6.1
Mapping Paragraphs: Think You Get It?

Based on the five-point outline above, make a concept map of what a good paragraph comprises.

Another important part of becoming a strong writer is finding your voice. In many ways, this may be the most difficult aspect of writing. It is something all writers struggle with. It comes with practice, with reading academic journals, and with writing and revising, rewriting and revising, and so on and so forth. In general you need to be able to make an argument in a way that makes sense to you. Although you should always acknowledge the work of others, you can provide evidence for your thesis while discussing counterevidence in an original way. Don't copy a style from someone else, never overquote, and don't rehash old arguments. Try to bring something new to the table! As you read through your paper for the final time, think about voice. In fact, use your voice. Does your paper sound like you? Many writers read their papers aloud and make corrections as they go. Listen for the rhythm of your writing, and focus on ensuring each sentence is clear and concise (Germano, 2005).

USING THE VEE HEURISTIC DIAGRAM TO REFLECT ON THE RESEARCH PROCESS

Visual representations of data have been used in the past to present information through charts, graphs, or tables. In this chapter we have discussed how maps can be used to brainstorm, organize your paper, and test your ability to summarize or paraphrase cited sources. It may be useful to consider other sorts of diagrams that can help you reflect on the research process as a whole. One such approach is based on the Vee diagram developed by Bob Gowin. Gowin, you may remember, was a colleague of Joseph Novak, who developed the most common form of concept maps as discussed in Chapters 2 and 3.

In their seminal book, Novak and Gowin (1984) originally used three terms for what is now known as the Vee diagram. The first was the Vee heuristic, the second was Gowin's Vee, and the third was the V diagram. They all share common features and were designed to enable students to understand how events, processes, and objects are meaningfully related (Gowin & Alvarez, 2005). The Vee diagram's name is derived from its shape. At the top of the V, there is a focus question that helps to organize the rest of the diagram. Traditionally, one side includes the conceptual or knowledge-based aspects, and the other includes the methodological or process-based components (Alvarez & Gowin, 2009). They are connected by a central event located at the bottom of the V, where the two sides meet. Figure 6.7 presents the traditional elements of Gowin's Vee diagram.

There is no question of the pedagogic value of the traditional Vee diagram (Gowin, 1981; Novak & Gowin, 1984); however, it might be usefully revised when being applied to the research process. Although Alvarez and Gowin (2009) continue to use the traditional Vee diagram to help students understand the research process in basic terms, other refinements have been attempted. One was developed by Åhlberg, who has used a revised Vee to assist students to plan, implement, and evaluate the research process, including their own role in the process (Åhlberg, Äänismaa, & Dillon, 2005; Åhlberg & Ahoranta, 2002). To avoid confusion, he titled his revised Vee the "Vee heuristic diagram." In many ways the revised Vee maintains the focus of the original, but Åhlberg is interested in how thinking, doing, and evaluating can be interrelated throughout the entire research process. In Table 6.1, we present some of the differences between the Vee diagram and the Vee heuristic diagram.

Perhaps the most important difference between the two is that instead of having an event or object serve as the focal point, the Vee heuristic diagram considers what was

Figure 6.7 Traditional Vee Diagram

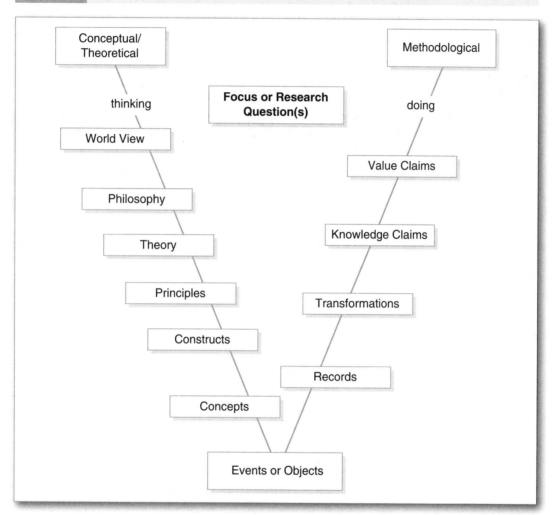

Table 6.1 Comparing Key Aspects of the Vee and the Vee Heuristic

Key Aspects of the Traditional Vee Diagram (Gowin, 1981)	Key Aspects of the Vee Heuristic Diagram (Åhlberg, 1993)
Conceptual/Thinking	Planning
Events and/or Objects	Implementation
Methodological/Doing	Evaluation

done in order to answer the main research or focus question. Although it makes sense to divide a question into aspects of knowledge and aspects of action, Åhlberg argued both sides of the Vee heuristic diagram require thinking, doing, and reflecting. Other differences are related to the main elements of each. Table 6.2 provides a useful outline.

Table 6.2 Detailed Differences Between Gowin's Vee and Åhlberg's Vee Heuristic

Key Aspects of the Traditional Vee Diagram (Gowin, 1981)	Key Aspects of the Vee Heuristic Diagram (Åhlberg, 1993)
1. Focus question	1. Focus question/research problem
2. World view	2. Value basis: Consider why it is worthwhile to use your time, energy, and resources to answer the focus question. Why do you care?
3. Philosophy/Epistemology	3. Theoretical basis: This combines epistemological aspects with specific theories relevant to answering the research problem.
4. Theory	
5. Principles	
6. Constructs	
7. Concepts	4. Conceptual basis: Based on Number 3, these are the main concepts, ideas, and/or viewpoints that are relevant to answering the research problem.
	5. Methodological basis: What are the main methods and tools you will use/have used in answering the research problem?
8. Events and objects	6. Implementation: Include here a description of what should be done or has been done to answer the research question(s).
9. Records	7. Which kinds of data were you able to collect? List here all data types you used (notes, audio or video recordings, concept maps, mind maps, drawings, photos, documents, discourse, Internet content, etc.).
10. Transformations	8. Which kinds of analysis did you use to draw conclusions from your data? List here approaches such as frequencies or more advanced statistical tools, thematizing, or more detailed content analysis.
11. Knowledge claims	9. Knowledge claims: Include what you consider the most important results of your research and if/how you answered your research question(s).
12. Value claims	10. Value claims: Include here the value of your research as a whole.

As discussed in this chapter, organizing the major elements of your paper can be a useful structural tactic and can help you plan your project. This has been done using Gowin's traditional Vee diagram (Alvarez & Gowin, 2009), yet Åhlberg's approach may assist students in planning in a different way. Using the Vee to outline the different phases involved in a research project, students first filled in the left, "Planning" side as they developed their project. At the end of the research project, they were instructed to complete the "Implementation" and "Evaluation" areas. In this way, the Vee heuristic diagram can operate throughout the research process and provide a means to reflect on how one's views changed and how early decisions influenced later outcomes. Figure 6.8 provides an example of a Vee heuristic diagram created by a student.

There are many other published examples of improved Vee heuristics created by students (Äänismaa, 2002; Åhlberg, 2005; Åhlberg & Ahoranta, 2002). A useful recent example is by Dr. Päivi Immonen-Orpana, who used the Vee heuristic diagram in her doctoral studies supervised by Dr. Åhlberg. Today, she teaches the improved Vee heuristics to her students and asks them to monitor and evaluate their research and the learning process associated with using it (Immonen-Orpana, 2009; Immonen-Orpana & Åhlberg, 2010). For this book she created a Vee heuristic of her learning process in doctoral studies (see Figure 6.9).

STUDENT ACTIVITY

Find a recent academic study of specific interest, using the suggestions presented in this chapter. As you read the study, consider the following questions: Are the sections usefully organized? Are they presented in ways that are similar to the format in this chapter? How are they the same, and how are they different? Read through the introduction section slowly. Does the author's voice lend credibility to the study? How? Once you have read the study, create a Vee heuristic diagram based on how the author described his or her work. Is it possible to complete all sections? If not, which sections are missing? What does this suggest about the researcher, the journal, or the academic field? Do you think credible research should address all elements located in the Vee heuristic diagram?

CONCLUSIONS

Maps, alongside a variety of other visual aids, can be used to help you organize, write up, and reflect on your research project. Writing up research is a complex process that involves a number of elements. Yet a student's ability to review, assess,

Figure 6.8   Example of Doctoral Student's Vee Heuristic Diagram

PLANNING

2. Value basis:

Professional development and R and D of own work. Promoting pupils' learning motivation and skills of learning to learn. Enhancing quality of learning and self esteem. Sustainable Development and Good Life.

3. Theoretical basis:

My own developing theory which is built using Åhlberg's theories of integrating education, high quality learning, continual quality improvement and sustainable development. Teacher as a researcher and developer of her own work.

4. Conceptual basis:

High quality learning, metalearning, deep and meaningful learning. Contextuality. Developing own work theory. Sustainable Development.

5. Methods basis:

Multiple case study, action research, design experiments, research literature, concept maps and Vee heuristics. Collaboration. Discussions with experts and pupils. Building own work theory. Observation.

1. Focus question:

What do I think about my research project as the whole?

EVALUATION

10. Value claims:

My research is valuable thinking of both results and the whole research process. It is possible to apply the developed model both in schools and in teacher education.

9. Knowledge claims:

My own theory of education became more organized. I developed a model of how use of concept maps and Vee heuristics can be integrated. I developed also my own version of Vee heuristics, suitable for my pupils

8. How did I make conclusions from my data?

Using tables, inferring and concept mapping.

7. What kind of data did I get?

Concept maps from the beginning and end of learning projects, Vee heuristics, own records, images and expertise.

IMPLEMENTATION

6. What did I do in order to answer the research problem?

I discussed with experts and read research literature. I thought, reflected and planned design experiments. I asked my pupils to construct concept maps and Vee heuristics. I analyzed data they created. I observed pupils' working. I lectured them when needed.

Source: Ahoranta (2004).

Figure 6.9   Example of Improved Vee Heuristic Diagram on Teaching and Learning

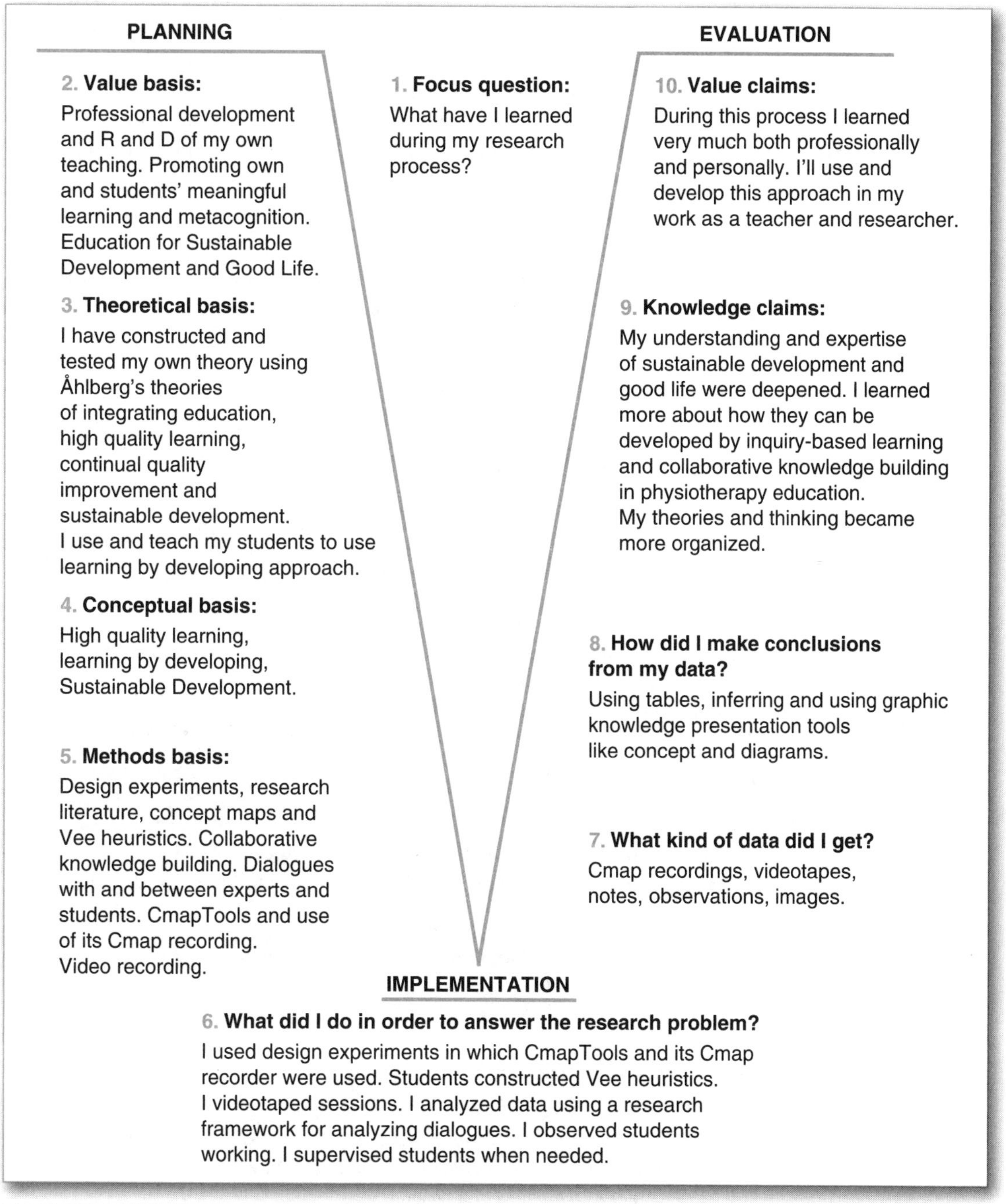

PLANNING   EVALUATION

2. Value basis:

Professional development and R and D of my own teaching. Promoting own and students' meaningful learning and metacognition. Education for Sustainable Development and Good Life.

3. Theoretical basis:

I have constructed and tested my own theory using Åhlberg's theories of integrating education, high quality learning, continual quality improvement and sustainable development. I use and teach my students to use learning by developing approach.

4. Conceptual basis:

High quality learning, learning by developing, Sustainable Development.

5. Methods basis:

Design experiments, research literature, concept maps and Vee heuristics. Collaborative knowledge building. Dialogues with and between experts and students. CmapTools and use of its Cmap recording. Video recording.

1. Focus question:

What have I learned during my research process?

10. Value claims:

During this process I learned very much both professionally and personally. I'll use and develop this approach in my work as a teacher and researcher.

9. Knowledge claims:

My understanding and expertise of sustainable development and good life were deepened. I learned more about how they can be developed by inquiry-based learning and collaborative knowledge building in physiotherapy education. My theories and thinking became more organized.

8. How did I make conclusions from my data?

Using tables, inferring and using graphic knowledge presentation tools like concept and diagrams.

7. What kind of data did I get?

Cmap recordings, videotapes, notes, observations, images.

IMPLEMENTATION

6. What did I do in order to answer the research problem?

I used design experiments in which CmapTools and its Cmap recorder were used. Students constructed Vee heuristics. I videotaped sessions. I analyzed data using a research framework for analyzing dialogues. I observed students working. I supervised students when needed.

Source: Immonen-Orpana (2009).

Note: Cmap = concept map.

and conduct research remains a central feature of master's- and doctoral-level academic work. It is increasingly being used as a means to engage students and offers a practical way to teach students about the role of theory in research and illustrate the practical challenges all researchers face. By organizing papers in sections, as described in this chapter, students can ensure they cover major elements in a research project. By using maps to chart these sections and the major components that they comprise, these sorts of visual representations offer a way to help students organize, structure, and revise their work. The use of charts, graphs, tables, and maps to present research findings is common, but the potential for maps to be used in other areas of research remains underexplored. Don't be afraid to use maps to help you brainstorm, plan your paper's structure, consider your paragraphs, or outline your approach. The utility of maps, including the Vee heuristic diagram introduced in this chapter, is that they offer another means to help you develop, organize, and reflect on your paper.

REVIEW

1. How can maps be used to design, organize, and write up your project? Provide examples for each.

2. Why are sources, structure, style, and voice integral considerations as you write up your research project?

3. What are the main structural elements of a research paper? Explain the purpose of each.

4. How can maps be used to test your ability to summarize and paraphrase cited academic sources?

5. How can the use of these maps help researchers present their approach and analysis strategies in new ways? How can the Vee heuristic diagram help in describing the research process as a whole?

SUGGESTED ADDITIONAL READINGS

Cryer, P. (1996). *The research student's guide to success.* Buckingham, UK: Open University Press.

Gowin, D. B. (1981). *Educating.* Ithaca, NY: Cornell University Press.

Hart, C. (1998). *Doing a literature search.* London: Sage.

REFERENCES

Äänismaa, P. (2002). Ympäristökasvatusta kehittämässä kotitalousopettajien koulutuksessa: kestävän kehityksen mukaisen asumisen ajattelu- ja toimintamallin kehittämistä toimintatutkimuksen avulla vuosina 1995–1998 [Promoting environmental education in home-economics teacher education] [Published, reviewed, and defended doctoral dissertation, University of Joensuu, Finland]. *Publications in Education, 0781-0334,* No. 74.

Åhlberg, M. (1993, August 3–5). *Concept maps, Vee diagrams and rhetorical argumentation (RA) analysis: Three educational theory-based tools to facilitate meaningful learning.* Paper presented at the Third International Seminar on Misconceptions and Educational Strategies in Science and Mathematics, Ithaca, NY.

Åhlberg, M. (2005). Integrating education for sustainable development. In W. Leal Filho (Ed.), *Handbook of sustainability research* (pp. 477–504). Frankfurt am Main, Germany: Peter Lang.

Åhlberg, M., Äänismaa, P., & Dillon, P. (2005). Education for sustainable living: Integrating theory, practice, design and development. *Scandinavian Journal of Educational Research, 49*(2), 167–186.

Åhlberg, M., & Ahoranta, V. (2002). Two improved educational theory based tools to monitor and promote quality of geographical education and learning. *International Research in Geographical and Environmental Education, 11*(2), 119–137.

Ahoranta, V. (2004). Oppimisen laatu peruskoulun vuosiluokilla 4–6 yleisdidaktiikan näkökulmasta käsitekarttojen ja Vee-heuristiikkojen avulla tutkittuna [Quality of learning in a primary school grades 4–6 from the viewpoint of general didactics using concept maps and Vee heuristics] [Published, reviewed, and defended doctoral dissertation, University of Joensuu, Finland]. *Publications in Education, 0781-0334,* No. 99.

Alasuutari, P. (1995). *Researching culture: Qualitative method and cultural studies.* Thousand Oaks, CA: Sage.

Alvarez, M. C., & Gowin, B. D. (2009). *The little book: Conceptual elements of research.* Lanham, MD: Rowman & Littlefield Education.

Blum, S. D. (2009). *My word! Plagiarism and college culture.* Ithaca, NY: Cornell University Press.

Cryer, P. (1996). *The research student's guide to success.* Buckingham, UK: Open University Press.

Germano, W. (2005). *From dissertation to book.* Chicago: University of Chicago Press.

Gowin, D. B. (1981). *Educating.* Ithaca, NY: Cornell University Press.

Gowin, D. B., & Alvarez, M. C. (2005). *The art of educating with V diagrams.* Cambridge, MA: Cambridge University Press.

Hart, C. (1998). *Doing a literature search.* London: Sage.

Immonen-Orpana, P. (2009). *Onnistuneen ikääntymisen ymmärrystä rakentamassa: Fysioterapeuttiopiskelijoiden oppiminen kestävää kehitystä edistävän kasvatuksen kehyksessä* [Building an understanding of successful ageing. Physiotherapist students' learning in a framework of education for sustainable development] [Published, reviewed, and publicly defended doctoral dissertation, University of Helsinki, Finland]. Retrieved November 25, 2010, from http://hdl.handle.net/10138/20023

Immonen-Orpana, P., & Åhlberg, M. (2010). Collaborative learning by developing (LbD) using concept maps and Vee diagrams. In P. Torres & R. Marriott (Eds.), *Handbook of research on collaborative learning using concept mapping* (pp. 215–235). Hershey, NY: IGI Global.

Latour, B. (2005). *Reassembling the social.* New York: Oxford University Press.

McShane, M. D., & Williams, F. P. (2008). *A thesis resource guide for criminology and criminal justice.* Upper Saddle River, NJ: Prentice Hall.

Nightingale, D. J., & Cromby, J. (Eds.). (1999). *Social constructionist psychology: A critical analysis of theory and practice.* Buckingham, UK: Open University Press.

Novak, J. D., & Gowin, D. B. (1984). *Learning how to learn.* Cambridge, UK: Cambridge University Press.

Office for Human Research Protections. (2011). *Policy and guidance on human subjects research.* Retrieved March 1, 2011, from http://www.hhs.gov/ohrp/policy/index.html

Portillo, S., Wheeldon, J. P., & Williams, T. M. (2008). *George Mason University ADJ writing guide.* Fairfax, VA: George Mason University. Retrieved February 27, 2011, from http://classweb .gmu.edu/WAC/adjguide/index.html

Silverman, D. (2005). *Doing qualitative research.* Thousand Oaks, CA: Sage.

Teddlie, C. B., & Tashakkori, A. (2009). *Foundations of mixed methods research: Integrating quantitative and qualitative approaches in the social and behavioral sciences.* Thousand Oaks, CA: Sage.

7

Maps, Limitations, and Considerations

New Directions in Social Science Research

CHAPTER OVERVIEW AND OBJECTIVES

As discussed in Chapter 6, a key element in writing up and presenting social science research is acknowledging limitations. Indeed, all research is limited in one way or another. One way to assess the quality, credibility, and utility of social science research is to consider the extent to which it addresses its limitations directly and transparently. This book should be no different. In this chapter, a number of conceptual and practical limitations to existing uses of concept maps and mind maps are discussed. In addition, this chapter considers old approaches and new questions related to reliability and validity, both for social science research generally and for the use of concept maps and mind maps specifically.

Finally, and by way of conclusion, this chapter considers new directions in social science research, including systematic review and participatory action research (PAR), and offers some suggestions about how both concept maps and mind maps might be used in the future. Maps may offer a way to combine the clarity of counts with the perspective and nuance of individualized meaning. This may be especially relevant as part of new research designs in the fields of education and justice reform.

Of specific interest is how maps can be used to showcase integrated approaches to PAR and to combine evidence-based policies with practice-based evidence.

As you read this chapter, consider your own experience using maps, and reflect on the following:

- Are the limitations that are expressed familiar? Are other limitations relevant?
- Consider how new approaches to reliability and validity might influence your own future research. What else would you like to know?
- What are the benefits of systematic reviews and meta-analyses to guide evidence-based practices?
- What is the value of more participatory approaches to social science research?
- How might maps be used to address concerns about objectivity, transparency, and reflexivity?

MAPS AND LIMITATIONS

Throughout this book, we have suggested that the use of maps can greatly assist students, instructors, researchers, and readers to understand and engage in social science research. This is because maps (a) provide a useful and novel way to communicate meaning and knowledge and (b) can serve both as a means to collect data and as a means to facilitate understanding. However, as with other social science research tools, the use of maps comes with some inherent limitations. These may usefully be organized into categories. In addition to the limitations included as part of the research examples discussed in Chapters 3, 4, and 5, in this chapter we consider both conceptual challenges and practical considerations. Their existence should not undermine the use of concept maps or mind maps, but as discussed in Chapter 6, all honest research acknowledges its limitations. Academic inquiry is based on doubt, and to be credible, social scientists must acknowledge what their research does not say, does not consider, and cannot know. This is not always easy. First, let's consider some of the challenges associated with using maps in general.

Conceptual Challenges

One concern strikes at the very justification offered for this book. There may be a danger that the suggestion that students, instructors, and researchers use more maps would result in the replacement of traditional forms of reflection with a sole focus on maps. If students who use maps begin to see them as more important than writing in visualizing our understanding of the social world, we may be seduced by the idea that research is a destination and not a journey. This might be connected to the mapping metaphor used throughout this book. Whereas concept maps and mind maps are reminiscent of *mappa mundi,* or early European maps of the world, it is not possible to say with a cartographer's confidence that maps always offer accurate depictions of reality.

This critique, although useful to consider, may be less important given the approach that has been developed throughout this book. We should always prefer accurate data-collection means and measures; however, maps that are inaccurate can also be of interest. They can lead to additional research questions to explore how and why misunderstandings exist. In this way, it might be better to think of maps as tools to represent the complex process of making, creating, or constructing meaning. For some researchers and as part of some research designs, maps offer a useful social science tool to discover general truth, based on the extent to which maps correspond to reality. For others, this focus on general truth is misplaced. Instead, maps offer a means to learn how people represent their individual understanding of reality and/or truth. It is this flexibility that is of interest. It is also the source of some important limitations.

One important challenge is connected to how one should define maps and mapping in social science research. As discussed in Chapter 2, there does seem to be some definitional confusion in existing studies and discussions of concept maps and mind maps. One solution might be to expand the definition of maps to include a wide variety of visual representations of experience (Wheeldon & Faubert, 2009). As presented in Chapter 2, Åhlberg (1993) has compared different graphical knowledge-representation tools such as mind maps, clustering, knowledge maps and concept maps, which are used in education and psychology. He demonstrated that there is an order from associative and flexible maps to more accurate and structured ones. However, as we have noted, this solution is at odds with the most recent work by leaders in the field. Yet conventional wisdom or popularity may not be an indicator of truth or utility. Some researchers continue to contend that concept maps must be narrowly construed, formally structured, and hierarchically organized (Novak & Cañas, 2008). Of course, this approach may be appropriate in certain situations, but as researchers and educators, we prefer the more tolerant, open, and flexible approach described in the previous chapters.

Although using traditional definitions of concept maps does not rule out their applicability in qualitative methods (Daley, 2004), the formality of concept maps may be at odds with the focus on precision, credibility, and transferability as they relate to capturing individual experiences and perceptions in qualitative research (Tattersall, Watts, & Vernon, 2007). In this book, we have tried to show how some approaches to mapping may be better suited to some kinds of research problems and less well suited to others. As we argued in Chapter 3, concept maps may be more appropriate for certain kinds of quantitative research designs, whereas Chapter 4 presented mind maps as better suited to qualitative research. However, it should be noted that the most recent elucidation of mind maps (Buzan & Buzan, 2010) appears to step back from the flexibility that would make mind maps relevant to qualitative researchers. Perhaps the most important takeaway from this limitation is a reminder to be clear about what kind of maps you are using and why you are using them and to show how your approach builds on past research. Don't forget to acknowledge that a debate exists about how to see, use, and rely on different kinds of graphic representation.

Another challenge is connected to the question of what maps actually represent. This book, of course, is based on an assumption that maps and other graphic tools are a useful means to capture experience. Although it seems clear that how people visualize relationships between various concepts or ideas can suggest more dynamic schemes of understanding (Mls, 2004), concepts and ideas are often difficult to map. They may occupy imagined rather than actual space and may be highly contested. Some concepts may have both *cognitive* and *emotive* aspects that are regarded very differently by a variety of communities and individuals. Different people find themselves in different, difficult, or heretofore unknown circumstances and contexts. Can maps be used to consider concepts with multiple aspects? This remains an open question. In forthcoming research, Wheeldon shows how students confronted questions of law and society in an era of terrorism through pre/post mind maps and how they viewed their own transformation through their course (Wheeldon, 2011). This exploratory study is by no means conclusive, and more research is needed to flesh out the utility of using maps in this way. However, there is no reason—in principle—that maps cannot be used to help focus our attention on the need to gather more user-generated and unsolicited reflections. In addition to these conceptual concerns, a number of practical considerations should also be acknowledged.

Practical Considerations

Linked to the conceptual challenge associated with how people see maps, there is evidence that whereas the graphic representation of experience may serve certain populations, it may alienate others. Indeed for some, maps may not be acceptable data-collection tools for certain people, groups, and personalities. Learning styles can limit the utility of maps in gathering data (Rohm, 1994) if maps are used alone. This need not be the case. People can always be interviewed before, during, or after constructing a map. For example, Åhlberg, Turja, and Robinson (2003) have demonstrated in their research on city development a method that involves first interviewing city decision makers, then transcribing the tapes, and finally transforming this text into concept maps. Using this approach, interview data were reconceived and presented as propositions within concept maps that could be validated by the participants themselves. In this way, maps can be used to allow participants to visualize multiple views of the complex, real-world practical problems involved in sustainable community development. Yet other challenges exist as well.

Czuchry and Dansereau (1996) found that women identified the mapping assignment as easier than did men. In some studies, participants suggested that making maps of their experience was "odd," "strange," and "very difficult," and this may have limited participation (Wheeldon, 2009). One challenge that was identified in Chapter 4 is what one should do with maps that fail to include key concepts requested by the researcher. How should one treat absence of evidence? Does it signify evidence of absence or something else entirely? As Tomas has suggested in her work on visual maps, "recall of experience is always selective and there will be many absences or gaps. People forget things or choose not to tell things or are not aware of things—for all sorts of reasons" (1997, p. 75).

Another important consideration is how researchers should analyze maps. In quantitative research with its focus on comparability, analysis may be limited by the complexity of the maps, the number of concepts or ideas included, or the unique ways in which they were constructed. Using the step-by-step islands and bridges process outlined in Chapter 3 can reduce these challenges. Another option for researchers interested in using concept maps might be free computer software—such as CmapTools (http://cmap.ihmc.us/download/), among other software—to create a defined interface with which participants can create their maps. This can better ensure consistency, concept quantification, and map-to-map comparisons (Bayram, 1995; Safayeni, Derbentseva, & Cañas, 2005). In qualitative research, maps make the general difficulty of data analysis (Chenail, 1995, p. 2) even more complex. However, there are structural constraints that can greatly mitigate this challenge. The mapping procedure in Chapter 4 suggests limiting the map to one page, and in Chapter 5 we show how maps can be used as part of mixed-methods research to provide a more nuanced and detailed understanding of a research problem.

Each of the studies discussed in the book contain limitations; this does not mean this research is of no value, nor does it mean that the findings should be discarded. However, it does provide a justification for the need to remain skeptical about maps as a panacea or cure-all for the challenges faced in social science research. Although all of these research examples have been published and presented elsewhere, as authors we take seriously the responsibility to present our research warts and all. Social science research requires an ability to work hard to investigate a phenomenon while remaining humble about what is found. It is this humility that advances our understanding and allows studies to be built, one on top of the other, toward a more complete understanding of the world. One important area to remain humble about is related to reliability and validity, and these can serve as limitations to the kind of measures and methods one uses to collect data, to one's research design, and to the practical value of the inferences that can be drawn.

RELIABILITY AND VALIDITY

Unlike research in the natural sciences, social science research attempts to measure what some consider intangibles. These include perceptions, behaviors, emotions, and/or personalities. A major challenge associated with social science research is whether we are truly capturing what we say we are capturing. There are two central concepts to understand in this regard. An important starting point is to consider the characteristics of a measure and whether our measurements are meaningful. In social science research, *reliability* considers the consistency of one's approach to measurement, and *validity* involves assessing its accuracy.

A recent approach to these issues involves reframing traditional concerns about validity and reliability into questions about the quality of the research inputs (design, data, analysis) on the one hand and the integrity of the process that interprets results and conclusions on the other. This has the effect of refocusing validity and reliability questions into practical but distinct steps that consider design quality and interpretative rigor separately (Teddlie & Tashakkori, 2009, p. 286). The value in reorganizing questions about validity in this manner is in assisting researchers to examine the quality of their inferences in a relatively straightforward manner. For now, let's explore reliability and validity in general and as they might be specifically applied to maps in social science research.

Reliability, Measures, and Maps

In quantitative research, reliability is concerned with questions of stability and consistency. In short, reliability asks if the same measurement tool can yield stable and consistent results when repeated over time. Administering the same measurement tool multiple times and comparing the results is one way to assess reliability. This *test/retest* method is based on the idea that you should get the same score on Test 1 as you do on Test 2. Another issue is related to *internal consistency*. This estimates reliability by grouping questions in a questionnaire or a survey that measure the same concept. The idea here is that if we ask one question in three ways in a survey, we can say a survey has internal consistency if participants answer each of the three questions in the same or similar ways.

In qualitative research, the focus is a bit different. As discussed in Chapter 4, qualitative research is based on constructivist accounts of human knowledge in which all interpretations are subjective and one cannot separate his or her own feelings and opinions from the research question and data. This requires some careful consideration about how to turn documents, interviews, observations, or other means of data collection into data that can be analyzed. At issue is the extent to which your interpretation would be similar to the interpretation of another researcher looking at the same data. One useful approach to reliability in qualitative methods is to use several approaches that can provide complementary data relevant to the subject under investigation. This process, called *triangulation,* is often used to apply more than two methods in a study to triple-check results. The idea is that one can be more confident with a finding if different methods lead to the same result. By using three methods to attempt to answer one question, the hope is that two of the three will produce similar answers. If three clashing answers are produced, the investigator knows that the question needs to be reframed, the methods reconsidered, or both.

Applying traditional understandings of reliability to concept maps and mind maps may be difficult. Based on the test/retest idea, one approach has been to consider reliability the degree to which the concept and connections in a participant's map would be repeated in a second map (Trochim, 1989). Yet for Trochim, reliability assessments should speak to the reliability of the map as a whole, not necessarily the individual concepts or propositions within the map. This means that in some cases, participant maps will demonstrate a similar understanding of the topic even though the maps themselves include different concepts and interconnections (Trochim, 1993).

Studies that focus on the reliability of scoring concept maps have shown that it is possible to reliably score concept maps and assess an individual's knowledge structure (Srinivasan, McElvany, Shay, Shavelson, & West, 2008). A better approach to reliability might be the one discussed in Chapter 4. Instead of using the maps as the sole means of data, they can be used to structure additional interview questions. In this way, maps are combined with additional data collection that puts those concepts in context and validates, challenges, or clarifies their meaning.

Validity, Methods, and Maps

Within quantitative research, validity has a number of elements, traditionally developed based on the positivist tradition, as discussed in Chapter 1. Cook and Campbell (1979) defined validity as the best available approximation of the truth or falsity of a given inference or conclusion. Validity can consider whether there is a relationship between the intervention and the observed outcome, known as *conclusion validity,* and whether the relationship is causal, known as *internal validity.* As discussed in Chapter 3, this is an important distinction. A *causal relationship* means that one thing directly causes another, whereas a *correlational relationship* is simply one in which two things change together but one does not necessarily directly cause the other. In social science research, there are far more phenomena that appear correlated than those that can be said to have a direct cause-and-effect relationship. There are also a number of threats to internal validity. Some of these are the failure to include a control group, the inclusion of a control group that is too dissimilar from the treatment group, unforeseen events affecting the treatment and control groups differently, and social interactions altering the way the groups operate or perceive the experiments. These threats were also discussed in the Chapter 3 research example.

Another element of validity concerns how well we *operationalized* the concepts under investigation. This refers to the process of defining variables in ways that can be gathered and measured. As a component of validity, it can be connected to data-collection means and measures because it considers how well we were able to design methods or measures to investigate the broader constructs under investigation. This is commonly referred to as *construct validity*. A final question to be considered is to what extent the findings of one study can be generalized. In addition to the discussion above, this depends on the quality of your design, the number of cases you were able to analyze, and the geographic dispersal of your sample. Known as *external validity*, this suggests that the findings in one study would be consistent in other places, in other times, and among different people.

In qualitative research, validity often refers to the appropriateness of the method to the research phenomenon under consideration, the approach to data analysis, and the credibility of the research process undertaken. This can involve some justification about why one approach makes more sense than another and the ability to locate the approach employed within other accepted designs. One way a literature review can be useful is the extent to which it addresses past approaches undertaken. In addition, qualitative researchers accept the idea that all interpretations are subjective. Thus, it is essential that we transparently outline how we arrived at a particular interpretation of the data. This can be difficult and involves a constant justification of one's interpretation and a reflexive evaluation of one's own motives for interpreting things in one way instead of another. As discussed in Chapter 4, *reflexivity* refers to awareness of the researcher's contribution to the construction of meaning and the improbability of remaining neutral, impartial, and unconnected to one's subject (Nightingale & Cromby, 1999).

Another way of increasing the validity of your research consists of showing your research participants excerpts of your interpretation of their interviews. The idea behind this way of increasing validity is that research participants are in a position to corroborate or challenge your interpretations. This additional step can assist in contextualizing your interpretation, although it has its own challenges. Participants might disagree with your interpretation because it places them in a difficult position, because they have changed their own views, or because your findings point to some uncomfortable conclusions. This may not mean your interpretation is wrong. If this were to occur, an honest qualitative researcher might use the validation exercise and the resultant disagreement as data themselves, to provide additional insight into the project, or to acknowledge that different views about the data exist. Using this more flexible approach to research might require some additional justification for sticking with your analysis approach in the face of interpretive variance.

Questions about maps and validity might refer to the degree to which a map accurately reflects reality (Trochim, 1989). One way to consider the validity of mapping as a data-collection tool is to compare concept maps with comparable information generated by some other method. According to Åhlberg (1993), validity estimates of concept maps have two phases. The first estimates how accurately a concept map as an external representation corresponds to its constructor's internal understanding. The second is to estimate how well the created concept map corresponds to reality. It may not always be possible to speak about definite social scientific truth, but we can make good estimates based on the views of subject matter experts. This approach was done in the research example in Chapter 3. In that case, the concept maps were compared with interviews and short-answer tests. This suggested the benefit of concept maps in education while providing a basis for some doubt about whether maps, interviews, and tests captured the same sort of data.

The second is connected to Trochim's (1989) view that validity can be assessed based on whether participants, when given a choice, can identify the difference between maps that present concepts in more accurate ways and other maps that connect concepts in less accurate ways. For example, three maps might be created with the same concepts, but arranged in different ways, with one presenting a clear view of the topic and another containing misconceptions. Participants could be asked to identify the map that most accurately reflects their thinking. If people could not identify the more accurate maps, the validity of research might be in doubt. A final consideration would be to explore whether concept maps confirm or challenge theoretically expected differences. Trochim (1989) suggested that in situations in which we have two groups of participants whom we might expect to differ in important ways, we compare the maps created by each group to see whether the maps are more or less like one group rather than another. This example would be well suited to two groups of teachers and students. Like in the Chapter 3 research example, pre/post maps could be compared to other sorts of maps, for example, made by a teacher or based on an end-of-unit test. Validity would involve seeing to what extent pre/post maps changed and/or to what extent they began to appear closer to a teacher's map.

The above discussion provides us with some conceptual tools to assist us to plan, design, undertake, and evaluate social science research; more study is needed to fully connect reliability and validity to the use of concept maps and mind maps as data-collection measures as well as the broader inferential considerations about the ultimate social value and applicability of studies that rely on maps. One clear observation is that both the reliability and the validity of maps can be strengthened when combined with other data-collection techniques. What then of the inferential and interpretative questions posed by Teddlie and Tashakkori (2009)? Although they offer a useful conceptual contribution to the understanding of reliability and validity, we believe their contribution should be explored, tested, and considered in more detail through future research. There are two research areas of immediate interest. Based on the number of people involved and who is affected, as well as on the growing costs of each and the clear need for more rigorous study, maps may have immediate relevance for studies into education and criminal justice reform.

NEW DIRECTIONS IN SOCIAL SCIENCE RESEARCH

A number of important new developments and directions in social science research have emerged in the past decade. Of interest is how maps might be used within these new models, approaches, methodologies, and methods. In our discussion below, we highlight education and criminal justice reform. However, there are a number of fields that can benefit from these new directions in social science research. Two methodological developments of specific interest are systematic review and PAR.

Systematic Reviews, Meta-Analyses, and Evidence-Based Policy

A *systematic review* is a comprehensive literature review that is focused on answering a single question. As we discussed in Chapter 6, as part of a research project literature reviews try to identify and evaluate credible sources. A systematic review attempts to synthesize only quantitatively rigorous research evidence that is relevant to a single question. In this way, evidence about issues of public concern are informed by peer-reviewed data gathered by independent researchers. The roots of this approach come from medicine, with its use of randomized controlled trials to identify effective treatments for disease. By challenging accepted practice and replacing assumptions with rigorous study, evidence-based medicine has led to improved health outcomes and reduced costs. Systematic reviews of high-quality, randomized, controlled trials are crucial to evidence-based practices, and their use is becoming increasingly important for health care professionals (Oliver et al., 2008).

Through rigorous data analysis, systematic reviews try to discover what works, expand the approaches that work best, fine-tune the ones that get mixed results, and shut down those that are failing (Orszag, 2009). As a result they have become increasingly popular in other disciplines within the social sciences, such as psychology (Lane, Millane, & Lip, 2005), education (Higgins, Baumfield, & Hall, 2007), and sociology (Garcia et al., 2006). For example, in the field of criminal justice, these approaches appear to offer a means to reform justice policies in ways that save money and improve outcomes. Criminologists and other researchers have provided important insights about how one might evaluate the effectiveness of a variety of criminal justice system practices (Lipsey, Landenberger, & Wilson, 2007) and the role of method in treatment effectiveness (Wilson & Lipsey, 2001).

The use of quantitative methods to assess the effectiveness of programs within the criminal justice system was developed by a group of researchers at the University of Maryland. These researchers were commissioned by the U.S. Congress to compile a report about "what works" in criminal justice (Sherman et al., 1997). This report examines not only the statistical significance and direction of a number of studies but also their level of scientific rigor (MacKenzie, 2006). To do this, the researchers attempted to locate as many studies as possible about specific interventions and programs less than 10 years old. A coding system was used to judge various aspects of each study, and each aspect was then assigned a score from 1 to 5 based on the level of methodological rigor in the study, with those at Level 3 and greater considered to be of good quality.

Based on the level of methodological rigor derived from the coding scheme and the strength and direction of the results, interventions can be placed into one of four categories. If an intervention had at least two Level 3 studies with positive results and a preponderance of the evidence from the other studies was positive, the intervention was thought to be effective and was categorized as something that "works." If at least two Level 3 studies were negative and other less rigorous studies showed negative results, the intervention was labeled "not working." Interventions were viewed as "promising" if most studies showed positive results but only one had a Level 3 rating. Interventions lacking quality research were categorized as "unknown" (MacKenzie, 2006).

Systematic reviews have become the basis for a number of other *meta-analyses* that have been undertaken, and they synthesize and summarize many research findings in a consistent and coherent way. Using this approach allows researchers to focus on the direction and magnitude of effect through the use of an effect size index rather than statistical significance. By estimating the average overall effect of an intervention through a comparison of numerous individual studies, this approach provides a means to explore average overall effects, variability in effects, and potential explanations of that variability. The Campbell Collaborative's use of meta-analysis relies on systematic, quantitative reviews of existing studies to provide empirical evidence about what works. Although steps are taken to ensure the quality of study inputs as described above, the value of this approach is that it provides policy makers with clear, empirically tested options to address identified social problems and issues.

USING CONCEPT MAPS

There are a number of ways concept maps and systematic reviews might be connected. The first was discussed in Chapter 2. You may recall that Nesbit and Adescope (2006) undertook a systematic review to identify more than 500 publications that referred to concept or knowledge maps and summarized the value of graphic organizers in educational research. Other, more recent reviews have considered diagrams and data collection (Umoquit, Tso, Burchett, & Dobrow, 2011). In addition to using meta-analyses to explore the prevalence of maps and diagrams in research, we think there are at least two ways that maps might be used as part of this approach. The first is related to how data are presented. The nature of meta-analysis often results in the presentation of long tables of data and related statistical information. In keeping with the potential of this approach to influence policy makers, researchers might consider mapping key findings and using visual shortcuts to make the results more easily understood. For example, based on a review of four meta-analyses, together comprising hundreds of studies, Gerald Gaes (2008) explored the role of prison education programs on postrelease outcomes. In his useful paper, he compiled a number of existing meta-analysis tables, compared and contrasted different education programs, and adjusted effect sizes for the reduction of recidivism. One immediate use for maps would be in the presentation of those data. By presenting the most effective programs (Gaes, 2008) most prominently in a map, this approach provides an accessible means to gather substantive information about types of relevant programs and their relative effectiveness. Figure 7.1 provides an example.

Figure 7.1 Prison Programming and Reducing Recidivism Based on Meta-Analyses

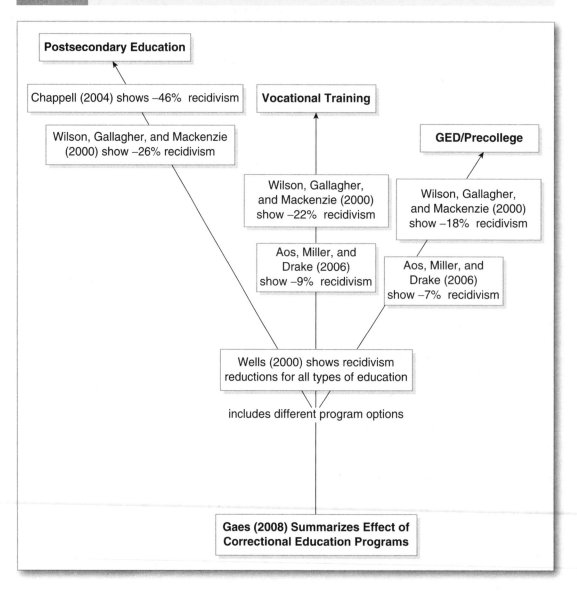

Another approach is to consider the connection between concept maps and education more broadly. Based on calls for more in-depth study, the use of concept maps in future systematic reviews of educational research requires first that they become part of research designs for upcoming studies. Some have begun to explore how maps can be used with special needs populations (Alkahtani, 2009); a more coherent meta-analysis would necessitate a common methodology and a more universalized approach to the construction and scoring procedure of concept maps. We presented one approach in Chapter 3, but adoption will require buy-in by those funding research and those collecting data. The use of computer software such as CmapTools may be useful in this regard. In addition to assisting in the creation of more structured concept maps, software could be readily accessed online and easily scored from a central location based on clearly predefined categories. As presented in Chapters 3 and 5, pre/post data could then be used to assess the effectiveness of different educational interventions, programs, and/or practices. New developers would have to build on existing software to develop programs that could score concept maps, which would represent an important means to collect student-centric data.

Beyond practical data-collection considerations, however, the use of maps might be justified on a pedagogical basis as well. There is evidence that concept maps can assist students in learning and represent a more active approach to data collection and meaning making. Whether maps are used to validate other sorts of data or as a means to assess pre/post learning, it may be useful to combine standardized, fill-in-the-bubble tests with a more creative means to gather data. Although existing research has laid important groundwork in considering how this could work (Jonassen, Reeves, Hong, Harvey, & Peters, 1997), new approaches will need to integrate the use of concept maps into emergent research areas and questions. These include, among others, literacy levels comparisons between charter and public schools, inclusive education, and perhaps even performance-based pay for teachers. As discussed throughout this book, concept maps offer a unique means to capture data that can be quantified while providing a more participatory means to engage students in their own education.

Participatory Research and Visual Data Collection

Another methodological development in social science research is Participatory Action Research (PAR). PAR refers to research that focuses on addressing problems, issues, or concerns as expressed by the community members themselves. Of interest within these approaches are the effects of the researcher's actions. Unlike some traditional models that involve experts who study participants, these approaches seek to involve local people in all stages of the research process. Through more participatory approaches, researchers and community members together identify major issues, concerns, and problems; initiate research; undertake action(s); and learn about and reflect on what they did and what the outcomes were. Based on these reflections, a new cycle of action and research is agreed on and implemented. This approach is seen as a continuous process and a revisable endeavor (O'Brien, 2001). By using more collaborative methods to test new ideas and implement action through the active participation of community members, it is assumed more meaningful outcomes will result.

PAR is often associated with the work of social psychologist Kurt Lewin, and it focuses on relationships within and between communities, groups, and researchers. As a means to flatten traditional hierarchies within research, PAR focuses on critical pedagogy that seeks to assist people to take control of their own educations and futures (Freire, 2000). Researchers often play a dual role, serving as observers and facilitators, and seek to decentralize the research process by shifting ownership of the project to the local people. In this way, PAR is interested in how people learn, engage, and reflect on the process not only of action but also of investigation of that action. Based on Lewin's past work in social psychology and the importance of experiential learning and group dynamics, Lewin argued against research that produces books or rarefied knowledge locked away in ivory towers (Lewin, 1946). Instead he sought to develop an approach to research that would result in social action that could model participatory approaches to decision making. His approach involves a series of steps that might be divided into two stages. As outlined in Figure 7.2, the first involves a process to identify an issue, engage in fact finding, make a plan, and have it validated with and by the community before taking action.

Once a plan has been developed with, and validated by, the community, the second stage involves a series of steps that include action, evaluation, and a willingness to amend a developed plan based on the experiences of those involved. This new plan then feeds the next action step, which is in turn evaluated. Through this *iterative process,* results are achieved through a repeated cycle of operations in which the lessons from past experience are built into future actions. This process is represented in Figure 7.3. Based on this process, McIntyre (2008) provided a useful overview of a number of projects that can be defined as participatory. These include community projects focused on violence against women (Maguire, 1987), HIV treatment (Maglajlić, 2004), prison education (Fine & Torre, 2006), and practical matters such as water sanitation (Jackson & McKay, 1982) and improving communication and efficiency in a hospital emergency room (Eisenberg, Baglia, & Pynes, 2006).

As PAR has grown, so have the methods used to capture, analyze, and present the data collected through these approaches. Indeed one of the characteristics of

Figure 7.2   Stage 1 of Action Research: Planning and Validating

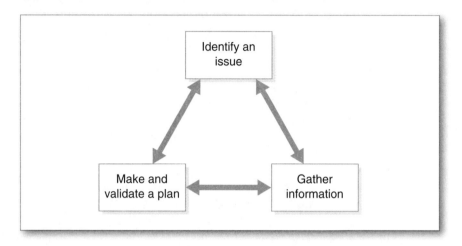

Figure 7.3   Stage 2 of Action Research: Action, Evaluation, and Experience

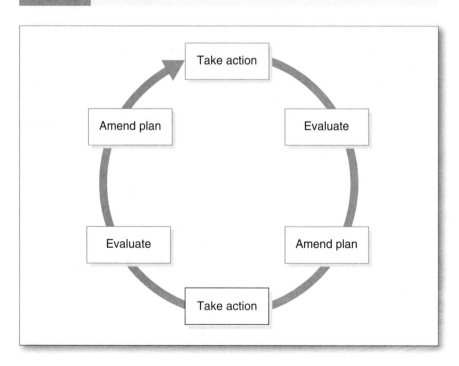

participatory approaches lies in innovative adaptations of methods drawn from conventional research and their use in new contexts, in new ways—often by, as well as with, local people. Of immediate interest is the increasingly visual nature of these methods. One approach of interest explored how a group of working-class women from Belfast, Northern Ireland, experienced the place(s) in which they lived (McIntyre, 2003). Using an approach called photovoice, participants were encouraged to use documentary photography to explore their own perceptions of relationships between place and their everyday lives. As a means of building community among this group, a photo-text exhibit provided a means for the women to share their photographs and their recorded reflections on the meaning(s) associated with the places photographed.

Others are built on more traditional approaches to data collection such as interviews. For example, Tomas and Dittmar (1995) described a process called the visual life history interview to explore the experience of housing and the meaning of home for homeless women in Brighton, United Kingdom. The maps were created by first encouraging participants to make timelines of their lives and then encouraging them to draw in all the places they lived along the timelines, using markers such as birthdays, celebrations, the first day at school, and so forth to jog the participants' memories. Using this approach, Tomas (1997) suggested these visual representations of home can be used as a means to identify friends, family, school, work, major life events, and other information participants wish to include. After this initial stage in which people, places, ages, and events converge chronologically, these constructed life maps can become a database to add to, reflect on, and see one's visual life history. Another recent slant on this autobiographical approach asks individuals to engage in a process of collage making as a means to allow autobiographical memories to emerge based on the pictures. This process provides another layer to traditional attempts to situate qualitative research into the meaning individuals provide when telling their own life stories (van Schalkwyk, 2010).

Yet another approach is based on maps and mapping. Participatory approaches to international development involved the construction of maps of watersheds, fields, and other relevant agricultural features (McCracken, 1988) and their construction as part of rural development appraisals (Chambers, 1994). These early experiences were augmented by the use of maps to consider issues of social significance. Maps have been used to study the uptake of health services and evaluations of disease prevention programs. Based on exploratory maps made by patients of their own bodies, warts and all (Cornwall & Jewkes, 1995), new participatory public health research methods have been explored (Burke et al., 2005). Another useful example used participant diagramming as data (Kesby, 2000), and participant concept maps have been used to explain PAR methods (Åhlberg, Äänismaa, & Dillon, 2005). In general, the utility of participatory mapping is that it can provide useful data while explicitly valuing the local sources of those data.

USING MIND MAPS

Mapping is a well-established means in PAR, and it may be useful to consider how maps could be applied to a practical issue of emergent interest. As discussed in Chapter 5, mind maps may offer an important means to collect data in more participatory ways and can be used as part of mixed-methods research to develop measures of association and identify issues of salience (Wheeldon, 2010). This may be of some value when considering how best to implement criminal justice reform. As discussed above, systematic review has provided important data about which specific kinds of programs work, based on more comprehensive analyses than have been previously attempted. However, although this approach has become increasingly popular, the sole focus on outcomes often comes at the expense of other important intervention aspects, such as the mechanisms at work in the program and the context in which the program is delivered (Pawson, 2002).

Understanding the contextual challenges inherent in applying the programmatic lessons of systematic review may require a means to gather data in more participatory ways from the people expected to implement these reforms. Paul Knepper (2005) offered an important contribution that focuses on two models of transferring criminological knowledge into the policy-making context. Knepper considered the evidence-based model, advocated by the Campbell Collaborative, and the reflexive model, envisioned by the Open Society Institute. On one view, the most common approach to evidence-based practices, as presented by the Campbell Collaborative, focuses on outcomes instead of processes and assumes that positivistic ideas about the nature of knowledge and reality should be favored over more qualitative, interpretive, and participatory approaches. In contrast, Knepper presented the Open Society Institute's reflexive model based on Karl Popper's emphasis on the social situation. He argued that the reflexive model provides a better means to engage research participants by emphasizing participation, social interaction, and the understanding that social tinkering and local innovation can best promote sustainable reform.

Research processes must consider how to better involve those who are affected by reform initiatives. Instead of seeing reforms as something that are instituted, they can be used as a way to identify and develop local champions who are willing to try new things and learn from past mistakes. Through iterative and participatory processes that include social engagement, reforms are a means to an end, not the end themselves. To give practical effect to the Open Society Institute's reflexive model, it may be useful to reconsider which aspects of a program or intervention researchers should focus on and how those data should be collected. Indeed, an understanding of the importance of context, process, and personalities requires a more robust definition that can ground theory in practice.

Mind maps could be used as part of data gathering to help identify issues of common concern when attempting to implement evidence-based reforms. In addition to providing a novel means to gather data as part of fact finding, maps can be combined with the results of subsequent evaluations to guide the iterative approach to action research by providing a means to assess outcomes and revise future activities. Using a version of a mixed-methods score, as outlined in Chapter 5, areas of concern identified in mind maps and through subsequent data collection could be quantified, combined, and analyzed. New approaches to mind maps and mapping analysis may offer a means to better clarify mechanisms at work in the criminal justice system and uncover pressures and processes at work within it. In this way, local experimentation on how best to implement evidence-based reforms can be used to model different approaches and attempts. Mind maps can be used to capture more nuanced qualitative data so implementation processes can be better understood. This information can assist policy makers, professionals, and citizens about the underlying logic of how their criminal justice system works. It can also provide a window into the personalities that are so often more important to successful interventions than simplistic programs, manuals, and top-down reform models.

AN INTEGRATED APPROACH TO SYSTEMATIC REVIEW AND PARTICIPATORY IMPLEMENTATION

As we have discussed throughout this book, mixed approaches to research offer important practical benefits for social science research. By combining a rigorous understanding of the *what*, mixed methods can also tell us about the *why* and the *how*. The focus on education and criminal justice reform may be useful for the reason provided above; there are a number of issues within social science research that might benefit from mixing more systematic and participatory approaches. Although it is too early to say with certainty how these approaches to research can inform new developments in systematic review and PAR, or even if, how, or when maps should be used, nonetheless we present the following model for consideration. Figure 7.4 provides an example of an integrated action approach.

This integrated action research model is based on past pragmatic approaches to public policy issues, and it provides a means for social science researchers to combine

Figure 7.4   Integrated Action Research Model

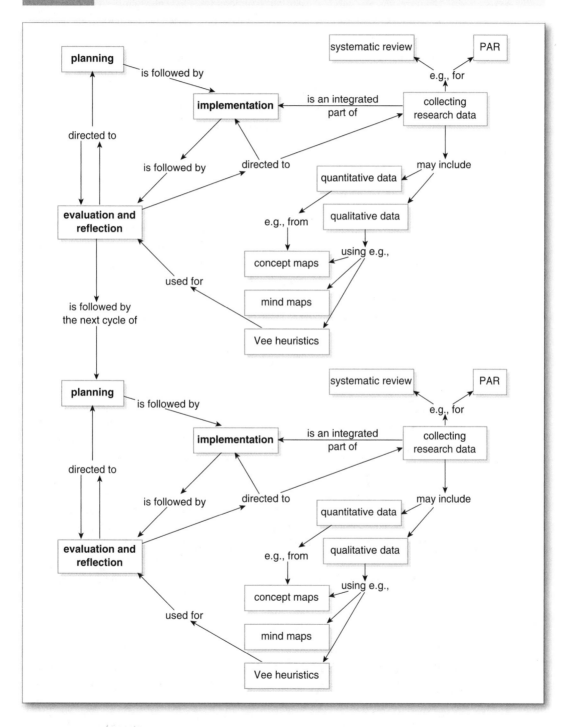

LIBRARY, UNIVERSITY OF CHESTER

systematic reviews with participatory implementation strategies using maps and diagrams. As an example, we might imagine that a rigorous quantitative analysis has identified a worthy program that ought to be more widely implemented. Participatory implementation strategies based on action research models could help us learn not only what works but also what doesn't and why. This exploration could focus on place-based research to understand the difference between institutions, organizations, geographic variations, and cultural dynamics. Combining quantitative counts with qualitative nuance, social scientists can better investigate how and under which conditions policy reforms result in practical and socially useful outcomes (Berman & Fox, 2010). In this way, evidence-based policy can be combined with practice-based evidence to make research findings more relevant in real-world/work situations (Olsen, Aisner, & McGinnis, 2007).

For all the reasons discussed throughout this book, concept maps and mind maps may be invaluable tools in this regard. Our colleagues; our past, present, and future students; and of course our readers, we encourage you to test, validate, revise, or reject the ideas in this book and to engage in your own exploration of social science research. This field cannot grow without your input. We hope you will return to this book, but for now, we humbly suggest you put down this book and get busy. There is plenty of work to do, and unfortunately, there are too few of us with the energy, inclination, and imagination to do it.

CONCLUSION

In this chapter, we have examined some of the limitations of using maps in social science research and provided concrete examples of how the research presented in past chapters was limited. We have suggested that the acknowledgment of limitations is central to all honest research and integral within the social sciences. In addition, we have explored how questions of reliability and validity are connected to the quality of inferences one can make about the results of his or her research. Although the more widespread use of maps in social science research is to be encouraged, issues of map validity and reliability require more study. Finally, in this chapter we have explored two emergent research areas of interest. Building on the call for more pragmatic approaches to social science research, we have discussed how systematic reviews and PAR offer a means to identify general program principles based on empirical evidence and how, by using an integrated approach to implementation, maps can be used to explore what works along with how and why. Concept maps and mind maps might be usefully applied in both of these scenarios. It is our hope that more researchers, educators, and students begin to consider, test, and revise the approaches provided in this book to build better theories and practical approaches for the use of maps to visualize social science research.

LIBRARY, UNIVERSITY OF CHESTER

REVIEW

1. Discuss some of the limitations of the research examples outlined in this chapter. Why does all good research acknowledge its limitations?

2. Define validity and reliability. How are they connected, and how are they different?

3. Why might traditional notions of validity and reliability need to be revised when considering their applicability to maps? Do maps provide data in sufficiently different ways to justify this qualification?

4. What is a systematic review? Find a systematic review in your field, and consider both the method used and the conclusion reached. Why is this approach central to getting a better understanding of "what works"?

5. What is participatory action research? How does it build on the theoretical approach explored in Chapter 4? How might this approach be used to explore how evidence-based reforms are implemented between and among agencies, people, and groups?

SUGGESTED ADDITIONAL READINGS

Åhlberg, M., Äänismaa, P., & Dillon, P. (2005). Education for sustainable living: Integrating theory, practice, design and development. *Scandinavian Journal of Educational Research, 49*(2), 167–186.

McIntyre, A. (2008). *Participatory action research.* Thousand Oaks, CA: Sage.

Pawson, R. (2002). Evidence-based policy: In search of a method. *Evaluation, 8,* 157–181.

REFERENCES

Åhlberg, M. (1993, August 1–5). *Concept maps, Vee diagrams and rhetorical argumentation (RA) analysis: Three educational theory-based tools to facilitate meaningful learning.* Paper presented at the Third International Seminar on Misconceptions in Science and Mathematics, Ithaca, NY.

Åhlberg, M., Äänismaa, P., & Dillon, P. (2005). Education for sustainable living: Integrating theory, practice, design and development. *Scandinavian Journal of Educational Research, 49*(2), 167–186.

Åhlberg, M., Turja, L., & Robinson, J. (2003). Educational research and development to promote sustainable development in the city of Helsinki: Helping the accessible Helsinki Programme 2001–2011 to achieve its goals. *International Journal of Environment and Sustainable Development, 2*(2), 197–209.

Alkahtani, K. (2009). *Creativity training effects upon concept map complexity of children with ADHD: An experimental study.* Unpublished doctoral dissertation, University of Glasgow, Scotland.

Aos, S., Miller, M., & Drake, E. (2006). *Evidence-based public policy options to reduce future prison construction, criminal justice costs, and crime rates.* Olympia: Washington State Institute for Public Policy.

Bayram, S. (1995). *The effectiveness of concept and software mapping for representing student data and process schema in science.* Unpublished master's thesis, University of Pittsburg, PA.

Berman, G., & Fox, A. (2010). *Trial and error in criminal justice reform: Learning from failure.* Washington, DC: Urban Institute.

Burke, J. G., O'Campo, P., Peak G. L., Gielen, A. C., McDonnell, K. A., & Trochim, W. M. K. (2005). An introduction to concept mapping as a participatory public health research methodology. *Qualitative Health Research, 15,* 1392–1410.

Buzan, T., & Buzan, B. (2010). *Mind map book: Unlock your creativity, boost your memory, change your life.* London: Pearson International.

Chambers, R. (1994). Participatory rural appraisal (PRA): Analysis of experience. *World Development, 22*(9), 1253–1268.

Chappell, C. A. (2004). Post-secondary correctional education and recidivism: A meta-analysis of research conducted 1990–1999. *Journal of Correctional Education, 55*(2), 148–169.

Chenail, R. J. (1995, December). Presenting qualitative data. *Qualitative Report, 2*(3). Retrieved December 11, 2009, from http://www.nova.edu/ssss/QR/QR2–3/presenting.html

Cook, T. D., & Campbell, D. T. (1979). *Quasi-experimentation.* Boston: Houghton Mifflin.

Cornwall, A., & Jewkes, R. (1995). What is participatory research? *Social Science Medicine, 41*(12), 1667–1676.

Czuchry, M., & Dansereau, D. F. (1996). Node-link mapping as an alternative to traditional writing assignments in undergraduate psychology courses. *Teaching of Psychology, 23*(2), 91–96.

Daley, B. (2004, September 14–17). *Using concept maps in qualitative research.* Paper presented at the First International Conference on Concept Mapping, Pamplona, Spain.

Eisenberg, E. M., Baglia, J., & Pynes, J. E. (2006). Transforming emergency medicine through narrative: Qualitative action research at a community hospital. *Health Communication, 19,* 197–208.

Fine, M., & Torre, M. E. (2006). Intimate details: Participatory action research in prison. *Action Research, 4*(3), 253–269.

Freire, P. (2000). *Pedagogy of the oppressed.* New York: Continuum International.

Gaes, G. (2008, March 31–April 1). *The impact of prison education programs on post-release outcomes.* Paper presented at the Reentry Roundtable on Education, John Jay College of Criminal Justice, New York.

Garcia, J., Sinclair, J., Dickson, K., Thomas, J., Brunton, J., Tidd, M., et al. (2006). *Conflict resolution, peer mediation and young people's relationships* [Technical report]. London: EPPI-Centre, Social Science Research Unit, Institute of Education, University of London.

Higgins, S., Baumfield, V., & Hall, E. (2007). *Learning skills and the development of learning capabilities.* London: EPPI-Centre, Social Science Research Unit, Institute of Education, University of London.

Jackson, T., & McKay, G. (1982). Sanitation and water supply in Big Trout Lake: Participatory research for democratic technical solutions. *Canadian Journal of Native Studies, 2*(1), 129–145.

Jonassen, D., Reeves, T., Hong, N., Harvey, D., & Peters, K. (1997). Concept mapping as cognitive learning and assessment tools. *Journal of Interactive Learning Research, 8*(3/4), 289–308.

Kesby, M. (2000). Participatory diagramming: Deploying qualitative methods through an action research epistemology. *Area, 32*(4), 423–435.

Knepper, P. (2005). Crime prevention in a multinational open society. *International Criminal Justice Review, 15*(1), 58–74.

Lane, D. A., Millane, T. A., & Lip, G. H. (2005). Psychological interventions for depression in adolescent and adult congenital heart disease. *Cochrane Database of Systematic Reviews,* Issue 2. Retrieved November 3, 2010, from http://www2.cochrane.org/reviews/en/ ab004372.html

Lewin, K. (1946). Action research and minority problems. *Journal of Social Issues, 2,* 34–46.

Lipsey, M. W., Landenberger, N. A., & Wilson, S. J. (2007). Effects of cognitive-behavioral programs for criminal offenders. *Campbell Systematic Reviews,* Issue 6. Retrieved December 2, 2010, from www.campbellcollaboration.org/lib/download/143/

MacKenzie, D. L. (2006). *What works in corrections: Reducing criminal activities of offenders and delinquents.* New York: Cambridge University Press.

Maglajlić, R. A. (2004). Right to know, UNICEF BiH—Developing a communication strategy for the prevention of HIV/AIDS among young people through PAR. *Child Care in Practice, 10*(2), 127–139.

Maguire, P. (1987). *Doing participatory research: A feminist approach.* Amherst, MA: Center for International Education.

McCracken, J. A. (1988). *Participatory research in Gujerat: A Trial Mmh'l/or the Aga Khan Rural Support Program (Italia).* London: International Institute for Environment and Development.

McIntyre, A. (2003). Through the eyes of women: Photovoice and participatory research as tools for reimagining place. *Gender, Place, and Culture, 10*(1), 47–66.

McIntyre, A. (2008). *Participatory action research.* Thousand Oaks, CA: Sage.

Mls, K. (2004, September 14–17). *From concept mapping to qualitative modeling in cognitive research.* Paper presented at the First International Conference on Concept Mapping, Pamplona, Spain.

Nesbit, J. C., & Adescope, O. O. (2006). Learning with concept and knowledge maps: A meta-analysis. *Review of Educational Research, 76*(3), 413–448.

Nightingale, D. J., & Cromby, J. (Eds.). (1999). *Social constructionist psychology: A critical analysis of theory and practice.* Buckingham, UK: Open University Press.

Novak, J. D., & Cañas, A. J. (2008). *The theory underlying concept maps and how to construct and use them.* Pensacola: *Florida Institute for Human* and *Machine Cognition.*

O'Brien, R. (2001). An overview of the methodological approach of action research. In R. Richardson (Ed.), *Teoria e Prática da Pesquisa Ação* [Theory and practice of action research]. João Pessoa, Brazil: Universidade Federal da Paraíba. Retrieved March 2, 2011, from http://www.web.ca/~robrien/papers/arfinal.html

Oliver, S., Bagnall, A. M., Thomas, J., Shepherd, J., Sowden, A., White, I., et al. (2008). *RCTs for policy interventions? A review of reviews and meta-regression.* Birmingham, UK: University of Birmingham.

Olsen, L. A., Aisner, D., & McGinnis, J. M. (2007). *Institute of Medicine Roundtable on Evidence-Based Medicine: The learning healthcare system, workshop summary.* Washington, DC: National Academies Press.

Orszag, P. R. (2009). *Building rigorous evidence to drive policy.* Washington, DC: Office of Budget Management.

Pawson, R. (2002). Evidence-based policy: In search of a method. *Evaluation, 8,* 157–181.

Rohm, R. (1994). *Positive personality profiles.* Atlanta, GA: Personality Insights.

Safayeni, F., Derbentseva, N., & Cañas, A. J. (2005). A theoretical note on concept maps and the need for cyclic concept maps. *Journal of Research in Science Teaching, 42*(7), 741–766.

Sherman, L., Gottfredson, D., MacKenzie, D. L., Eck, J., Reuter, P., & Bushway, S. (1997). *Preventing crime: What works, what doesn't, what's promising.* Washington, DC: National Institute of Justice.

Srinivasan, M., McElvany, M., Shay, J., Shavelson, R., & West, D. (2008). Measuring knowledge structure: Reliability of concept mapping assessment in medical education. *Academic Medicine, 83*(12), 1196–1203.

Tattersall, C., Watts, A., & Vernon, S. (2007). Mind mapping as a tool in qualitative research. *Nursing Times, 103*(26), 32–33.

Teddlie, C. B., & Tashakkori, A. (2009). *Foundations of mixed methods research: Integrating quantitative and qualitative approaches in the social and behavioral sciences.* Thousand Oaks, CA: Sage.

Tomas, A. (1997). *The visual life history interview.* Retrieved March 2, 2009, from www.colinwat sonleeds.co.uk/RMarticles/ReadingG.pdf

Tomas, A., & Dittmar, H. (1995). The experience of homeless women: An exploration of housing histories and the meaning of home. *Housing Studies, 1466–1810, 10*(4), 493–515.

Trochim, W. (1989). An introduction to concept mapping for planning and evaluation. *Evaluation and Program Planning, 12,* 1–16.

Trochim, W. (1993, November). *Reliability of concept mapping.* Paper presented at the annual conference of the American Evaluation Association, Dallas, TX.

Umoquit, M. J., Tso, P., Burchett, H. E., & Dobrow, M. J. (2011). A multidisciplinary systematic review of the use of diagrams as means of collecting data: Techniques, challenges and recommendations. *BMC Medical Research Methodology, 11,* 11. Retrieved March 2, 2011, from http://www.biomedcentral.com/1471-2288/11/11

van Schalkwyk, G. J. (2010). Collage life story elicitation technique: A representational technique for scaffolding autobiographical memories. *Qualitative Report, 15*(3), 675–695.

Wells, R. E. (2000). *Education as prison reform: A meta-analysis.* Unpublished doctoral dissertation, Louisiana State University, Baton Rouge.

Wheeldon, J. P. (2009). *Mapping international knowledge transfer: Latvian-Canadian cooperation in justice reform.* Unpublished doctoral dissertation, Simon Fraser University, Burnaby, Canada.

Wheeldon, J. P. (2010). Mapping mixed methods research: Methods, measures, and meaning. *Journal of Mixed Methods Research, 4*(2), 87–102.

Wheeldon, J. P. (2011). *Mapping law and society in an age of terror* (Working Paper No. 321). Washington, DC: Center for Justice, Law, and Development.

Wheeldon, J. P., & Faubert, J. (2009). Framing experience: Concept maps, mind maps, and data collection in qualitative research. *International Journal of Qualitative Methods, 8*(3), 68–83.

Wilson, D., Gallagher, C. A., & Mackenzie, D. L. (2000). A meta-analysis of corrections-based education, vocation, and work programs for adult offenders. *Journal of Research on Crime and Delinquency, 37*(4), 347–368.

Wilson, D. B., & Lipsey, M. W. (2001). The role of method in treatment effectiveness research: Evidence from meta-analysis. *Psychological Methods, 6,* 412–429.

Appendix A

Example Research Participant Protection Form Checklist

CHECKLIST TO BE SUBMITTED WITH RESEARCH PROJECT

I, _____, am a student at _____ and have completed this research as part of my coursework.

I hereby pledge (check all)

- I will not and have not used vulnerable populations (children, prisoners, probationers, or any other vulnerable population) in this study.
- The project will be or was of minimal risk to participants.
- No deception will be or was employed.
- Consent will be or has been obtained from each participant.
- Confidentiality of participants will be or has been ensured.
- Any data collected will not be used for publication or public presentation or other research purposes without approval.

Print Name: _____

Student #: _____

Date: _____

Signature: _____

Appendix B

Example of Informed Consent Form

(TITLE OF RESEARCH STUDY)

RESEARCH PROCEDURES

This research is being conducted to (state purpose of research) _____.
If you agree to participate, you will be asked to (include information on participation—interview or survey) _____.

RISKS

There are no foreseeable risks for participating in this research.

BENEFITS

There are no benefits to you as a participant other than to further research related to _____.

CONFIDENTIALITY

The data in this study will be confidential. (a) Your name will not be included on the surveys and other collected data; (b) a code will be placed on the survey and other collected data; (c) through the use of an identification key, the researcher will be able to link your survey to your identity; and (d) only the researcher will have access to the identification key.

PARTICIPATION

Your participation is voluntary, and you may withdraw from the study at any time and for any reason. If you decide not to participate or if you withdraw from the study, there is no penalty or loss of benefits to which you are otherwise entitled.

CONTACT

This research is being conducted by (investigator's name and department) _____ at (university name) _____ as part of a course taught by (instructor's name) _____. He or she may be reached at (phone number) _____ for questions or to report a research-related problem.

CONSENT

I have read this form and agree to participate in this study (for nonexempt research projects, include this statement and a place for the participant's signature and the date of signature).

_____

Name

_____

Signature

_____

Date of Signature

Index

SAGE Research Methods Online
The essential tool for researchers

Sign up now at
www.sagepub.com/srmo
for more information.

An expert research tool

- An **expertly designed taxonomy** with more than 1,400 unique terms for social and behavioral science research methods
- **Visual and hierarchical search tools** to help you discover material and link to related methods

- Easy-to-use navigation tools
- Content organized by complexity
- Tools for citing, printing, and downloading content with ease
- Regularly updated content and features

A wealth of essential content

- The most comprehensive picture of quantitative, qualitative, and mixed methods available today
- More than **100,000 pages of SAGE book and reference material** on research methods as well as editorially selected material from SAGE journals
- More than **600 books** available in their entirety online

Launching 2011!

 SAGE research methods online

D1352017